The City of Philadelphia, Plaintiffs in Error, vs. John Augustus Girard, and others, Defendants in Error.

Anonymous

The City of Philadelphia, Plaintiffs in Error, vs. John Augustus Girard, and others, Defendants in Error.
City of Philadelphia vs. Girard
HTR00104
32
Court Record
Yale Law Library
c.1862

The Making of Modern Law collection of legal archives constitutes a genuine revolution in historical legal research because it opens up a wealth of rare and previously inaccessible sources in legal, constitutional, administrative, political, cultural, intellectual, and social history. This unique collection consists of three extensive archives that provide insight into more than 300 years of American and British history. These collections include:

Legal Treatises, 1800-1926: over 20,000 legal treatises provide a comprehensive collection in legal history, business and economics, politics and government.

Trials, 1600-1926: nearly 10,000 titles reveal the drama of famous, infamous, and obscure courtroom cases in America and the British Empire across three centuries.

Primary Sources, 1620-1926: includes reports, statutes and regulations in American history, including early state codes, municipal ordinances, constitutional conventions and compilations, and law dictionaries.

These archives provide a unique research tool for tracking the development of our modern legal system and how it has affected our culture, government, business – nearly every aspect of our everyday life. For the first time, these high-quality digital scans of original works are available via print-on-demand, making them readily accessible to libraries, students, independent scholars, and readers of all ages.

bibliolife
old books. new life.

The BiblioLife Network

This project was made possible in part by the BiblioLife Network (BLN), a project aimed at addressing some of the huge challenges facing book preservationists around the world. The BLN includes libraries, library networks, archives, subject matter experts, online communities and library service providers. We believe every book ever published should be available as a high-quality print reproduction; printed on-demand anywhere in the world. This insures the ongoing accessibility of the content and helps generate sustainable revenue for the libraries and organizations that work to preserve these important materials.

The following book is in the "public domain" and represents an authentic reproduction of the text as printed by the original publisher. While we have attempted to accurately maintain the integrity of the original work, there are sometimes problems with the original work or the micro-film from which the books were digitized. This can result in minor errors in reproduction. Possible imperfections include missing and blurred pages, poor pictures, markings and other reproduction issues beyond our control. Because this work is culturally important, we have made it available as part of our commitment to protecting, preserving, and promoting the world's literature.

GUIDE TO FOLD-OUTS MAPS and OVERSIZED IMAGES

The book you are reading was digitized from microfilm captured over the past thirty to forty years. Years after the creation of the original microfilm, the book was converted to digital files and made available in an online database.

In an online database, page images do not need to conform to the size restrictions found in a printed book. When converting these images back into a printed bound book, the page sizes are standardized in ways that maintain the detail of the original. For large images, such as fold-out maps, the original page image is split into two or more pages

Guidelines used to determine how to split the page image follows:

- Some images are split vertically; large images require vertical and horizontal splits.
- For horizontal splits, the content is split left to right.
- For vertical splits, the content is split from top to bottom.
- For both vertical and horizontal splits, the image is processed from top left to bottom right.

James H. Campbell

SUPREME COURT,

IN BANC.

JULY. 1862   No 32.

THE CITY OF PHILADELPHIA,

PLAINTIFFS IN ERROR

vs

JOHN AUGUSTUS GIRARD, and others,

DEFENDANTS IN ERROR

PAPER BOOK OF THE CITY OF PHILADELPHIA

INDEX TO PAPER BOOK

Docket Entries,	1–3
History of Case,	4–7
Charge of Court	7
Specifications of Error	7–8
Argument for Plaintiffs in Error,	9–31
Exemplification of Record in the Court below, commences at page 101 and ends at page	128
Agreement as to evidence,	129

Bill, Answer and Opinion in a case in the C C, in which a judicial construction was given to the Will of Stephen Girard, commence, . 133

Bill, . 133–198

Will of S Girard, . . . 199–227

Report of Examiner, . 228–262

Answer, . 263–310

Opinion of Judge Grier, 311–317

Act of March 24, 1832, . 318–325

Exemplification of Pleadings in case of Vidal and others against the City of Philadelphia, commence at page . . 327
and continue to the end

The names of the Parties as they stood on the Record below at the time of the Trial, and the Form of the Action.

JOHN AUGUSTUS GIRARD, JOHN FABRICIUS GIRARD, MARGARET P LARDY, LEWIS F DEVOUX and MARIE, his wife, in right of said MARIE, ALFRED DE LENTILHAC and ANNIE, his wife in right of said ANNIE MADALINE H GIRARD, PARMIELE DUVARS DUMAINE, FABRICIUS DUVARS DUMAINE, FRANCOIS C VIDAL, JOHN F CLARK, and and HARRIET, his wife, in right of said HARRIET, MARIE A HEMPHILL, FRANKLIN PEALE and CAROLINE E, his wife, in right of said CAROLINE,

F W & J HUGHES
582.
CAMPBELL

vs

THE CITY OF PHILADELPHIA

An Abstract of the Proceedings showing the Issue and how it was made.

DOCKET ENTRIES

JOHN AUGUSTUS GIRARD, JOHN FABRICIUS GIRARD, MARGARET P LARDY, LEWIS F DEVOUX, and MARIE, his wife, in right of said MARIE, ALFRED DE LENTILHAC and ANNE C, his wife, in right of said ANNE MADALINE H GIRARD, PARMIELE DUVARS DUMAINE, FABRICIUS DUVARS DUMAINE, FRANCOIS C VIDAL, JOHN F CLARK and HARRIET his wife in right of said HARRIET MARIE A HEMPHILL FRANKLIN PEALE and CAROLINE E his wife, in right of said CAROLINE,

HUGHES
PARRY

Ejectment

vs

THE CITY OF PHILADELPHIA.

D W S—1

Summons in Ejectment against the above defendants for all that certain tract and body of lands situate in the townships of Butler and Mahonoy, in the county of Schuylkill, and surveyed under warrants respectively in the several names of Daniel Reese, Samuel Reese, James Chapman, Thomas Grant, Samuel Scott, William P. Brady, John Brady, Edward Lynch, Thomas Paschall, Joseph Paschall, John Howell, John Blackey, Nathan Beach, Israel Cope, James McNeal, Jeremiah Jackson, Josiah Haines, William Steadman, John Lockhart Nathan Brown, containing in all about eight thousand five hundred acres,—the title, and right of possession to which the said demandants say is in them, and not in the said defendant returnable the day next preceding the 1st day of December Term, 1859.

14 August, 1860. Defendants plead not guilty.

22 November, 1860. Affidavit filed.

22 November, 1860. On motion of Mr. Bannan and affidavit filed. Rule on plaintiffs' counsel to show cause why the names of Alfred De Lentilhac and Annie Stephanie, his wife, and Miss M. H. Girard, Mrs. M. P. Lardy, and P. Dumaine and F. Dumaine, heirs of Stephen Girard, should not be stricken from the above action of ejectment, returnable on the first day of next term.

8 February, 1861—continued. 14 March, 1861—continued, on payment of costs by defendants. 6 August, 1861—continued. 10 December, 1861—rule discharged. 22 March, 1862—Court direct this case to be placed at the head of Trial List for third week of April next, and now, April 21st, 1862, a jury being called, the following persons came: Charles Maurer, Josiah Stees, Michael J. Thomas, Adam Cressman, Solomon Shellhammer, Daniel G. Herb, Abraham Baughner, Plaukinton W. Harvey, Philip Steinbach, William Biddle, Philip M. Barrow and Isaac Harvey, twelve free, honest and

lawful men, who, after having been first duly ballotted, challenged, sworn, and 25 April, 1862, charged, do say that they find for the plaintiffs.

Entered in Judgment Doc 13, 1842

25 April, 1862 Before verdict, defendants' counsel except to so much of the charge of the Court as answers the fourth point of plaintiff in the affirmative, and to so much of the charge as refuses to answer the second, fifth and sixth points of defendants in the affirmative, and to so much thereof as declares that the testator devised a trust for an indefinite accumulation of income into capital, and to so much as declares that there is a direction in the will that the rents of the real estate shall be applied to the repair and improvement of testator's real esate and that the same is a trust for an indefinite accumulation of capital in the shape of buildings, and renders the will void as intending to create a perpetuity and that, on the whole evidence of the case, the plaintiffs are entitled to recover Defendants' counsel ask the Court to file their charge and answers to the points made, in writing, and to file their notes of testimony with the record in the cause

25 April, 1862 Defendants' exceptions plaintiffs' and defendants' points and offers filed with præcipe

25 April, 1862. Notes of evidence and charge of the Court filed

30 April, 1862 Writ of error filed.

History of Case.

This was an action of Ejectment, brought by the heirs of Stephen Girard, against the City of Philadelphia, to recover possession of twenty tracts of unseated land in Schuylkill County

The plaintiffs (below) claimed as heirs of Mr. Girard the defendants (below) as his devisees

Upon the trial of the case it was agreed that the plaintiffs were the heirs and next of kin of Mr Girard, and that Mr. Girard was the owner of the premises previous to the date of the last codicil to his will

It was also admitted that the plaintiffs or their ancestors had received and receipted for the legacies respectively bequeathed to them by Mr Girard

To the claim of title and possession made by the defendants, as devisees of Mr. Girard, the plaintiffs interposed the objection, and the devise to them was in trust, to create and maintain a perpetuity and therefore void

This allegation by the defendants, was made upon the following provisions of the will·

'I do give, devise and bequeath *all the residue and re-*
"*mainder of my real and personal estate* of every sort and kind
'wheresoever situate, unto the Mayor, Aldermen and Citizens
'of Philadelphia their successors and assigns *in trust*, to
"and for the several uses, intents and purposes hereinafter
"mentioned and declared of, and concerning the same, that
"is to say so far as regards my real estate in Pennsylvania,
"in trust that no part thereof shall ever be sold or alienated
"by the said Mayor, Aldermen and Citizens of Philadelphia,
"or their successors, but the same shall forever thereafter be
"let from time to time, to good tenants, at yearly or other
"rents, and upon leases in possession and not exceeding five

"years from the commencement thereof, and that the rents,
"issues and profits arising therefrom *shall be applied towards*
"*keeping that part of the said real estate situate in the City and*
"*liberties of Philadelphia constantly in good repair,* (parts else-
"where situate to be kept in repair by the tenants thereof
"respectively,) *and towards improving the same, whenever*
"*necessary by erecting new buildings*, and that the net residue
"be applied to the same uses and purposes as are herein
"declared of and concerning the residue of my personal
"estate".

The uses and purposes of the residue of the testator's personal estate were declared to be (1) as to $2,000,000 thereof to erect the College buildings described in the will and (2) as to $500,000 to improve the eastern front of the city. And as to the remainder to apply the same (1) to the further improvement and maintenance of the said College (2) to enable the city corporation to improve their police and (3) to municipal purposes generally.

The plaintiffs showed that among the property so devised to the defendants, was 567 acres of farm land in the southern part of the City of Philadelphia, in what was before the year 1854, the township of Passyunk, and the district of Moyamensing. That the same was rented for farms and truck gardens, part of it was subject to overflow from the river, and that an annual bank tax was paid to bear part of the expense of damming out the river from this and the neighbouring lands.

The argument of the plaintiffs was, that the first trust of the income of the real estate in Pennsylvania, was one to cover this farm land with buildings, and they asked the Judge to charge, "That the devise in trust to apply the
"rents of the real estate in Pennsylvania, first to the erec-
"tion of new buildings upon so much thereof as is situate
"in the City and liberties of Philadelphia from time to
"time as the same may be necessary, has no limitation as to
"the time when such filling up of capital by the accumula-

"tion as aforesaid is to cease, but the same may continue "beyond the period fixed for the vesting of an executory "limitation, and is therefore void"

The court affirmed this point and instructed the jury, that upon the evidence the plaintiffs were entitled to recover: and added, ' this instruction renders it unnecessary to answer "the other points put by the plaintiffs' counsel or the points "of the defendants' counsel"

The points of the defendants counsel were

1st That the trust of the residuary estate created by the will of Stephen Girard is not void as creating a perpetuity

2d That the trust of the residuary estate created by the will of Stephen Girard is not a trust for accumulation

3d That the direction in restraint of alienation attendant on the devise to the City, if void, does not affect the validity of the devise itself

4th. That if the restraint on alienation should be void, the devise will be sustained for the charity, unclogged by the condition

5th That the plaintiffs cannot recover, and the verdict should be for defendants

The defendants excepted, as appears by the record, as follows

Before verdict the defendants excepted to so much of the charge of the Court as answers the fourth point of the plaintiffs in the affirmative

And to so much of the charge as refuses to answer the second, fifth and sixth points of the defendants in the affirmative

As to so much thereof as declares that the testator devised a trust for an indefinite accumulation of income into capital

And to so much as declares that there is a direction in the will that the rents of the real estate shall be applied to the repair and improvement of the testator's real estate and that the same is a trust for an indefinite accumulation of capital in the shape of buildings, and renders the will void as intending to create a perpetuity, and that on the whole evidence of the case, the plaintiffs are entitled to recover.

Charge of the Court

The Judge charged, "That the devise in trust to apply the "rents of the real estate in Pennsylvania, first to the erec-"tion of new buildings upon so much thereof as is situate in "the City and liberties of Philadelphia, from time to time as "the same may be necessary, has no limitation as to the time "when such filling up of capital by the accumulation as afore-"said is to cease, but the same may continue beyond the period "fixed for the vesting of an executory limitation, and is "therefore void."

"And that upon the evidence, the plaintiffs were entitled to "recover, and that this instruction renders it unnecessary to 'answer the other points put by the plaintiffs' counsel or the "points of the defendants' counsel."

Specifications of Error.

1. The Court below erred in charging "That the devise "in trust to apply the rents of the real estate in Pennsyl-"vania, first to the erection of new buildings upon so much "thereof as is situate in the City and liberties of Philadel-"phia, from time to time as the same may be necessary, has "no limitation as to the time when such filling up of capital "by the accumulation as aforesaid is to cease, but the same

"may continue beyond the period fixed for the vesting of an "executory limitation, and is therefore void."

2. In declining to charge as the counsel for defendant's requested, that is to say in not charging

1st. That the trust of the residuary estate created by the will of Stephen Girard is not void as creating a perpetuity.

2d. That the trust of the residuary estate created by the will of Stephen Girard is not a trust for accumulation.

3d. That the direction in restraint of alienation attendant on the devise of the City, if void, does not affect the validity of the devise itself.

4th. That if the restraint on alienation should be void, the devise will be sustained for the charity, unclogged by the condition.

5th. That the plaintiffs cannot recover, and the verdict should be for defendants.

6th. That the acceptance of the legacies by the parties and privies under the will of Stephen Girard, and the ratification of said will by the acts of the General Assembly of March 24 and April 4, 1832, which are in evidence in this cause, prevents a recovery by the plaintiffs, and the verdict should be for defendants.

Argument for Plaintiffs in Error

Mr. Girard, by his will, after making certain bequests to trustees or corporations for charitable purposes, and bequests and devises to his relations and friends, disposed of the residue of his estate as follows:

XX. And, whereas, I have been for a long time impressed with the importance of educating the poor, and of placing them, by the early cultivation of their minds and the development of their moral principles, above the many temptations, to which, through poverty and ignorance, they are exposed, and I am particularly desirous to provide for such a number of poor male white orphan children, as can be trained in one institution, a better education, as well as a more comfortable maintenance, than they usually receive from the application of the public funds and whereas, together with the object just adverted to, I have sincerely at heart the welfare of the city of Philadelphia, and as a part of it I am desirous to improve the neighborhood of the river Delaware, so that the health of the citizens may be promoted and preserved, and that the eastern part of the city may be made to correspond better with the interior. Now, I do give devise and bequeath, *all the residue and remainder of my real and personal estate* of every sort and kind wheresoever situate (the real estate in Pennsylvania charged as aforesaid,) unto ' the Mayor Aldermen and Citizens of Philadelphia," their successors and assigns, in trust, to and for the several uses, intents and purposes hereinafter mentioned and declared of and concerning the same, that is to say so far as regards my real estate in Pennsylvania, in trust, that no part thereof shall ever be sold or alienated by the said Mayor, Aldermen and Citizens of Philadelphia, or their successors, but the same shall forever thereafter be let from time to time, to good tenants, at yearly or other rents, and upon leases in possession not exceeding five years from the commencement thereof, and that the rents, issues and profits arising therefrom shall be applied towards keeping that part of the said real estate situate in the City *and Liberties* of Philadelphia constantly in good repair, (part elsewhere situate to keep in repair by the tenants thereof respectively) and towards improving the same, whenever necessary, by erecting new buildings, and that the nett residue (after paying the several annuities hereinbefore provided for) be applied to the same uses and purposes as are herein declared of and concerning the residue of my personal estate, and so far as regards my real estate in Kentucky, now under the care of Messrs Triplett & Brumley in trust, to sell and dispose of the same, whenever it may be expedient to do so, and to apply the proceeds of sale to the same uses and purposes as are herein declared of and concerning the residue of my personal estate.

He then proceeds to the disposition of the personal residue —

"XXI And so far as regards the residue of my personal ' estate in trust, as to two millions of dollars, part thereof to ' apply and expend so much of that sum as may be necessary " in erecting, as soon as practicably may be in the centre of " my square of ground between Chestnut and High Streets," a college with outbuildings sufficiently spacious for the accommodation of at least three hundred scholars, " poor white male orphans of the City of Philadelphia,' &c, and the requisite teachers and persons necessary to the management of the institution, and in supplying it with furniture, books, &c The plan of the college is described in detail, and as soon as it shall have been completed he directed " the income, issues ' and profit of so much of the said sum as shall remain un- " expended, shall be applied to maintain the said college, " according to his directions '

The last paragraph of this section provides as follows

"If the income, arising from that part of the said sum of
"two millions of dollars remaining after the construction and
"furnishing of the college and out buildings, shall, owing to
"the increase of the number of orphans applying for admis-
"sion, or other cause, be inadequate to the construction of
"new buildings, or the maintenance and education of as many
"orphans as may apply for admission, then such further sum
"as may be necessary for the construction of new buildings,
"and the maintenance and education of such further num
"ber of orphans as can be maintained and instructed within
"such buildings, as the said square of ground shall be ade-
"quate to, shall be taken from the final residuary fund here-
"inafter expressly referred to for the purpose comprehending
"the income of my real estate in the city and county of Phila-
"delphia, and the dividends of my stock in the Schuylkill
"Navigation Company—my design and desire being that the
"benefits of said institution shall be extended to as great a
"number of orphans as the limits of the said square and
"buildings therein can accommodate"

The next section (22d) declares a further trust of five hun
dred thousand dollars part of the residue of his personal
estate, to be invested, and the income applied to the opening
of Delaware Avenue and the further improvement of the
eastern front of the city

The 23d section is a bequest of three hundred thousand
dollars to the Commonwealth, to be paid as soon as the neces
sary laws to enable the corporation of the City to carry into
effect the improvements mentioned in the 22d section, are
enacted provided the same should be passed within one year
after his decease

The final residue is then disposed of thus.

XXIV. And as it regards *the remainder of said residue* of
my personal estate, in trust to invest the same in good securities, and in like manner to invest the interest and income

thereof from time to time, so that the whole shall form a permanent fund, and to apply the income of said fund,

1st. To the further improvement and maintenance of the aforesaid College, as directed in the last paragraph of the XXIst clause of this Will.

2d. To enable the Corporation of the City of Philadelphia to provide more effectually than they now do for the security of the persons and property of the inhabitants of the said city, by a competent police, including a sufficient number of watchmen, really suited to the purpose, and to this end, I recommend a division of the city into watch districts, or four parts, each under a proper head, and that at least two watchmen shall, in each round or station, patrole together.

3d. To enable the said Corporation to improve the city property, and the general appearance of the city itself, and, in effect, to diminish the burden of taxation, now most oppressive, especially on those who are the least able to bear it —

To all which objects, the prosperity of the city and the health and comfort of its inhabitants, I devote the said fund as aforesaid, and direct the income thereof to be applied yearly, and every year forever, after providing for the College as hereinbefore directed, as my primary object. But, if the said City shall knowingly and willfuly violate any of the conditions hereinbefore and hereinafter mentioned, then I give and bequeath the said remainder and accumulations to the Commonwealth of Pennsylvania, for the purpose of internal navigation, excepting, however, the rents, issues and profits of my real estate in the city and county of Philadelphia, which shall forever be reserved and applied to maintain the aforesaid College, in the manner specified in the last paragraph of the XXIst clause of this will, and if the Commonwealth of Pennsylvania shall fail to apply this or the preceding bequest to the purposes before mentioned, or shall apply any part thereof to any other use, or shall, for the term of one year from the time of my decease, fail or omit to pass the law hereinbefore specified for promoting the improvement of the City of Philadelphia, then I give, devise and bequeath the said remainder and accumulations (the rents aforesaid, always excepted and reserved for the College as aforesaid,) to the United States of America, for the purposes of internal navigation and no other

By a codicil forty five acres of land in Penn Township were substituted for the square of ground in the city of Philadelphia, whereon to place the College buildings.

I.

The Court below charged that there was a trust to apply the rents of the real estate in Pennsylvania, first and above all other purposes, to erect new buildings upon so much thereof as was situate in the City and Liberties of Philadelphia, and that as there was no limitation, as to time when such erection of new buildings should cease—or in the language of the Court—the piling up of capital by accumulation, the time might continue beyond a lawful period, and the devise was, therefore, void

The proof in the case was, that the testator devised to the defendants, and that the latter held about five hundred and sixty-seven acres of farm lands south of Philadelphia in the late Township of Passyunk, and District of Moyamensing, unimproved except for farming purposes and the argument at bar, was that the testator designed that this land should be improved by building city houses thereon that a period beyond the legal limit would be consumed in thus improving the property, add to which there would be a dangerous accumulation of capital in the shape of houses The plaintiff's Fourth point was shaped to this state of things and the charge of the Court was in accordance with it The point and the charge could apply to nothing else. It could not have been directed to a supposed injunction, to replace old houses, with new ones, whenever necessary, because that is part of every trust which embraces improved real estate. The defendants hold no other, or at least a very small quantity of unimproved property in the city or county of Philadelphia.

The plaintiffs make no distinction between the *City and County* of Philadelphia and *the City and Liberties* of Philadelphia. The testator knew they were not the same. In the 20§ of his will he speaks of the City and Liberties, and in the 21§ and 24§ he speaks of his real estate in the City and County of Philadelphia.

The *Liberties* of the City of Philadelphia, are or were, a well known territory, situated north and west of the city. There were no liberty lands south of Philadelphia.

The history of these "Liberties" is this. William Penn agreed with his purchasers, that for every 500 acres of land purchased in the province there should be allotted 10 acres in the city which it was intended to lay out. But it being ascertained that to comprehend the proportion mentioned, or the 6 or 7000 acres which the land sold must have required, the town would have covered such an extent of ground as would have frustrated the main object of a city, that of nearness of residences and conveniences of intercourse.

The plan of the site of the city was abandoned, and one extending from river to river and from Vine to South streets was laid out. The purchasers received lots in the town, and their proportion was made up of liberty lands. These were embraced in a circuit of territory embracing five or six miles northward and westward of the city.

Sergeant's Land Law of Pennsylvania, 225, 2 Smith Laws, note, p. 106.

The land south of Philadelphia was owned and inhabited by the Swedes and Dutch, before William Penn's arrival, and there was none unappropriated.

If it be alleged that sometimes in popular language the

whole surrounding neighborhood of the city was called "Lberties," in the same manner that the built up neighborhood of the city was called "the City of Philadelphia." Yet in official or legal instruments, the distinction was necessarily observed.

In this very will, Mr. Girard provides that children born in the City of Philadelphia, shall have a preference of admission into his College; but it was never doubted that the testator meant the corporate city, and not what was called in popular language, the City of Philadelphia. Soohan vs. The City of Philadelphia, 9 Casey, 9—

The doctrine that words or description in a will which may be applied both to a popular and a legal or technical meaning, are to be construed to mean the latter, seems to have been established in Blenon's Estate, Brightley, p. 338. In that case, Mr. Blenon, a resident of the District of West Philadelphia, devised the residue of his estates ' to the dif-"ferent institutions of charity and beneficence, constituted "and established *at Philadelphia* for the unfortunate, &c.,' and this court decided that only societies, located within the corporate limits of the City of Philadelphia were entitled to take; reversing the court below which construed the words "at Philadelphia,' the City of Philadelphia, as popularly understood to mean the city proper and the adjoining built up districts.

II

The Legislature of the Commonwealth, by an act approved March 24, 1832, entitled "An Act to enable The Mayor, Aldermen and Citizens of Philadelphia, to carry into effect certain improvements and execute certain trusts," *Provided* that it should be "lawful for the Mayor, &c, to exercise all ' such jurisdictions, enact all such ordinances, and to do "and execute all such acts and things whatsoever as may "be necessary and convenient for the full and entire accept-"ance, execution and prosecution for any and all devises, "bequests and provisions contained in the said will," to carry into effect which the testator had desired the Legislature to enact the necessary laws. And by a Supplement approved April 4, 1832 "The Select and Common Coun-"cils of the City of Philadelphia" were "authorized to pro-"vide by ordinance or otherwise, for the election or "appointment of such officers or agents as they may deem "essential to the due execution of the *duties and trusts en-*"*joined and created* by the will of the late Stephen Girard" Pamph Laws, 1831-32, p 176, p 275

By these acts, the Legislature show a legislative opinion of the validity and legality of the trusts in Mr Girard's will and though not a judicial decision and entitled to weight and confidence as such, yet if the question be a doubtful one, such legislative opinion should be of value

III.

The Argument of the other side is, that this will contains a trust to apply the income of the real estate to cover with buildings the vacant land of the testator, situate in the late County of Philadelphia Assuming for the sake of the argument, that the testator knew or meant no distinction between the County of Philadelphia, and the "Liberties," of Philadelphia, yet the language of the will does not authorize the construction sought to be put upon it

The latter is, "the rents   *   *   shall be applied "towards keeping that part of the real estate situate in the "City and Liberties of Philadelphia, constantly in good re-"pair, (parts elsewhere situate to be kept in repair by the "tenants thereof, respectively,) and towards *improving the* "*same, whenever necessary by erecting* new buildings," &c

Now there is not a word here about improving unimproved property. The spirit of the language is to the contrary. The words "new buildings" is put as the opposite of old building. The testator meant that buildings becoming old or dilapidated or old in the sense of not being suited to the necessities or conveniences of business were to be replaced with new ones.

The testator had a number of houses and stores in the City and *Liberties* of Philadelphia, and he directed, what the law would have done for him, that his trustees should keep the property in repair and rebuild when necessary. He also owned farm land south of the city, and as to that, he made the exception in his will, namely, that "parts elsewhere situate," that is elsewhere than in the City or Liberties of Philadelphia, "should be kept in repair by the tenants." As to the farm land he made no provision for improvement, at the time of death thirty years ago, the prospect of this land being needed for buildings was very remote, it is still far distant. Their improvement the testator left to the chances happening in distant generations.

But suppose the testator meant what the other side say he did, namely, *that the rents of his improved property should be applied to covering with buildings his unimproved property.* What is there unlawful in it? If the income ultimately is appropriated to a charitable or public purpose?

The Court say that such a thing—or in their own language, such piling up of capital by accumulation—may continue beyond the period fixed for the vesting of an executory limitation, and is therefore void.

But this is not a piling up of capital by accumulation. If the direction had been, *to purchase lands or make new acquisitions* with the rents, it might be obnoxious to the objection mentioned. But here the property is already owned by the devisee in trust and the direction is to improve it only.

The objection to trusts for indefinite accumulation is, that

D W S—2

eventually they would absorb an amount of property dangerous to the Commonwealth But certainly a trust to improve unimproved property and render it available for the business of life, especially when the income is to be appropriated to charitable uses, is a benefit instead of an injury to the Commonwealth

And although the Court cannot judicially know that the unimproved property can be covered with buildings within the legal period, yet they cannot judicially know to the contrary.

In the case in hand the unimproved property consists of three lots The rent applicable to their improvement amount to the annual gross sum of about $150,000

The time within which the improvements, said to be directed to be made by the testator, is necessary to be ascertained before it is decided, that it is or is not within the transgressive period of limitation It must be shown that the improvements cannot be made within the time fixed for the vesting of an executory limitation, before it is declared that a devise, such as is objected to, is void

The statement is shown to be law by the following authority.

" A class of limitations which it has generally been sup-
" posed are exempted from the operation of our laws against
" remoteness, consists of those, *the nature of whose subject*
" *matter* is such as to render it necessary (it is said) for them
" to take effect, if at all, within the period prescribed by the
" rule for the prevention of perpetuities, and which, therefore,
" in themselves, preclude any question of remoteness " "Thus,
" let it be supposed that A being a tenant under a freehold
" lease for three lives, devises the property of which he is
" lessee, after the death of B without issue, to C Taking
" the event and the limitation expectant upon it, abstractedly,
" or dissociated from the nature and circumstances of the estate,
" the former is unquestionably, too remote, and the latter,
' therefore void But, considering them in reference to or in

'connection with the peculiar character of the subject of the
'gift, the applicability of the rule seems at least, doubtful"
  Lewis on Perpetuities, [p 627]
  Butler's Note to Fearne, 500

Low v Burron, 3 P Ws 262 Testatator seized of an estate for three lives in the property in question, devised it to his daughter M M for life, remainder to her issue male, and for want of such remainder to L One of the questions being, whether the remainder to L was good, it was held, by Lord Chancellor, in the affirmative, he observing that there could be no danger of a perpetuity for all these estates would determine on the expiration of the lives of the *cestuis que vies* and so likewise would it have been, had there been twenty lives pending at the same time

Wastneys v Chappell, 1 Bro Parl Ca 457 Where it was decided, though the will in terms tended to create a perpetuity yet the nature of the estate devised prevented it

Bengough v Edridge, 1 Simon, 173 The question, whether limitations in a will tending to perpetuity could be judged of by the quantity of the interest out of which they were to issue, or were to be judged solely by their legal effect, was discussed The Chancellor decided in favor of the limitations

Mr Lewis, (Perpetuities, p 680,) says the rule above stated has, besides the authorities above cited, the assent of Mr Butler, Mr Peere Williams, Mr Fearne, and Mr Preston

The reasonableness of this rule seems clear and to extend it to cases like the present, seems to be warranted by every consideration of equity

If where the language of a will declares a trust of the application of the income of improved property to the improvement of unproductive estate is to be declared to be within the rules of law against perpetuity, without considering other circumstances, then where a testator leaves but a single lot of ground and directed it to be improved, he has made as great a violation of the rule as if he had left a thousand

In reference to the magnitude of the estate of Mr Girard, no more time would be occupied in covering his vacant land of 500 acres with buildings, than would be consumed in the case of most estates in building up a few city lots

IV.

Mr Girard's will has been likened to the one which was the subject of the case of Hilliard *vs* Miller, (10 Barr, 326,) and that case was considered by the Judge below as deciding this one

But in Miller's will the charitable object was remote, uncertain and subordinate in Mr Girard's, it is immediate and paramount

In Miller's will there was a devise of the residue of his estate to trustees to invest his personal estate in mortgage securities and to apply the income thereof and the rents of his real estate to making loans to farmers and mechanics as often as application was made and the funds admitted And when (1) an accumulation existed beyond the application for loans, (2) when such accumulation was likely to remain, (3) when the amount should justify the undertaking, and (4) when mechanics wanted employment, the trustees were authorized to endow a hospital But the trust for loaning money was not to cease even after the hospital should be endowed

This trust the Court declared to be one for the perpetual accumulation of income, and void because it fell within the rule against perpetuities

In Mr Girard's will the gift to charities is immediate The College buildings are to be erected "as soon as practicably may be," and the sum of $2,000,000 is given for such erection. After the buildings are completed and furnished the whole of the income of his residuary estate is to be applied if necessary towards its further efficiency. Till the contingencies should happen of using the income of the residuary for the uses of the College, the income was given so the city for public purposes.

A gift to a charity is necessarily a perpetuity, for it is the very nature of such gift to withdraw the thing given from commerce and circulation, since its alienation would be inconsistent with the use to which it is dedicated. And such gifts are not within the rule against perpetuities.

If the internal structure and constitution of a charitable trust are not conformable to the rule on the subject of perpetuities, yet if the trust is for a charitable purpose, the trust will not fail.

Martin vs Maugham, 14 Simons, 230. S B bequeathed his property to trustees, to convert into money and invest the proceeds, and after paying annuities, to add the dividends to the capital till it should produce an annual income of £600—when, as the testator expressed it, he hoped that every five years receipt of that income would produce an increase of income of £150 a year, and his will was that every such increase of income should be appropriated for the benefit of certain parish charity schools. Before the Vice Chancellor, (Shadwell) it was argued for the next of kin, that the accumulation directed by the testator was perpetual—*that regard being had to the amount of the estate, to the price of stocks and to the annuities, the accumulation must necessarily continue for a much larger time than the law permitted,* and therefore the direction to accumulate and all the ulterior gifts must fail.

The Vice Chancellor. "Although the particular mode in "in which the testator meant the benefits to be doled out to ' the objects of his bounty, cannot take effect, yet as there is "confessedly a devotion of his personal estate to charitable "purposes, my opinion is that his next of kin have no claim "at all to his property. I conceive that if a testator has 'expressed his intention that his personal estate shall be, 'in substance, applied for charitable purposes, *the particular mode which he may have pointed out for effecting those purposes has nothing to do with the question whether the devotion* for "charitable purposes shall take place or not, and that, "whatever the difficulty may be, the Court, if it is com- "pelled to yield to circumstances, will carry the charitable intention into effect, through the medium of some other 'scheme."

Where the purpose of the accumulation directed is such that an end can be put to the accumulation by satisfying that purpose, the trust is valid. Bateman v Hotchkin, 10 Bevan, 426.

The trust was for raising and accumulating a sinking fund for payment of mortgages (either existing at the testator's death or made pursuant to his will,) was held not void for remoteness, though the period during which the accumulation might last was indefinite.

Where there is a discretion in the trustees to stop the accumulations, a trust for such is valid.

Ewen v Bannerman, 2 Dow & Clark, 74. A trust deed provided that a fund should accumulate with the interest arising thereon until the principal sums should amount to the sum of £——, when it was to be applied to the building of an hospital, and to the maintenance of —— boys, leaving blanks as to the amount of the accumulation, and as to the number of boys, it was held that the deed was void, on the ground that it was too uncertain to be carried into execution, although it was admitted that the gift would have been good if *a discretion had been given to the trustees to begin to build as soon as they should have accumulated such a fund as they should think equal to the donor's purpose.*

The power to act at discretion may be implied from the nature of the trust. Peckerine v Shotwell, 10 Barr, 23.

V.

If there is any one principle of the law, more thoroughly and universally established and settled than another, it is that, if possible, a devise for charitable uses shall be sustained

In 4 Cruise, 25, §43, it is said that the statutes of Mortmain did not extend to charitable uses, nor the statute of wills 1 Eden, 10, 1 W. Bl, 90, Attorney General v Tancrede

The execution of a power by will, defectively executed, is good, if the appointment is to charitable uses Margaret Pepper's will, 1 Parson's, p 446

A direction in a will that the devised estate should not be alienated, makes no perpetuity in the sense forbidden by the law, if the devise be upon trust for charities

Perin et al, v Carey et al, 24 Howard, p 507

McDonough v Murdock, 15 Howard p 363

Girard v The City of Philadelphia, C C U S Opinion by Grier, J

Case of Thetford School, 4 Coke Rep, 131, part VIII

Sir T M devised land of the value of £35, for the maintenance of a preacher, of a master of a school, and of certain poor people and a special distribution was made by the testator himself, by his will among them Afterwards the land increased to a yearly value of £100 Two questions were moved (1) Whether the preacher, shoolmaster and poor, should have only the sum appointed to them by the founder, or that the revenue and profit of the land should be employed to the increase of the stipend of each of them? (2) If any surplus remained, how it should be employed? Resolved by the two Chief Justices and Walmsley, J, That the revenue and profit of the land should be employed to the increase of the stipend of the preacher, &c And if any surplus remained, it should be expended for the maintenance of a greater number of the poor, &c., and nothing shall be converted by the devises of their own use.

Magill v. Brown, Brightley, 396. Baldwin says the above case and the statute of Templars, declared the common law to be, that the appropriation of increased profits and revenues of land, charged with a specific sum of charities, should go to the same objects as those specified, and no part should go to the heir or any other use than the charity.

So in Brown's C. Cases. Lord Commissioner Eyre, "Surplus results to the charity, not necessary to look further than the objects. It must be applied to its benefits."

To the same point is 3 Bro. Ch. Cases, 373; 2 Vesey, 1 Attorney General v. Tonna.

These cases, showing how favorably charitable dispositions by will are regarded by the Courts, might be multiplied *ad infinitum*. The citations from the text books would present the same views. This rule is to be found in the civil law, and in the common law. There was a time when a portion of the residue of every man's estate was applied to charity and the ordinary thought himself obliged so to apply it.

If there is any doubt in the mind of the Court, as to the construction of the will in this case, we claim the benefit of these decisions. But we submit that the reasonable and legal interpretation of the devise in question, is in favor of the construction put upon it by the plaintiffs.

The other side argue that Mr. Girard devised to the City of Philadelphia a large improved and unimproved real estate *in the city and county of Philadelphia*, in trust, to cover the unimproved real estate with buildings from the rents derived from the improved estate, and that after such buildings were erected, then the income of all the estate is to be applied to the charities mentioned in the will. They then assume that the time which will be occupied in constructing such buildings will exceed the time allowed for the vesting of an executory limitation, and that the devise is void.

We submit, with great confidence that the will admits of no such interpretation

The testator's object was to devote the residue of his estate to charitable use. He calls the building and endowment of his college his "primary object." He declares that he devotes the residue of his estate "to the prosperity of the city and the health and comfort of its inhabitants." That in the event of the city forfeiting his bequest, still "the rents, issues and profits of" his "real estate in the city and county of Philadelphia" "shall *forever* be reserved and applied to maintain" the college.

In the introductory section to that in which he provides for the erection of the college, he declares that he has been for a long time impressed with the necessity of educating the poor, and placing them beyond temptations early in life, and that he has sincerely at heart the welfare of the city of Philadelphia

His direction that his real estate shall not be sold—the large endowment provided for the college—the provision for forfeiture if the city wilfully violate the conditions on which it was to administer his bequest—are all expressive that his charities were intended to be real and substantial.

That his charities were to have immediate effect is not less explicitly expressed. The college is to be erected "as soon as practicably may be." The bequest to the city of the residue for municipal purposes, till the necessities of the college require it, is to enable the corportion to 'provide more effectually than they *now* do for the security" of persons and property—"to diminish the burden of taxation, *now* most oppressive." To these purposes, and the college, the income of the residue is "to be applied yearly and every year forever."

Mr Girard's gift was of real estate in the city and county of Philadelphia, on which were erected buildings, and of farm land in what, at the time of his death, were the district of Moyamensing and the township of Passyunk, in a high state of cultivation and improvement, having thereon all the buildings and fixtures needful for conducting farming operations. If it be conceded that Mr Girard meant, when he spoke of the "liberties" of Philadelphia, the "county" of Philadelphia, and that it is of the land of the latter he speaks, when he directs that the real estate shall be kept in good repair and improved by erecting new buildings, what is the true construction of that part of his will? Now, if Mr Girard had said nothing about improving by building upon his real estate, his trustees, with the approbation of a Court of Chancery, would be authorized to apply the income of the trust estate for the purposes of improvement. The law puts these words in the will. But Mr Girard indicates the *fund* which shall bear the expense of the improvement, namely, the income of the real estate, thus intending to exclude what would most probably be the direction of a Chancellor, namely, to apply the income of the personalty.

A trust to keep unimproved land perpetually unimproved would be a perpetuity of the worst kind, and obnoxious to the objection against perpetuities in a high degree, namely, withdrawing property from the uses of trade. The argument on the other side seems inconsistent. If land is not to be improved, then it is a perpetuity; if it is to be improved, out of the funds of the estate, it is still a perpetuity. In fine, the owner of unimproved property cannot give it in charity, if the argument is correct.

The direction in the will is, that the trustees shall apply the income of the real estate towards improving it, when necessary, by erecting new buildings. The phrase, "when necessary," indicates the large discretion given to the trustees. If never necessary, then never to be improved. The necessity must exist. If the trustees should attempt to apply the rents, to the detriment of the charity, to the covering the five hundred and odd acres with new buildings, a Chancellor would require them to show the necessity.

It is submitted, with great confidence, that the correct interpretation of this part of the will is, that the trustees are authorized, when the interests of the trust would be promoted, to replace old buildings with new ones, and to pay expenses of such renewal out of the income of the real estate. That such renewals were to be made from time to time as the necessity therefor became apparent, and that it was not the design of the testator, nor has he expressed any such, to create a trust for the improvement of any part of his estate in such manner as is forbidden by law.

VI.

It was in evidence in the case, that the plaintiffs (below,) or their ancestors, received from the executors of Mr Girard's will the several legacies bequeathed to them respectively. This, the defendants argued, estopped the plaintiffs from recovering in the suit, and they asked the Judge so to charge, which he refused.

No person is permitted to claim under any instrument, deed, or will, without giving full effect to it in every respect, so far as such person is concerned. He cannot avail himself as to part, and then defeat the provisions of any other part.

City of Philadelphia *v* Davis, 1 Wharton, 502.

Kennedy J. The doctrine of equitable election is founded on the intention of the author of the instrument, which must be collected from the face of the instrument itself. When the intention necessary to raise the question of election is clearly expressed or necessarily implied, the party to whom a benefit is given by the instrument, but claiming a right adverse thereto, may either be compelled to make his election, or otherwise to make compensation out of what is thereby given to him.

This case of the City *v* Davis, was a suit by Mr Girard's heirs, to recover possession of property acquired by the testator after the making of his will. The city set up the defence that the heirs had accepted legacies under the will. But the Court decided that it was not a case where the heirs must be put to an election, because, the will and codicils were inoperative and invalid as to the lands in dispute, that in fact they had no existence as regarded the testator at the time of making his will or codicils

In that case the question of claiming under and against the will did not arise

Irwin v Tabb, 17 S & R 423 A debtor made a mortgage to secure the payment of a sum of money to three absent persons in different proportions expressed in the mortgage— two had paid up the sums expressed—the third had not at the time of the execution of the mortgage, but did so by advances soon after all joined in a suit to sell the mortgaged premises, the proceeds of the sale were not sufficient to pay the whole sum mentioned in the mortgage, one of the mortgagees insisted that the fund must be divided in the proportions of the money advanced at the time of the mortgage. held, that as this creditor claimed under the mortgage, he must take according to the proportions mentioned in the mortgage, because he had elected to claim under it the Court saying, (p 423,) "there is no rule of equity more universal in its application, or more just in its consequences, than that a party shall not claim in repugnant rights, and that he who takes the benefit shall also bear the burden" And ' the books are full of cases to show that a party shall not contest the validity of an instrument from which he draws a benefit, or affirm it in part and disaffirm it in part"

Adlum v Yard, 1 Rawle 171 The Court declared that the plaintiff might have repudiated an assignment, for it was to delay creditors, but that having taken a dividend he should not question its validity The doctrine of election is more analogous to *estoppel* than confirmation.

Trustees Bank U S, 2 Parsons, 147 A creditor who sought to draw a benefit from one assignment not allowed to destroy another

Festermacher v Moyer, 11 Casey, 356

"A testator devised his real estate to his two nephews (whom he also appointed his executors), and charged the same with the payment of a sum of money to other relatives, and gave the residue of his personal property to the same persons in whose favor the legacy was so charged on the real estate Held, that one of the said legatees, by his receipt to the executors, for a sum of money ' for inheritance" was estopped from setting up an adverse claim to the testator's real estate"

Fulton v. Moore, 1 Casey, 468 " Where a person accepts a legacy bequeathed, it is an election to stand by the provisions of the will"

The rule against perpetuities is founded on the reason that they are against public policy The defendants claim to recover this property because one of the trusts of it, is against this policy. But the Commonwealth by the Acts of the General Assembly, of March 24 and April 4, 1832, (p 111) declared the trusts in this will lawful This Act of the Commonwealth could, not of course, divest the heirs of Mr Girard of their rights then existing But it declared so far as the Commonwealth was concerned, the objections to the will on the ground of being obnoxious to public policy should no longer exist If there was a perpetuity in the part of the will complained of, the Commonwealth declared that the perpetuity was not illegal With this objection then, removed by the Act of the Commonwealth, the heirs of Mr Girard, elected to receive their legacies under his will Their making their election to accept under it, after the Commonwealth had removed a supposed objection to its validity These Acts of Assembly were approved March 24, 1832, and April 4, 1832, and the heirs, as shown by their receipts, (p 129,) received their legacies July 5, 6, and 7, 1832, August 21, 1832, September 1, 1832, and January 4 nd 23, 1833

It is submitted that they could have not more fully consented to the establishment of the will, if they had executed a deed to the Trustee in the will, conveying all their interest in their ancestor's estate.

VII

The defendants (below) also put in evidence the record of the Supreme Court of the United States, between the same parties or their privies, to show an adjudication in their favor on this will for the premises in question inter alia.

This case is reported in 2 *Howard* 17. Judge Grier, says of it, it has put an end to any further controversy as to the *validity of the Trusts*, and the power of the City to execute them. Girard *v* The City, C C U S. (See record, p 311)

The maxim *expedit respublicæ ut sit finis litium*, is as old as the law itself, and a part of it. Marsh *v* Pier, 4 Rawle, 288, same case. Whenever, on the trial of a cause from the state of the pleadings in it, the record of a judgment rendered by a competent tribunal upon the merits in a former action for the same cause, between the same parties or those claiming under them, is properly given in evidence to the jury, it ought to be considered conclusively binding on both Court and jury, and to preclude all further inquiry in the cause.

Wilson *v* Hamilton, 9 S & R 428. Duncan, J, "to "permit a plaintiff to prosecute in a second action, what "was included in and might have been recovered in the "first action, would be unjust and against the policy of the "law, because it would harass a defendant and expose him "to double costs. This is the doctrine in Hesse *v* Heeble, "6 S & R. 57"

Man *v.* Drexel, 2 Barr, 205. The Court, citing the opinion of Lord Chief Justice De Gray, in the Duchess of Kingston's case, "that the judgment of a Court of concurrent jurisdiction, directly upon the point, is, as a plea, a bar, or, as evidence, conclusive between the same parties, upon the same matter directly in question in another Court,' say thus declaring that the proper deduction to be drawn from all the civil cases on the subject, was, that the judgment of a Court of concurrent jurisdiction between the same parties, upon the same point, deciding the same matter, was conclusive, as well when given in evidence without being pleaded as when pleaded."

In Pennsylvania, an action of ejectment upon an equitable title, is in substance a bill in equity, and a judgment on such title is a bar to further suits to recover the same lands, between the same parties. Peterman *v* Huling, 7 Casey, 432.

DAVID W SELLERS,
JAMES H. CAMPBELL,
EDWARD OLMSTED,
CHARLES E LEX,
F CARROLL BREWSTER,
WILLIAM M MEREDITH
Counsel for City of Philadelphia

Additional Argument

Additional argument upon the question of former recovery, being the plaintiffs' (in error) 5th point

1. The dismissal of a bill in equity is a final judgment, and pleadable as such   Saylor's Appeal, 3 Wright, 495

2. A decree of a Court of Equity is of as high a dignity and character as a judgment of a Court of Law, and may be given in evidence on the same footing   Owen v. Dawson, 1 Watts, 151, Montford v. Hunt, 3 W C C R 28

3. The judgment of a Court of concurrent jurisdiction directly upon the point, is a plea, a bar or as evidence, conclusive between the same parties upon the same matter directly in question in another Court   Kelsey v. Murphy, 2 Casey, 80

1. The parties to the bill and in this suit are the same

2. Is the subject matter the same?

The bill was brought to have the devise of the residue and remainder of the real estate, to the city of Philadelphia in trust, declared void for want of capacity of the devisees to take lands by devise—or if taking generally by devise for their own use and benefit, for want of capacity to take such lands as devisees in trust, and because the objects of the charity for which the lands were devised in trust were altogether vague, indefinite and uncertain, and so no trust was created by the will, which was capable of being executed or of being cognizable at law or in equity nor any trust estate devised, that could vest at law or in equity in any existing or possible *cestui que trust, and therefore, the bill insisted that as the trust was void there was a resulting thereof* for the testator's heirs at law, and the bill accordingly sought a declaration to that effect, and the relief consequent thereon, and for a discovery and account, and for other relief.

The above summary of the contents of the bill, with the description of the relief prayed for, is from Judge Story's opinion in the case of Vidal *v* The Mayor, &c, 2 Howard.

In the suit now before the Court the plaintiffs seek to recover part of the same residuary estate which was the subject of the bill.

The doctrine that a judgment in a Court of concurrent jurisdiction upon the point, is conclusive between the same parties in a subsequent suit upon the same subject, was also a rule of the Civil law, where it was called the plea of *exceptio rei judicata*.

Story Eq. Pleadings, p 798, No 5 ' Voet collects the "effect of many passages, scattered in different parts of the ' *Corpus Juris Civilis,* in the following extract, speaking "with express allusion to the *exceptio litis finitæ Non aliter* "*tamen huic exceptioni locus est, quam si lis terminata denuo* "*moveatur inter easdem personas, de eadem re, et ex eadem* "*petendi causâ Sic ut uno ex his tribus deficiente, cesset*"

In 7 Johnson Ch 1. Naefie *v* Naefie, The syllabus is, ' a bill regularly dismissed on its merits, may be pleaded in "bar of a new bill for the same matter, but to make a "a decree of dismissal of a bill on its merits a bar, it must "be an absolute decision upon the same *point or matter,* and "the new bill must be brought by the same plaintiff or his "represensatives against the same defendant or his repre- ' sentatives If the defendant in the original suit, having "since acquired a legal estate or legal advantage, files his ' bill against the former plaintiff, the cause is opened on its "merits."

In the case of Kelsey *v* Murphy, it is said the first judgment must be upon "*the point*" In Naefie *v* Naefie, upon "the same point or matter." In the Civil law, "the same course of action."

Now, the "point," the "matter," the "cause of action" in the bill was a claim that the devise to the city of the real estate, was void, and that the same passed to the testator's heirs. The point was, under the will, did the real estate pass to the devisee or were the heirs its owners? And as between the parties to the bill, the decision was that the city was entitled.

The *reasons* set up by the heirs to establish their claim, was not the *subject* of the controversy, and now their claim being put upon a reason that they did not allege in their bill, does not make a new cause of action.

Suppose there are two judgments in ejectment the same way and the losing party brings a third suit, will it be pretended that the point is not the same, because he seeks to recover for a reason which existed, but was not urged by him on the previous trials? If this can be done, there can be no settlement of controversy.

To permit a plaintiff, said Judge Duncan, in Wilson v. Hamilton, 9 S. & R., 429, to prosecute in a second action what was included in, and might have been recovered in the first, would be unjust, and against the policy of the law.

The cases in Pennsylvania, in which a judgment in a first suit were held not to bar a second suit, were cases in which the second suit as for instalments or claims, or parts of claims not embraced in the first suit. Wilson v. Hamilton, 9 S. & R., 424, Croft v. Steele, 4 Watts, 373, Steiner v. Gower, 3 W. & S., 136.

In these cases each instalment, or each distinct claim was capable of being the subject of a separate suit.

The two following cases show what is the distinction between suits wherein the title of the party is the "point," and those wherein the second suit relates to matters growing out of his title, but in which the first decision is not a bar.

Spark v. Walton, D. C.

Sharswood, P. J.—This was an ejectment. The plaintiff

had the legal title. The defendant claimed under a contract of sale with a former owner, and purchase money paid, with notice to plaintiff. The jury found for the defendant, under a reservation of two questions: 1. Whether the contract under which defendant claimed was sufficient within the statute of frauds. And 2. *Whether the defendant was bound by a decree of the Court of Common Pleas in equity, dismissing his bill for a specific performance.*

We do not consider it necessary to decide the first reserved question. It appears to have been that which was passed upon by the Court of Common Pleas. Such a defence as that set up by the defendant, is a purely equitable defence. It would not be listened to in a court of law. But in the mixed jurisdiction exercised by the courts in Pennsylvania, it was allowed, in order to obtain substantial justice before a court of chancery existed, or before chancery powers were directly conferred upon the courts. The general principle was adopted, that whatever a chancellor would decree to be done, should be considered as though it were actually done. Upon this only ground was it held that ejectment might be maintained upon an equitable title against the holder of the legal title in possession. If the vendee, under written articles, had paid the purchase money, and tendered a deed to be executed by the vendor, and if the case was such that a chancellor would have decreed a conveyance of the legal title, he could recover possession just as if such a deed had been executed. Hawn v Norris 4 Binn 77. Vincent v Huff, 4 S & R, 301. Our books are full to the same effect. In like manner the defendant in possession under an equitable, may defend against the holder of the legal title. If he shows a right to the legal title, it is the same as though it had actually been conveyed to him. This was the precise position in which the defendant had claimed to be. *But he had himself presented that question to a tribunal having jurisdiction, competent to give him the precise relief which he is now claiming here, though in a different form, and that tribunal has decided against him.* Had his bill been dismissed for want of prosecution, or for any other cause than a decision against him upon the merits, it would appear upon the decree. Even if the bill had been dismissed without prejudice to the legal rights of the parties, it may be doubted whether that would leave it open to them to assert in another mixed tribunal, whether by way of action or defence, a purely equitable case. Seitzinger v Ridgway, 9 Watts, 496, and Kelsey v Murphy, 2 Casey, 78, are authorities in following which, we think, we are bound to give judgment for the plaintiff upon the reserved point

Rule dismissed, verdict set aside, and judgment for plaintiff upon the reserved points. Legal Intelligencer Vol XVII, No 29, p 228

Kelsey v Murphy, 2 Casey, 28

The question was whether the plaintiffs' bill in the New York Chancery dismissed on final hearing and duly pleaded was a bar to the suit

The court said—The bill was between the same parties as the present action "Was it directly upon the same point? Was the present cause of action included, and might it have been recovered in that suit?"

The plaintiff, in his bill, described a sale of coal to West, and its fraudulent transfer to Kelsey, and charged that West obtained the delivery of the coal with the intention to defraud the plaintiff by getting possession of it, and refusing to pay for it; and that he and Kelsey, pretending a bona fide sale and purchase between themselves persisted in keeping the coal without paying for it, all of which was fraudulent and passed no title. The bill prayed a decree that the coal belonged to the plaintiff, and that his lien for the value might be established

The bill was dismissed upon its merits.

The plaintiff then brought his suit at law in case, in the nature of a writ of conspiracy. The decree in the chancery suit was pleaded in bar

The court decided the latter to be no bar, because the

suit at law was quite another cause of action from that set forth in the bill in equity. That the bill claimed that he had never parted with his title to the coal, while the suit at law alleged that he had sold and delivered the property, but through a fraudulent combination had been cheated out of the price

In this case the proceedings resulted from the same transactions, but the case presented in the suit was not the same cause of action as that disclosed in the bill

The contrast is to be found in the case of Sparks v Walton, where the plea of former recovery prevailed, because the cause of action was the same in both cases.

Among the Records and Proceedings in the Court of Common Pleas of Schuylkill (SEAL) County, of December Term, 1859, No. 582, it is thus contained:

JOHN AUGUSTUS GIRARD, JOHN FABRICIUS GIRARD, MARGARET P LARDY, LEWIS F DEVOUX and MARIE, his wife, in right of said MARIE, ALFRED DE LENTILHAC and ANNIE, his wife, in right of said ANNIE, MADALINE H GIRARD, PARMIELE DUVARS DUMAINE, FABRICIUS DUVARS DUMAINE, FRANÇOIS C VIDAL, JOHN F CLARK and HARRIET, his wife, in right of said HARRIET, MARIE A HEMPHILL, FRANKLIN PEALE and CAROLINE E, his wife, in right of said CAROLINE,

F W & J HUGHES 582. CAMPBELL

vs.

THE CITY OF PHILADELPHIA

Served a true and attested copy of this writ personally on F B 'Kaercher, ag't for the City of Philadelphia, Dec'r 1, 1859

Summons in Ejectment, issued 29th Nov'r, 1859

21 April. The Court direct, on motion of plaintiffs' attorney, that the warrantee name of John Howell, in the præcipe count, be changed to Joseph Howell, and that the name of John Augustus Girard be amended and changed by striking out John (Amendment filed)

D W. S—14

14 August, 1860 Defendants plead not guilty.

22 November, 1860. Affidavit filed

22 November, 1860 On motion of Mr Bannan and affidavit filed Rule on plaintiffs counsel to show cause why the names of Alfred De Lentilhac and Annie Stephanie, his wife, and Miss M H Girard, Mrs M P Lardy, and P Dumaine and F Dumaine heirs of Stephen Girard, should not be stricken from the above action of ejectment, returnable on the first day of next term.

8 February 1861—continued 11 March, 1861—continued, on payment of costs by defendant 6 August, 1861—continued 10 December, 1861—rule discharged 22 March, 1862—Court direct this case to be placed at the head of Trial List for third week of April next, and now, April 21st, 1862, a jury being called, the following persons came: Charles Maurer, Josiah Stees, Michael J Thomas, Adam Cressman, Solomon Shellhammer, Daniel G Herb Abraham Baughner, Plankinton W Harvey Philip Steinbach, William Biddle, Philip M Barrow and Isaac Harvey, twelve free honest and lawful men, who, after having been first duly ballotted challenged, sworn, and, 25 April, 1862, charged, do say that they find for the plaintiffs.

Entered in judgment doc 13, 1842

25 April, 1862 Before verdict, defendant's counsel except to so much of the charge of the Court as answers the fourth point of plaintiff in the affirmative, and to so much of the charge as refuses to answer the second, fifth and sixth points of defendants in the affirmative, and to so much thereof as declares that the testator devised a trust for an indefinite accumulation of income into capital, and to so much as declares that there is a direction in the will that the rents of the real estate shall be applied to the repair and

improvement of testator's real estate, and that the same is a trust for an indefinite accumulation of capital in the shape of buildings, and renders the will void as intending to create a perpetuity, and that, on the whole evidence of the case, the plaintiffs are entitled to recover. Defendants' counsel ask the Court to file their charge and answers to the points made, in writing, and to file their notes of testimony with the record in the cause.

25 April, 1862. Defendants' exceptions, plaintiffs' and defendants' points and offers filed with præcipe.

25 April, 1862. Notes of evidence and charge of the Court filed.

30 April, 1862. Writ of error filed.

Judgment Docket Entry.

AUGUSTUS GIRARD, JOHN FABRICIUS GIRARD, MARGARET P. LARDY, LEWIS F. DEVOUX and MARIE, his wife, in right of said MARIE, ALFRED DE LENTILHAC and ANNIE, his wife, in right of said ANNIE, MADALINE H. GIRARD, PARMIELE DUVARS DUMAINE, FABRICIUS DUVARS DUMAINE, FRANCOIS C. VIDAL, JOHN F. CLARK and HARRIET, his wife, in right of said HARRIET, MARIA A. HEMPHILL, FRANKLIN PEALE and CAROLINE E., his wife, in right of said CAROLINE, 1842. *vs* THE CITY OF PHILADELPHIA	From December Term, 1859. 582 25 April, 1862 — Judgment sur verdict in favor of the plaintiffs

SCHUYLKILL COUNTY, *ss*

    I, Charles Frailey, Prothonotary of the Court [L S] of Common Pleas of Schuylkill County, do hereby certify that the foregoing writing is a true and perfect copy of the Appearance and Judgment Docket Entry of the case therein stated, wherein Augustus Girard *et al* are plaintiffs, and the City of Philadelphia defendant, of December Term, 1859, No. 582.

In testimony whereof, I have hereunto set my hand and affixed the seal of said Court, at Pottsville, this twenty-seventh day of May, A. D. 1862.

        CHAS. FRAILEY, *Proth'y*,
            Pro S. B. SHOENER

JOHN AUGUSTUS GIRARD, JOHN FABRICIUS GIRARD, MARGARET P LORDY, LEWIS F DEVOUX and MARIE, his wife, in right of said MARIE, ALFRED DE LENTILHAC and ANNE C, his wife, in right of said ANNE, MADALINE H GIRARD, PARMIELE DUVARS DUMAINE, FABRICIUS DUVARS DUMAINE, FRANCOISE C VIDAL, JOHN F CLARK and HARRIET, his wife, in right of said HARRIET, MARIE A HEMPHILL, FRANKLIN PEALE and CAROLINE E, his wife, in right of said CAROLINE,

vs

THE CITY OF PHILADELPHIA,

} Ejectment

Issue Summons in Ejectment against the above defendant for all that certain tract and body of lands situate in the townships of Butler and Mahanoy, in the county of Schuylkill, and surveyed under warrants respectively in the several names of Daniel Reese, Samuel Reese, James Chapman, Thomas Grant, Samuel Scott, William P Brady, John Brady, Edward Lynch, Thomas Paschall, Joseph Paschall, John Howell, John Blackey, Nathan Beach, Israel Cope, James McNeal, Jeremiah Jackson, Josiah Haines, William Steadman, John Lockhart and Nathan Brown containing in all about eight thousand five hundred acres,—the title as right of possession to which the said demandants say is in them, and not in the said defendant, returnable the day next preceding the last day of December Term, 1859

F. W & J HUGHES,
Pro Plaintiffs

DANL. H SHOENER, *Proth'y*

SCHUYLKILL COUNTY, ss.

[L S] The Commonwealth of Pennsylvania, to the Sheriff of Schuylkill county greeting You are hereby commanded, that you summon the City of Philadelphia to appear before the Judges of the Court of

Common Pleas, in and for said county, to be holden at Pottsville, on the day next preceding the last day of December Term next, then and there to answer to a certain complaint, made by John Augustus Girard, John Fabricius Girard, Margaret P. Lardy, Lewis F. Devoux and Marie, his wife, in right of said Marie, Alfred de Lentilhac and Annie, his wife, in right of said Annie, Madaline H. Girard, Parmele Duvars Dumaine, Fabricius Duvars Dumaine, Francoise C. Vidal, John F. Clark and Harriet, his wife, in right of said Harriet, Marie A. Hemphill, Franklin Peale and Caroline E., his wife, in right of said Caroline, that it, the said The City of Philadelphia now has in its actual possession all that certain tract and body of lands situate in the townships of Butler and Mahanoy, in the county of Schuylkill, and surveyed under warrants respectively in the several names of Daniel Reese, Samuel Reese, James Chapman, Thomas Grant, Samuel Scott, William P. Brady, John Brady, Edward Lynch, Thomas Paschall, Joseph Paschall, John Howell, John Blackey, Nathan Beach, Israel Cope, James McNeal, Jeremiah Jackson, Josiah Haines, William Steadman, John Lockhart, and Nathan Brown, containing in all about eight thousand five hundred acres,—the right of possession or title to which they, the said plaintiffs, say is in them, and not in the said The City of Philadelphia, all which they, the said plaintiffs, aver they are prepared to prove before our said Court. Hereof fail not. Witness the Honorable Charles W. Hegins, Esq., President of our said Court at Pottsville, the twenty-ninth day of November, A. D. one thousand eight hundred and fifty-nine.

DANL. H. SHOENER, *Prothonotary.*

[Endorsed 582. Dec. T. 1859. John Augustus Girard, John Fabricius Girard, Margaret P. Lardy, Lewis F. Devoux, *et al*, *vs* The City of Philadelphia. F. W. & J. Hughes. Summons in Ejectment. Served a true and attested copy of this writ personally on Franklin B. Kaercher, agent for the City of Philadelphia, Dec. 1st, 1859. So answers JOHN P. HOBART, *Sheriff*. Sheriff's fee, $112.]

JOHN A. GIRARD, et al., vs. THE CITY OF PHILADELPHIA	In the Common Pleas of Schuylkill County, of Dec Term, 1859 582. Ejectment

Affidavit of Alfred De Lentilhac

SCHUYLKILL COUNTY, ss

ALFRED DE LENTILHAC maketh oath and saith That he is married to Anne Stephanie Girard, one of the heirs of the estate of the late Stephen Girard That he has a regularly executed power of attorney to act for Miss M H Girard, Mrs M P Lardy, and P D Dumaine and F Dumaine, in all matters connected with any interest they may have in real or other estate in America, and is now in the State of Pennsylvania, attending to their business under the power aforesaid, and which has not been revoked by the above named persons The said parties above named are residents of France, and their interests have been committed by them to this deponent, and to no other persons, with the consent of this deponent or of the aforesaid constituents, within his knowledge and belief That the said deponent is now, as well for the benefit of his wife, above named, as for and in behalf of these other constituents, prosecuting a bill in equity against the City of Philadelphia, to recover from the City a certain part of the estate of the late Stephen Girard, and objections are being made to the said above-mentioned action of ejectment in their names, and this deponent saith that the institution of the above action of ejectment was not authorized by him, either in the name of his said wife, himself, or in the names of his constituents above named, but, so far as this deponent knows and believes it was at the instance of parties having no authority to act for them or either of the persons above named, and that the pendency of the said action of ejectment at this time is calculated to prejudice and affect their cause, pending by the said bill in equity.

A. DE LENTILHAC.

Sworn and subscribed before me, this
22d day of November, A D 1860
JACOB REED, J P
[Filed, 22 November, 1860]

HEIRS OF GIRARD
vs
THE CITY OF PHILADELPHIA. } 582 Dec. T 1859.

April 21st, 1862 The Court direct, on motion of plaintiffs' attorney, that the warrantee name of John Howell, in the præcipe and writ, be changed to Joseph Howell, and that the name of John Augustus Giraid be amended and changed by striking out John

[Endorsed Amendment to præc and writ Filed, 21 April, 1862]

GIRARD HEIRS
vs
THE CITY OF PHILADELPHIA. } 582. December T, 1859

Before verdict, the defendants except to so much of the charge of the Court as answers the fourth point of the plaintiffs in the affirmative.

And to so much of the charge as refuses to answer the second, fifth and sixth points of the defendants in the affirmative

And to so much thereof as declares that the testator devised a trust for an indefinite accumulation of income into capital

And to so much as declares that there is a direction in the will that the rents of the real estate shall be applied to the repair and improvement of the testator's real estate and that the same is a trust for an indefinite accumulation of capital in the shape of buildings, and renders the will void as intending to create a perpetuity, and that, on the whole evidence of the case, the plaintiffs are entitled to recover.

Defendants' counsel ask the Court to file their charge and answers to the points made, in writing, and to file their notes of testimony with the record in the cause.

      EDW. OLMSTED,
      CHAS. E. LEX,
      W. H. CAMPBELL,
         For Defendants.

April 25, 1862.

Additional point presented, April 24, 1862, on behalf of defendants.—That the acceptance of the legacies by the parties and privies under the will of Stephen Girard, and the ratification of said will by the acts of the General Assembly of March 24, and April 4, 1832, which are in evidence in this cause, prevents a recovery by the plaintiffs, and the verdict should be for defendants.

HEIRS OF GIRARD
vs
THE CITY OF PHILADELPHIA

The Court is respectfully requested by the plaintiffs to charge the jury upon the following points, viz.:

1. That the devise of the real estate in Pennsylvania in trust that no part thereof shall ever be sold or alienated, is a transgressive trust, and void, and therefore no title or estate in the lands passed to the City of Philadelphia under the will, but by operation of law the title to the real estate vested in the heirs of the testator upon his decease.

D. W. S.—15

2. That the devise of the lands described in the writ in trust that no part thereof shall ever be alienated, but the same shall forever thereafter be let from time to time to good tenants at yearly or other rents and upon leases in possession not exceeding five years from the commencement thereof, in connection with the provisions of the will directing the application of the income of the real estate and of the other trust funds, is transgressive and void, and that the title of the lands vested in the heirs of the testator at his death.

3. If the jury believe that the lands described in the writ are coal lands, and that by the terms and restrictions of the will the development and use thereof are so shackled and fettered that they cannot be used and enjoyed as such, the devise thereof is void, and the estate vested in the heirs of the testator at his death.

4. That the devise in trust to apply the rents of the real estate in Pennsylvania first to the erection of new buildings upon so much thereof as is situate in the City and Liberties of Philadelphia, from time to time as the same may be necessary, has no limitation as to time when such piling up of capital by the accumulation as aforesaid is to cease, but the same may continue beyond the period fixed for the vesting of an executory limitation, and is therefore void

5. That the devise in trust to invest the net residue of the rents of the real estate in the same manner as the residue of the remainder of the personal estate, and to apply the income only as directed by the will, is a transgressive trust, being a trust for accumulation beyond the period allowed by law ; rendering the devise of the lands to the City of Philadelphia void, so that no title passed to the City under the will, but by operation of law the title to the lands vested in the heirs of the testator upon his decease.

6. The devise of the real and personal estate is upon a trust which contemplates perpetual accumulation from the income thereof, and is therefore void.

Defendants request the Court to charge:

1st. That the trust of the residuary estate created by the will of Stephen Girard is not void as creating a perpetuity.

2d. That the trust of the residuary estate created by the will of Stephen Girard is not a trust for accumulation.

3d. That the direction in restraint of alienation attendant on the devise to the City, if void, does not affect the validity of the devise itself.

4th. That if the restraint on alienation should be void, the devise will be sustained for the charity, unclogged by the condition.

5th. That the plaintiffs cannot recover, and the verdict should be for defendants.

HEIRS OF GIRARD
vs
PHILADELPHIA
} Offer No. 1

Plaintiffs propose to prove, by Peter W. Shafer, that he is a professional and practical surveyor and geologist; that he has, under the direction and at the request of the Committee of the Girard Trust, appointed by the City Councils, made a survey and map of all the lands in Schuylkill and Columbia counties, including the lands described in the writ, claimed by said City under the will of Stephen Girard; and to show the character and extent of such lands,—that the principal part thereof, including the lands in suit, are coal lands, unimproved and undeveloped, that the greater part thereof are unfit for agricultural purposes, and that, after the coal is mined therefrom and the timber cut off, such lands will be valueless, or nearly so. And to be followed by the testimony of three witnesses skilled in the business of mining coal, that if used, as directed by the will, only by tenants upon leases for not exceeding five years, without any allowance for improvements and repairs usual and necessary for mining purposes that such lands will not be developed or improved, and that the lands are, by the said directions of the will, practically taken out of use and enjoyment for any of the purposes for which they are adapted, and for which the necessities of civilized life demand they should be used.

The defendants object, because the evidence offered is irrelevant.

That it is only the opinion of the witness, and to be followed by the opinions of other witnesses.

And because the offer assumes that the defendants are not authorized to allow for or to furnish means for improvements.

The Court overrule the objections and admit the evidence.

Defendants' counsel except, and the Court thereupon seal this bill.

C. W. HEGINS, *P. J.*

[Endorsed 582 Dec r T 1859 Augustus Girard *et al* vs Philadelphia City Defendants' exceptions, plaintiffs' and defendants' points and offers filed. Filed 25 April, 1862]

HUGHES
FOSTER
HIRST
PARRY

AUGUSTUS GIRARD, FABRICIUS GIRARD, MARGARET P. LARDY, LEWIS F DEVOUX and MARIE, his wife, in right of said Marie ALFRED DE LENTILHAC and ANNIE C, his wife, in right of said Annie, MADALINE H. GIRARD, PARMIELE DUVARS DUMAINE, FABRICIUS DUVARS DUMAINE, FRANÇOIS C VIDAL, JOHN F CLARK and HARRIET, his wife, in right of said Harriet, MARIE H. HEMPHILL, FRANKLIN PEALE and CAROLINE E, his wife, in right of said Caroline,

CAMPBELL
MEREDITH
LEX
OLMSTED
SELLERS

vs.

THE CITY OF PHILADELPHIA.

Dec T
1859.

No 582

Mr HUGHES opens for plaintiffs.

Nov 29, 1859 Writ of ejectment for a body of land in Butler and Mahanoy townships, Schuylkill county surveyed under warrants to Daniel Reese, Samuel Reese, James Chapman, Thomas Grant, Samuel Scott, William P Brady, John Brady, Edward Lynch, Thomas Paschall, Joseph Paschall, John Howell, John Blackey, Nathan Beach, Israel Cope, James McNeal, Jeremiah Jackson, Josiah Haines, William Steadman, John Lockhart, and Nathan Brown, containing in all about 8,500 acres

It is admitted that the title to the lands in question was vested in Stephen Girard at the time of the date of his will, and at the time of his death

It is also admitted that the plaintiffs are the heirs of Stephen Girard

Agreement, signed by Mr Olmsted and plaintiffs counsel, read in evidence (Vide agreement, page   )

Mr. OLMSTED opens for defendants·

Will of Stephen Girard, 16 Feb'y, 1830

First codicil, dated 24 Dec., 1830

Second codicil, dated 20 June, 1831

Probate of will, dated 31 Dec, 1831

Defendants offer certified record of suit in U. S. Circuit Court of Pennsylvania, and Supreme Court of United States, of suit between the plaintiffs, or their ancestors, and the defendants

The plaintiffs object to the admission of the evidence

The Court admits the evidence, and the Court notes an exception

Mr HUGHES opens for the rebutting evidence

Quotes Randall on Perpetuities, page 48.
    " Sanders on Uses and Trusts, page 196.
    " Ferne on Contingent Remainders, page 35
    " Hillyard *v* Miller, 10 Barr, 326.

Tuesday, April 22, 1862

Mr PARRY makes a further opening for the plaintiffs Written opening·

PETER W SHAEFFER, *affirmed*—I am a surveyor and geologist. I have practised as such since 1837. I have made a survey for the Girard Trust for their lands in Schuylkill and Columbia counties—about 20,000 acres. They are all connected; the land is generally mountainous; it is not generally adapted to agricultural purposes; a portion of the land is coal land—about one-third of the 20,000 acres. The land for which suit is brought is all embraced in the city lands; can't tell what proportion is coal land. The two Bradys' are partly coal land. The tracts of land embraced in suit were, two years ago, undeveloped and unimproved, but they were occupied by saw mills and buildings. The Daniel Reese tract had improvements on it.

GIDEON BAST (subject to the exception already taken) *sworn.*—Am a coal operator and coal land owner; have been an operator, engaged in mining coal, since 1830; am partly engaged in mining coal in Mahanoy coal region, on the Locust mountain, for six or seven years; the Girard lands adjoin the Locust mountain on the east; the veins run northeast and southwest; our leases generally run for ten years, with privilege of having them extended for five years longer; our lease with the Locust Mountain Company is for ten years, with privilege for ten years longer. We pay twenty five cents now, although when we leased we paid about twenty cents; the usual rate is twenty five cents there. For my part, I would not take a lease for five years, unless with privilege of renewing, because it always takes from one to two years to begin rightly in operation. I would not take a lease for five years, where I had to build the improvements, make the repairs, put up the houses, and work the mines in a miner-like manner, because the expenses of improvements are greater than most persons think, and the profits on the business for the last few years are too small—and then to surrender at the end of five years.

Cross-examined.—The Mine Hill railroad was made over into the Mahanoy region for five or six years; it does not reach the Girard lands. The Broad Mountain and Mahanoy and the East Mahanoy railroads are now building, which will make the lands accessible. If there had been tenants on the Girard lands then the Mine Hill railroad would have made branches. I am working on the Locust Mountain lands, below water level; some of the Girard lands might be worked above water level. I would not take a lease, above water level, on the Girard lands, for five years. I pay twenty five cents, with heavy improvements.

GEORGE W. SNYDER, *sworn.*—I have been engaged in the mining of coal about twenty years; have been operating in the Mammoth vein, in the Schuylkill basin; I have been in the Mahanoy coal field; I pay thirty-one cents at one of my places and twenty-five cents at another. I have not been in the habit of working lands under so short a term as five years; there might be cases where it could be worked for that time, where the vein was opened and known, and the locality favorable. I should hesitate about taking a lease for five years, where I had to make the improvements, build the houses and run the risks. If the vein had been known and opened, and above water level, I might take a lease for five years at a moderate rent. It generally takes a year or two to open a vein, put up the improvements; we have had no experience in so short a term; our leases are for ten, fifteen or twenty years. I think I could not take a lease for five years rent free, where I had to make the improvements, build the houses, make the lateral railroads, in a body of land of 20,000 acres.

Cross examined.—I have been on the Girard lands; they embrace some valuable veins of coal, some above water level; I think the rent would be worth one third more above water level than below; where I would be allowed to retain the cost of improvements out of the rent, there it would be more favorable; I might be induced to take a lease on such terms. In the past, leases were made for shorter terms than now; when I first came they were generally made for ten years, and now they are generally for fifteen or twenty years. I am mining coal now; I mined last year 130,000 tons of coal; my mines are on the Lee lands; there are veins on the Girard veins equally as good as mine, I have no doubt; I pay thirty-one cents. The perpendicular depth below water is about 160 feet, the slope about 1100 feet. I am working on the third lift, have three sixty-horse engines. The charge for transporting coal from Mahanoy is $1\frac{1}{2}$ cents per ton per mile; used to be $2\frac{1}{2}$ cents; I pay between fourteen and fifteen cents to Schuylkill Haven.

Examined in chief.—At Ashland, Mr. Bast, Mr. Bancroft, Mr. Potts, Mr. Reppher, each mined more than 40,000 tons from above water level in one year. I came here in 1833. When I came here they then began to put up machinery; before, they hauled it away in carts.

Cross-examined.—I think you would have to pay $8,000 or $10,000 for a breaker and improvements appertaining thereto (for an above water level), for miners houses, if there were none, you would have to lay out $5,000 or $6,000 more, and you would want $2,000 or $3,000 more to open the veins and make the water courses. It has been the habit for the lessee to make most of the improvements heretofore.

Examined in chief.—If the lease terminated at the end of the shipping season then you would have to leave the gangway, the breasts which were finished. In an extensive working, the tenant would have to leave several thousand dollars of expense, which would only be available to the next tenant. On a lease for five years, you could not take out 40,000 tons yearly; for one year you might do it but I question if it could be done yearly. If you had but a single gangway, going in one direction, with the work for operating to do, you would do well to take out 10,000 tons yearly. Above water level, the gangway goes only in one direction generally, because the drift opening is generally in a ravine. In five years, the gangway would not pass more than 10,000 tons yearly. If you would drive a tunnel the expense would be increased and the work delayed; the rock tunnel would cost from $25 to $50 per ton; one hundred yards rock tunnel would take twelve to fourteen months to drive.

CHARLES BAKER, *sworn.*—Came to Schuylkill county in 1830; have been engaged in coal mining; have put up improvements at collieries; am acquainted with the Girard lands. I would not like to put up improvements for the sake of a five years' lease, if I had to compete for a renewal with the highest bidder, after its termination, I would not have it.

D. W. S.—16

Enoch W. McGinnes, *sworn*—Have lived in Schuylkill county upwards of thirty years, have been mining coal sixteen or seventeen years, am acquainted with the Girard lands. I would not like to take a lease for five years, and put up the improvements, if at the end I were either compelled to take away the improvements, or be a competitor with others for a new term. It would cost about $8,000 to put up a breaker of 40,000 tons yearly capacity, including engine. It would cost about two dollars a yard to drive gangway and put down rails. It would cost about $20,000 to put up and prepare a colliery above water level, it would cost more below water level. It would cost about $35,000 for an operation for above and below water level. I have not included houses. It would cost $10,000 to build houses. I put up improvements on another tract, Bailow & Evans', to do about the same business, and they cost $47,000; it would cost about the same on the Girard lands. It is very doubtful whether the money could be got out of the operation on five years' lease to pay the improvements, unless we came across an 1854.

Cross-examined—I have had a number of leases, have had them for ten years and as high as twenty years, had one transferred which had seven years to run. Mammoth Vein is on the Girard lands. Perhaps an operation, economically constructed, could be put up, and, on a five years' lease, they might make some money. I should think there was a great deal of coal in these lands above the water level, ravines cut the veins and it would be easy to drive a drift. I think that, as a general thing, the veins are regular.

Examined in chief—We need not build houses at such a place as Pottsville or St. Clair, but if there are none, somebody must build them.

Charles Baker, *recalled by defendant*—I think money could be made on a lease for five years, on the Girard lands, at a moderate rent; a moderate rent would be ten or fifteen cents. I suppose the improvements would cost about $10,000, and do a business of about 40,000 tons. The improvements would be cheap, and would not be worth much at the end of the five years; the mines might be left in good condition: the man who came in after me could probably not pay as much rent.

PETER W. SHAEFFER, *recalled by plaintiffs.*—About one-third of the 20,000 acres is good workable coal land. The Daniel and Samuel Reese are about two-thirds in the coal measures; the James Chapman is all in the coal measures; the Thos. Grant is two thirds, Saml. Scott, all coal, Wm. P. and John Brady are good coal tracts two thirds of the Wm. P., and all the John Brady; the Edward Lynch is within the coal measures, Thos. Paschall is one-half coal, Jas. Paschall is all coal, Jos. Howell is mostly coal, John Blackey is one half coal, Nathan Beach, all coal, Israel Cope, partly coal, James McNeal is partly coal, Jeremiah Jackson, partly coal, Josiah Haines is little or no coal, Wm. Stedman is partly coal, John Lockhart is outside the coal measures, Nathan Brown is a little coal perhaps, doubtful. All the tracts within the Girard lands. The improvements I spoke of are on the Saml. Reese; it is a saw mill, there is a saw mill on the James Chapman, there are some houses on the Wm. P. Brady or on the Flower tracts, no other improvements. As a geologist, I should say that between one-third and one fourth of this coal is above the water level.

Cross examined.—The coal above water level can be mined at much less expense than below. The Mine Hill railroad was finished in 1854, it came within about two miles of these lands, they have been making four railroads within the last year in the Mahanoy coal region; the toll was before $2\frac{1}{4}$ cents per ton per mile, now it is $1\frac{1}{2}$ cents per ton, the distance by Ashland was 29 miles to Schuylkill Haven, the coal here can be mined with facility, the hills being cut with ravines, the veins are generally regular, the coal can be mined as cheaply as anywhere in the region. At Bear Ridge the breast is about 150 yards high; fine breasts also on the Skidmore and Primrose veins. The transverse cuts or ravines exist all through the coal region. The competition among the railroads, I suppose, is the reason of the reduction of tolls.

(Draft offered in evidence, and admitted.)

FRANCIS MCCORMICK, *sworn*.—I am the Superintendent of the Girard Estate, have been so about two months; I have the books concerning the Girard Estate; I have no statement of the amount of the cost of the Girard College; the books are in one of the offices in the Court House.

Statement presented in a former suit against the city by some of the heirs of Girard—parts on page 26—read in evidence.

City holds property in Philadelphia and other places, page 26.

In city of Philadelphia, 152 dwelling-houses and stores, Girard College and grounds, &c.

Reads also on page 28 to 39 inclusive, to end of figure column.

Page 39. total amount expended in building Girard College, $1,935,737 46.

Also, page 40-41, also on page 42, so far as the statement of the cost of improvement of the square is concerned.

The whole of pages 42, 43, 44, 45, 46, foot of page 48.

FRANCIS MCCORMICK *continued*.—Have no knowledge of the farm in Moyamensing and Passyunk. I am not aware that it has been ordered to be laid out in streets.

Certified copy of record in case of Vidal *vs* Girard admitted in evidence.

Henry W. Arey, *sworn.*—I am secretary of Girard College. In some streets up to the College they are curbed and paved; in Ridge Avenue it is curbed and paved; some property improved beyond the College; sparse buildings to the north of the College; city is improving in that direction; College lot extends from Eighteenth street to about Twenty-second; the passenger railways, Girard, extend beyond the buildings. Am somewhat acquainted with the farms in Moyamensing; northern part of the district is built up about as far down as the Moyamensing prison; the main body of Girard lands in the Neck, about three miles from Moyamensing prison; main portion between Schuylkill river and Broad street; partly grazing land, truck; partly subject to overflow; can't tell how much is subject to overflow; the body of land in the Neck lies principally together; the part of the farm rented to a man named Bastion is subject to overflow; it is the largest of the farms; about 150 acres in the farm; I have heard the tenant say that it was subject to overflow; the same tenant has been on that property for upwards of twenty years, I think; the progress of the city southward has been comparatively small recently; the progress is principally northward; the distance from Front and Chestnut to Moyamensing prison has been principally built up within the last century and a quarter; the depot of the Pennsylvania Railroad is on the Delaware front of Washington avenue; these lands are southwest, on the Schuylkill. It would seem likely that, within the next twenty-five years, the property in the neighborhood of the Girard College will be pretty much built and improved.

McCormick, *recalled.*—A tax is laid for preserving the bank, to prevent the land from being overflowed. My impression is that the tax is one dollar per acre.

Journals of the House of Representatives from 1832 down, containing the statement of the Girard Fund, in evidence.

Mr Campbell makes a further opening for the defence.

Burd Patterson, *sworn*—I am acquainted with that part of the Girard land which is coal land; have known them thirty three or thirty four years; owned a small portion at one time. have been engaged in buying and selling coal land in this county. There are plenty of good people who want leases on the Girard land, and are ready now to take them; they are ready to take them on the same terms as the lease of the city to James J. Connor. I think that plenty of tenants could be got to make all the improvements, on a five years lease, at fifteen cents per ton, and half of that for nut coal, not to build houses; think it would be a favorable lease; this would be only for above water level; the lands are favorably located; it is the nearest coal to Port Carbon in that valley; the veins are proven to be good, and it makes a favorable operation for any one to go there. I should say it would take $10,000 to build houses sufficient for a colliery in the Mahanoy valley; I do not include the cost of the houses in my estimate of the amount of rent. The city allowing $20,000 for improvements, as she now is doing, plenty of responsible persons could be found to take leases at twenty five cents per ton. If the tenant built the houses and improvements, then the rent might be twelve and a half cents per ton. My estimate is for 50,000 tons of coal, but the first year not much could be done. I think an operator could mine 50,000 tons yearly, four years out of the five. Connor & Patterson did it at Ashland, out of one drift, and Connor has four veins on which he can drive drifts, and he has only 300 yards from the first vein to the last, being the length of the drift roads outside from the first vein to the last. Connor's lease is for five years from the date of his lease. There is a perfect rush to get leases on the Girard land. Can't tell whether the Mahanoy operators made anything within the last three or four years, or not.

Cross examined—No money has ever been lost on these lands, because they have not been worked. I have heard that Mr Foulke has laid out a town near Girardville.

PETER W. SHAEFFER, *recalled*—I know that leases have been made on the terms stipulated by the city. I think that an operator could take a lease for five years, make the improvements, build the houses, at ten to fifteen cents rent; they could do a business of fifty thousand tons. The mines are not expensive to open; the run is for one or two miles, and the breast is one hundred yards and over.

Cross examined.—Have never mined any coal myself; have superintended mining. The coal operator ought to make twenty five cents a ton on such a lease. Graeff & Nutting made enough before the five years to pay for their improvements; no other case occurs to me now. I do not know of any one in the Mahanoy region who has made any money within the last four or five years; think Bast has. $20,000 will cover all the cost of the improvements. I am not accounting for any serious faults or accidents in my estimate. In the large vein there are very few faults; my estimate is not much for faults.

15th March, 1862. Lease, from the City of Philadelphia to James J. Connor, for five years, at twenty-five cents per ton, and ten cents for pea coal.

CORNELIUS TYSON, *sworn.*—I have been engaged in mining coal for the last five years in Llewellyn, but have been shafting in the Bear Ridge, Girard lands, for the Mammoth Vein; have come to nineteen feet of coal without finding bottom; would be willing to take a lease, the same as Connor's.

Cross-examined.—My experience has been in Llewellyn. I depend much on my partner, Mr. Kendrick, who is a practical miner. My application is for a lease above water level.

CHARLES M. HILL, *sworn.*—The difference in the rent for above and below water level should be ten to fifteen cents. Know the Girard lands. I would be willing to take a lease on the city lands on the same terms as Mr. Connor's.

Cross-examined.—What I say refers to a lease above water level. I think most of the coal on the Girard lands was above water level, more than one-third or one-fourth. I represent Mr. Dundas in this county; not his land in Mahanoy Valley; do not represent any land in that valley.

Examined in chief.—I should think there were 100 or 150 coal operators in this county.

Mr. McCormick, *recalled.*—We have applications from Messrs. Tyson & Kendrick and from J. W. Donaldson, which have been agreed to. we have also applications from A. W. Juvenal, T. W. Yardley, and Roland Jones. Juvenal resides in the city, and is a man of respectability. They propose to take on the same terms as Connor's.

James J. Connor, *sworn.*—Engaged in mining for twenty-five years; since '53, in Mahanoy basin, on Mammoth Vein. Have taken lease for five years on Girard lands, on Mammoth Vein.

A. W. Juvenal, *sworn.*—About one fifth of farms in Moyamensing.

Plaintiffs refer to page 8 of Answer in C C U S

Hughes for plaintiffs.

3 Watts, 440, Cassel *v* Spade
Lewis on Perpetuities, 1-46, 129-139, 164, 172, 478, 481
4 Kent, 264
3 Law Lib, 48, Cornish on Uses
Vernon Ch R 152
Lawyer on Trust, 24 L Lib 67
1 Jarmyn on Wills, 229
7 Harris, 41, Cond *v* Alien, held void
No prohibition in devise to charity is good
The prohibition is of the subject of the trust

If trust void by reason of restraint on alienation, the estate vests in heirs. 2 Story Eq., sec. 1183.

1 Jarmain, 182 (10 Law Lib., p. 82.)
3 Law Lib. 274
5 Paige, 172, Lorrillard v. Da Costa.
Disposition of charities by Chancellor.
  37 Law Lib., 407
  55 " " 632, Crabb on Real Prop.
  2 Prince Wm. 59
Doctrine of Cy Pres, or approximation
  Lewis on Perpet., 426-7-8, &c.
  1 Jarmain. 217
  17 S. & R. 93. Witman v. Lex.
  1 Watts, 226

W. L. HIRST, for plaintiffs.
1 Vernon, 161
10 Barr, 398 Hillyard v. Miller
16 Wendall, 60, Holly v. ———.

OLMSTED, for defendants.
10 Barr, 23, 11 Casey, 316, 1 Penna. 49, 1 Parsons, 436, 2 Bevan, 313
15 Howard, 564, McDonough v. Murdock
24 " 465, Canine v. Casey.
35 E. L. & Eq. 241, Hoch v. Gloucester

MEREDITH, for defendants.
1 Rawle, 163, 1 Wh. 699. Act 1853, Purdon, 649

FOSTER, for plaintiffs.
Statute of Elizabeth—Charitable Uses
6 Vesey, 404, 9 Vesey, 525. 6 Harris, 99

D W S—17

Charge

The Court affirm the plaintiffs' fourth point, and instruct the jury that, upon the evidence, the plaintiffs are entitled to recover the land demanded in the writ.

This instruction renders it unnecessary to answer the other points put by plaintiffs' counsel, or the points of the defendants' counsel.

Before verdict the defendants' counsel except to the charge of the Court, &c., the evidence to be made part of the record.

C. W. HEGINS, *P. J.*

[Endorsed: Notes of Evidence and Charge of Court Filed 25 April, 1862.]

The Commonwealth of Pennsylvania, to the Justices of the Court of Common Pleas for the County [L. s.] of Schuylkill greeting: Because in the record and process, and in rendering the judgment in a certain plaint, which was in our said Court, before the Judges of the same Court, by our writ between The City of Philadelphia, plaintiffs in error, and John A. Girard, John F. Girard, Margaret P. Lardy, Louis F. Deroux and Marie, his wife, in right of the said Marie, Alfred de Lentilhac and Annie C. his wife, in right of said Annie, Madeleine H. Girard, Parmele D. Dumaine, Fabricius Duvars Dumaine, Francoise C. Vidal, John S. Clark and Harriet, his wife, in right of the said Harriet, Marie Hemphill, Franklin Peale and Caroline E., his wife, in right of said Caroline, defendants in error, as it is said manifest error hath intervened, to the great damage of the said plaintiffs in error, as by the complaint of the same plaintiffs in error we have received information. We, willing that if any error be therein, it should be corrected, and that speedy justice be done to the parties in this part, *Do Command You*, that, if judgment as it is said, be rendered in the said plea, then the record and process and all things touching the same, under your seals, distinctly and openly you have before the Justices of our Supreme Court of Pennsylvania at a Supreme Court to be held at Philadelphia in and for the Eastern District of said Commonwealth, on the last Monday of July next, and this writ, that the record and process aforesaid being inspected, we may further cause to be done what of right and according to our laws and customs ought

WITNESS the Honorable WALTER H. LOWRIE, Chief Justice of our said Supreme Court at Philadelphia the twenty eighth day of April, in the year of our Lord one thousand eight hundred and sixty two, and of the Commonwealth the eighty sixth Allowed,

    JAMES ROSS SNOWDEN,
           Prothonotary

SCHUYLKILL COUNTY, ss

The record and process within mentioned, with all things touching the same before the Judges within named at the day and place within contained, in a certain record to this writ annexed, we do certify and send as within we are commanded

    C W HEGINS,
    JAMES FOCHT,
    BENJ HEILNER,
  Judges of the Common Pleas of Schuylkill Co

[Endorsed 32, July Term 1862 Supreme Court The City of Philadelphia, plaintiffs in error, *vs* John A Girard, *et al.*, defendants in error. (Decem., 59, 582.) Writ of error to the Court of Common Pleas for the County of Schuylkill, returnable the last Monday of July, 1862. Rule on the defendants in error to appear and plead on the return day of the writ.

I certify that James McClintock, No. 905 Walnut street, M. D., and Francis B. McCormick, No. 1005 Mellon street, Superintendent of the Girard Estate, are bail in error in the above case, in the sum of five hundred dollars.

J. R. SNOWDEN, *Proth'y*

C. E. LEX.
Filed 30 April, 1862.]

Agreement referred to in Record, at page 113

Girard *vs* The City of Philadelphia.	C P Schuylkill Co Sep T 1859

It is agreed that on the trial of the above case, the following facts be admitted, namely

1 That Augustus Girard, called in the writ John F Girard, and John Fabricius Girard are sons of Etienne Girard, deceased who was a brother of Stephen Girard of Philadelphia, deceased

That Margaret P Lardy, Maria De Roux, Anna C Lentilhac, and Madeleine H Girard are daughters of said Etienne Girard, deceased, who was a brother of said Stephen Girard, deceased

That Palmire DuVars Dumaine and Fabricius DuVars Dumaine are children of Ann H Girard (late Dumaine), deceased, who was a daughter of the said Etienne Girard, deceased, who was a brother of the said Stephen Girard, deceased

That Francoise C Vidal is a daughter of Sophia Girard, deceased, who was a sister of said Stephen Girard, deceased

That Harriet Clark, Maria A V Hemphill and Caroline E. Peale are daughters of John Girard, deceased, who was a brother of the said Stephen Girard, deceased

2 That on the 5th day of July, 1832, the said John Fabricius Girard received from the executors of the said Stephen Girard, deceased, his legacy of $5,000 under the will of said Stephen Girard, less the collateral inheritance tax of $125

That on the same day the said Augustus Girard received from the same parties his legacy of $5,000 under the said will, less the said tax of $125.

That on the same day the said Francoise C Vidal received from the same parties her legacy of $5,000 bequeathed to her by the said will under the name of Victorine Fenelon, less the said tax of $125

That on the 6th day of July, 1832, the said Harriet Clark received from the same parties her legacy of $10,000 under the said will, less the said tax of $250

That on the 7th day of July, 1832, the said Maria A V Hemphill received from the same parties her legacy of $10,000 under the said will, less the said tax of $250

That on the 21st day of August, 1832, the Trustees of the said Maria A V Hemphill received from the same parties her legacy of $50,000 bequeathed in trust for her, less the said tax of $2,250

That on the 1st day of September, 1832, the Trustees of the said Caroline E Peale (then Haslam) received from the said parties her legacy of $10 000 bequeathed in trust for her, in her then name of Haslam, by the said will, less the said tax of $250

That on the 2d January, 1833, the before mentioned Etienne Girard (now deceased) received from the same parties, by his attorney, John F Girard, his legacy under the said will of $5,000

That on the same day the said Margaret P Lardy, Maria De Roux and Anna H Girard (afterwards Dumaine) received from the same parties, by their attorney, John F Girard, their respective legacies of $5,000 under the said will, less the collateral inheritance tax And

That on the 24th January, 1833, the said Madeleine H Girard received from the same parties, by her guardian, John F Girard, her legacy of $5,000 under the said will, less the said tax of $125

     EDWARD OLMSTED,
      Attorney for Defendants
     W L HIRST,
      Attorney for Plaintiffs

BILL, ANSWER, AND OPINION,

IN A

Case in the Circuit Court,

IN WHICH

A JUDICIAL CONSTRUCTION

WAS GIVEN TO THE

WILL OF STEPHEN GIRARD,

APPLICABLE TO SOME OF THE POINTS

SUBMITTED BY THE

CITY OF PHILADELPHIA,

IN THIS CASE

Bill filed by some of the heirs of Stephen Girard, November 5, 1860. Circuit Court, October Session, 1860. No. 7.

To the Judges of the Circuit Court of the U. S, for the Eastern District of Pennsylvania

MADELEINE HENRIETTE GIRARD, MARGUERITE P LARDY ANNE STEPHANIE DE LENTILHAC, and ALFRED DE LENTILHAC, her husband, FABRICIUS DEVARS DUMAINE, a minor, and MARGUERITE PALMIRE DUMAINE a minor by their next friend John Devars Dumaine, all aliens, subjects of the Emperor of the French, bring this their bill against the City of Philadelphia, a municipal corporation, holding its franchises from the State of Pennsylvania. And thereupon, the said plaintiffs complain and say, that in the month of December, 1831, Stephen Girard, a native of France, and citizen of the State of Pennsylvania, resident in the City of Philadelphia, there died, seized and possessed of estates, personal and real, unmarried, without issue, and leaving neither father nor mother, but leaving a brother Etienne Girard, and the heirs and representatives of another brother, John Girard, then deceased, and the heirs and representatives of a sister, Sophia Girard, also then deceased. That of the said Etienne Girard, who died in the year 1837, the children living at the time of his death were Marguerite Chloe Girard, who has since died intestate, without issue and unmarried, John Fabricius Girard, Marguerite P Girard, one of these plaintiffs who married Louis Lardy, who is now deceased, Anne Henriette Girard, now deceased, who married John Devars Dumaine, also now deceased, and had issue

D W S—18

by him Fabricius Devars Dumaine a minor, under the age of twenty one years one of these plaintiffs and Marguerite Palmire Dumaine also a minor under the age of twenty-one years, one of these plaintiffs, John Augustus Girard, Madeleine Henriette Girard one of these plaintiffs, Marie Girard, afterwards married to Louis de Roux, and Anne Stephanie Girard one of these plaintiffs, afterwards married to Alfred de Lentilhac, one of these plaintiffs.

That the value of the estate real and personal, of Mr Girard, was estimated at and about the time of his death to be, and actually was, several millions of dollars, but that at this day owing to the enhancement of value of parts of the realty, namely certain portions of it in the City of Philadelphia, and all of that portion of it namely, about 30,000 acres, which contains mines of anthracite coal, and lies in the Counties of Schuylkill and Columbia, the present value of the entire estate is supposed to be, and is by the plaintiffs averred to be, and stated at upwards of thirty millions of dollars, which value is from year to year constantly increasing

That by the last will and testament of the said Stephen Girard which was proved at Philadelphia, the 31st of December, 1831 the testator, after bequeathing various legacies to individuals and bodies corporate, and providing for the building and endowment of a college, for the maintenance and education of certain poor white male orphan children devised to the municipal corporation known and then existing as the Mayor, Aldermen, and Citizens of Philadelphia, the ultimate residue of his estate, real and personal, to improve their police, to improve the city property, and the general appearance of the city itself, and to diminish the burden of taxation, which corporation, thus constituted the ultimate residuary devisee of the said testator, then comprised within its limits the territory and population of a portion of one of the Counties of the State, namely, that of Philadelphia, which included within its boundaries, also many other municipal corporations, each having separate and distinct corporate existence. And the plaintiffs show that by the proceedings of the corporators of the said city, under and by virtue of an act of the General Assembly of the Commonwealth of Pennsylvania, usually called the Consolidation Act, those different municipal bodies were cast into one, to which was given the name of the City of Philadelphia. And the plaintiffs are advised that by the operation and effect of the said Act of Assembly, and of the proceedings thereunder, as hereinafter fully explained the said municipal corporation, the Mayor, Aldermen, and Citizens of Philadelphia, the devisees of the said Stephen Girard, being extinct, and these defendants, the present City of Philadelphia, not being capable under his will to hold the said estates so devised to the late city, to the said uses of the improvement of the police the improvement of the property and to diminish the burden of taxation of the said late city, nor to comply with and perform the said municipal uses and conditions, nor to apply thereunto, according to the will of the testator, the surplus thereof beyond the wants of the said college the said surplus goes to the heirs at law, and they the said plaintiffs, as certain of the heirs-at law of the said Stephen Girard, became and now are entitled to their rateable portion in the said estates of the testator, which were so as aforesaid after the payment of legacies, and providing for the said College for Orphans, bequeathed for the said uses to the said Mayor, Aldermen and Citizens of Philadelphia. That the title of the heirs at-law of the testator is at this time, what that of the said Girard himself would be to the said ultimate residue of the said estates, had he made a gift or grant of them during his life, instead of a bequest to take effect after his death, and had the said Mayor, Aldermen, and Citizens of Philadelphia his grantees, been consolidated as aforesaid with the county in the lifetime of the said Girard.

And the plaintiffs are advised that their claim is not embarrassed by the question, if such be made whether in point of law the late corporation, the Mayor, Aldermen, and

Citizens of Philadelphia, has been dissolved, and ceased to have cognizable legal existence, or, on the contrary, has such existence, and has been enlarged and extended and not dissolved, if it be true, as in fact it is, that the effect of the act and the proceedings thereunder is to prevent the performance of the uses and conditions of the will, and to divert the bounty of the testator from the channel he appointed for it, into one which by the language and meaning of the will is contrary to his purposes. That if such be their effect, the defendants, though they may have artificial legal identity with the municipality called the Mayor, Aldermen, and Citizens of Philadelphia, are not the devisees of the testator, nor capable to hold the ultimate residue of the estates, so as aforesaid bequeathed, and to perform its uses and conditions, but the same goes to the heirs-at-law.

And the said plaintiffs proceed first to lay before the Court a summary of the will of the testator and such portions of its contents, either word for word, or by substantial statement, as may be necessary to be referred to, a full and complete copy of it in all its parts being hereto annexed marked A, which they pray may be taken as part of this their bill. It is divided by the testator into twenty-six *clauses* so styled by him, and added thereto are two codicils.

And the plaintiffs show that, by the first eighteen clauses he bequeaths various pecuniary legacies, and a house at Bordeaux, to different individuals, his relatives, friends, servants, and certain bodies corporate; the value of the said bequests, some of which were in the form of annuities, not being capable of exact ascertainment by the plaintiffs, but seeming to be of an amount of several hundred thousands of dollars. That by the nineteenth clause, he bequeaths certain property held by him near Ouachita, in Louisiana, consisting of a plantation and slaves, and a body of upwards of two hundred and eight thousand acres of land, "to the corporation of the City of New Orleans," and to the Mayor, Aldermen, and Citizens of Philadelphia, in designated proportions, subject to an interest for a term of twenty years in the plantation and slaves, should he so long live, to Mr. Henry Bree, whom the testator designates as his "particular friend." That the City of New Orleans is directed to apply the proceeds of their portion of the bequest, after having sold their interest in the lands, "to such uses and purposes as the said corporation may consider most likely to promote the health and prosperity of the inhabitants of the City of New Orleans," and the Mayor, Aldermen, and Citizens of Philadelphia to apply their portion of the proceeds of the same, after having sold their interest in the lands, "to the same uses and purposes declared and directed of and concerning the residue of my personal estate." That by the twenty second clause, he devises the sum of five hundred thousand dollars, which he calls "part of the residue of my personal estate," to be invested, and the income applied to three objects: the first being to lay out and regulate a street or passage on the eastern front of the City, "to be called Delaware Avenue, extending from Vine to Cedar Street," and "to completely clean and keep clean all the docks within the City." The second "to pull down and remove all wooden buildings" "within the limits of the City of Philadelphia and also to prohibit the erection of any such buildings within the said City's limits at any future time." The third "to regulate, widen, pave, and curb Water Street, and to distribute the Schuylkill water therein."

That by the twenty-third clause is bequeathed the sum of three hundred thousand dollars to the Commonwealth of Pennsylvania, "for the purpose of internal improvements by canal navigation," on condition of their enacting the laws necessary to enable the City to carry out the various improvements provided for in section twenty-second. That by the twenty fifth, direction is given to his executors not to interfere with a certain trust established for winding up the affairs of his banking-house. That by the twenty sixth, are appointed the executors of the will. That by the first codicil the will is republished, and by the second it is again republished and provision made for changing the site of the said College for Orphans, from a lot on Chestnut and Market Streets where it was originally directed to be placed, to a piece of ground in the Township of Penn, then recently and subsequently to the execution of his will, purchased by the testator. That by the twentieth clause, the testator devises the residue and remainder of his real and personal estate to the Mayor, Aldermen, and Citizens of Philadelphia, in trust for the uses, intents, and purposes to be declared by him, and directs that the residue of the realty be applied to the same uses declared for the residue of the personalty. And accordingly in those parts of the will which are subsequent to the twentieth clause, the whole residue real and personal, is denominated by the testator *personalty*. That by the twenty first clause, he appropriates, of his residuary estate, two millions of dollars, or "so much thereof as may be necessary," to building and fitting a College for Orphans, for the construction, organization, and government of which he gives directions; "The income, issues, and profits of so much of the said sum of two millions of dollars as shall remain unexpended," in building and fitting the college, to "be applied to maintain the said college according to the testator's directions." And that, in the concluding portion of the clause, he provides for the contrary case, namely, that of the two millions being found inadequate, after having built and fitted the college, to maintain it. "If the income arising from that part of the said sum of two millions of dollars, remaining after the construction and furnishing of the college and out-buildings shall, owing to the increase of the number of orphans applying for admission, or other cause, be inadequate to the construction of new buildings, or the maintenance and education of as many orphans as may apply for admission, then such further sum as may be necessary for the construction of new buildings, and the maintenance and education of such further number of orphans as can be maintained and instructed within such buildings as the said square of ground shall be adequate to, shall be taken from the final residuary fund, hereinafter expressly referred to, for the purpose, comprehending the income of my real estate in the City and County of Philadelphia, and the dividends of my stock in the Schuylkill Navigation Company,—my design and desire being that the benefits of said institution shall be extended to as great a number of orphans as the limits of the said square and buildings therein can accommodate."

That by the twenty fourth clause, the testator devises, "as it regards the remainder of said residue of my personal estate," which expression, *personal estate*, comprises, as aforementioned, both realty and personalty, "in trust, to invest the same in good securities, and, in like manner, to invest the interest and income thereof, from time to time, so that the whole shall form a permanent fund, and to appropriate the income of the said fund —

'*First.*—To the further improvement and maintenance of the aforesaid college, as directed in the last paragraph of the twenty first clause of this my Will

'*Second.*—To enable the corporation of the City of Philadelphia to provide more effectually than they now do for the security of the inhabitants of the said city, by a competent police, including a sufficient number of watchmen really suited to the purpose, and to this end, I recommend a division of the city into watch districts, or four parts, each under a proper head

"*Third.*—To enable the said corporation to improve the city property, and the general appearance of the city itself, and in effect, to diminish the burden of taxation, now most oppressive, especially on those who are the least able to bear it" "To all which objects, the prosperity of the city, and the health and comfort of its inhabitants, I devote the said fund as aforesaid and direct the income thereof to be applied yearly, and every year forever, after providing for the college, as hereinbefore directed as my primary object"

And the plaintiffs show, that the scheme of the said Will may be stated thus That the testator, after devising specifically his real estate in Louisiana and in France, and leaving certain pecuniary legacies, gives "all the residue and remainder" of his "real and personal estate" to "the Mayor, Aldermen, and Citizens of Philadelphia, their successors and assigns, in trust to and for the several uses, intents, and purposes" in the Will, "declared of and concerning the same," and so far as regards his "real estate in Pennsylvania, in trust, that no part thereof shall ever be sold or alienated." That he declares those uses, intents, and purposes to be, ' to apply and expend two millions of dollars, if so much should be required, to build and fit the college; to invest five hundred thousand dollars securely, and apply the income thereof in the manner prescribed, to improve, within the city limits, the wharves and Water Street, and to pull down and prevent the future erection of wooden buildings; to pay three hundred thousand dollars to the State, provided they passed, in one year after the death of the testator, such laws as might be necessary "to enable the constituted authorities" of the city to carry into effect the proposed improvements of the wharves and Water Street, and in the removal of wooden buildings and preventing their future erection; and, as regards the remainder of the said residue, to apply the income thereof—

First.—To the further improvement and maintenance of the College, "as directed in the last paragraph of the twenty-first clause" of the Will.

Second.—To enable the corporation to improve their police.

Third.—To enable the corporation to improve the "City property and general appearance of the City itself, and, in effect, to diminish the burden of taxation."

And the plaintiffs are advised that if it be a question, whether, by the terms of the will, the testator should be understood as bequeathing to be used, if necessary, in the support and maintenance of the College, the whole "remainder of the said residue of his estate," or less than the whole of it, the solution of such question, as will be hereinafter shown, cannot affect the claim of these plaintiffs.

But they are advised that the testator bequeathed to the support and maintenance of the College, beside the said two millions of dollars, not the whole "remainder of the said residue" of his estate, but only the income of his real estate in the City and County of Philadelphia and the dividends of his stock in the Schuylkill Navigation Company. That by the ninth section of the twenty-first clause of the will, as quoted at pages 5 and 6 of this bill in full so far as concerns the said question of the application of the residue of his estate to serve the College, the testator declares that in case of the inadequacy of the two millions of dollars to build the College and maintain it and to construct new buildings and maintain an increased number of orphans, in that event, "such further sum," "comprehending the income of my real estate in the City and "County of Philadelphia and the divideds of my stock in "the Schuylkill Navigation Company,' "shall be taken "from the final residuary fund' "as may be necessary for ' the construction of new buildings and the maintenance "and education of such further number of orphans.' That is, such further sum as may be necessary, comprehending these two sources of revenue, shall be taken from the residuary fund. And the plaintiffs are advised that it is the "further sum" "necessary for the construction of new buildings and the maintenance and education of such further number of orphans as can be maintained and instructed within" them, and not the "residuary fund," which the testator measures as comprehending the income of his real estate in Philadelphia and the dividends of his Schuylkill Navigation Company stock. That the residuary fund comprehended much more real estate of the testator than that in the City and County of Philadelphia, and many other stocks than his Schuylkill Navigation Company stock, and that, neither by inadvertence nor intentionally, does he otherwise suggest; but declares and devises that, should the two millions be exhausted, a further sum from his residuary estate, limited to the income of his realty in Philadelphia and

Schuylkill Navigation stock, may be taken and applied to the College. And that the testator, after so devising the said two millions of dollars and if need be the income of his real estate in the City and County of Philadelphia and the dividends of his Schuylkill Navigation Company stock, when he proceeds by the concluding words of the said twenty first clause to say ' my design and desire being, that " the benefits of said institution shall be extended to as great " a number of orphans as the limits of the said square and " buildings therein can accommodate,' did not mean, and could not have anticipated, even as a possibility, that his whole estate would be nor is it nor will it ever be required for supplying the wants of the College. That in endowing it with the two millions and the income of all his real estate in the City and County of Philadelphia and the dividends of his Schuylkill Navigation Company stock he necessarily supposed that he was making and he did in fact make, the amplest provision for the extension of "the benefits of said institution to as "great a number of orphans as the limits of the said square and buildings therein" or as the forty-five acres the present site of the College could "accommodate' That if in accordance with the intention of the testator and the expectations of the devisees the income only and not the capital of the said two millions of dollars, or but a moderate portion of it, had been expended on the College buildings, there would now be a large surplus income of the said two millions beyond the wants of the said College. That the income of the houses and other real estate in Philadelphia, at fair rents, is about two hundred and fifty thousand dollars ($250 000) that the income of the two millions of dollars, if the same were still in the hands of the devisees and invested according to the intention of the testator, would be about one hundred and twenty thousand dollars (120,000), and that the stock of the Schuylkill Navigation Company, of which there were transferred by the executors of Mr. Girard to the Mayor, Aldermen, and Citizens of Philadelphia twenty two hundred (2200) shares, was by the testator regarded as property of the utmost value and the same actually yielded dividends so considerable that the Mayor, Aldermen, and Citizens of Philadelphia must have received, and did receive, in the dividends of one year, the sum of fifty-five thousand dollars ($55,000) upon the testator's said investment of twenty two hundred shares. And that by means of the said provision beyond the two millions, so made for it, the said College must to the testator have seemed to be, and it actually was, and still remains, furnished with a contingent revenue ample enough to admit of the largest possible extension of the buildings and benefits of the institution and of the most lavish expenditure upon them.

And the said plaintiffs show that Mr Girard, in making his devisees, industriously excludes from participation in them the surrounding, and now with the said Mayor Aldermen, and Citizens of Philadelphia, consolidated municipalities, which, as hereinafter shown, must needs, by reason of such consolidation, take to themselves the almost exclusive benefit of them. That in every part of the will, an unvarying discrimination is observed by the testator between the City, and the City and suburbs. That the bequests are rigidly confined to the City proper, and bestowed on it by its correct corporate designation of the Mayor, Aldermen, and Citizens of Philadelphia, and that when, in the instance of the neighboring township of Passyunk, in which was situate Mr Girard's farm, where he sometimes sought relaxation from the cares of business, he provides, in the eighth clause, a fund of six thousand dollars, to buy a lot of ground there, and build a school-house, and schoolmaster's house, for educating the poor children of his neighbors, he bequeathes not to the township, but to trustees of his own selection. That it is only the unexpended balance of this small sum of six thousand dollars, which, after purchasing the ground, and erecting the buildings, must be little or nothing, that he authorizes those trustees to pay over to a board of directors chosen by the inhabitants of the township

That, with this single exception, if it be regarded as an exception, every portion of the territory and population of the twenty-eight municipalities, which, by the fact of their consolidation with the late city, become, as will be in the plaintiffs' bill shown, possessors of the whole ultimate residue of the testator's estate, were intended to be absolutely excluded from it. That when he leaves a legacy of ten thousand dollars by the fourth clause of the will, to "the Comptrollers of the Public Schools for the City and County of Philadelphia," functionaries who govern the Public Schools of the county, and who were and are not a city but a county establishment or foundation, including in common with the city all parts of the county, he declares that this sum shall be for the use of those schools only that are situate within the limits of the City, and excludes those of the suburbs. That when, by the twentieth clause, five hundred thousand dollars are appropriated "to pull down and remove" wooden buildings, and "to prohibit the erection of any such buildings" "at any future time," and for the improvement of Water Street and Delaware Avenue, these improvements are directed by the testator to be stopped when they arrive at the limits of the City, namely, at Vine Street on the north, and South Street on the south.

And the said plaintiffs show that the said corporation, the Mayor, Aldermen, and Citizens of Philadelphia, was known to the testator and had, in fact, no other existence or organization than as a municipality, whose territorial extent was limited to a front or breadth of about one mile on the River Delaware, from north to south, lying between east and west lines drawn through the centres of the said two streets, called Vine Street, its northern boundary, and South Street, its southern boundary, and extending in depth westward a distance of somewhat less than two miles to the River Schuylkill. And that the said corporation, until the second of February, 1854, when, by the said act of the General Assembly of the Commonwealth of Pennsylvania, entitled " A further supplement to an act entitled

'An Act to incorporate the City of Philadelphia,'" and the proceedings thereunder, it was consolidated with the surrounding suburbs and other municipalities, was one of twenty nine municipal corporations, each with a territory, population, and government of its own, and all of them, lying within the boundaries of the County of Philadelphia That the said twenty-nine bodies, so lying within the said county, and so the second of February, 1854, consolidated into one, had been incorporated at various dates, were of various territorial extent and population, differed in the details of their several organizations, and were respectively known by the following corporate names, namely —The Mayor, Aldermen, and Citizens of Philadelphia. The commissioners and inhabitants of the District of Southwark The inhabitants of the incorporated District of the Northern Liberties The commissioners and inhabitants of the Kensington District The commissioners of the District of Spring Garden The commissioners and inhabitants of the District of Moyamensing The commissioners and inhabitants of the District of Penn. The commissioners and inhabitants of the District of Richmond, in the County of Philadelphia The District of West Philadelphia. The District of Belmont The Borough of Manayunk The Borough of Germantown The Borough of Frankford The Borough of White Hall The Borough of Bridesburg The Borough of Aramingo The Township of Passyunk The Township of Kingsessing The Township of Blockley The Township of Roxborough The Township of Germantown The Township of Bristol The Township of Oxford The Township of Lower Dublin The Township of Moreland The Township of Byberry The Township of Northern Liberties. The Township of Delaware The Township of Penn

That the said twenty-nine municipalities of the said county occupied an area of upwards of one hundred and twenty-nine square miles of which the municipality styled the Mayor, Aldermen and Citizens of Philadelphia occupied less than two square miles, but in point of population, bore to the rest of the county a greater proportion the fifth, sixth, seventh, eighth ninth and tenth wards of the present or consolidated city, which cover the ground formerly governed by the Mayor, Aldermen and Citizens of Philadelphia, being entitled under the Consolidation Act to a representation in the Common Council of twenty members out of eighty-five, their entire number such representation being based upon taxable population, so that, while the territorial relation of the late city to all the other municipalities of the county was less than as two to one hundred and twenty seven, its relation in point of number of taxable inhabitants was as twenty to eighty five That the old city therefore, comprised less than a sixty fourth part of the territory of the new one, but between a fourth and a fifth part of its population

That of the said twenty-nine municipalities, the late city and those called districts, as the District of Kensington, the District of Southwark, and others, were, in greater or less measure built up and closely inhabited those called boroughs as the Boroughs of Manayunk Germantown, and others, were villages of the County of Philadelphia, and the townships, as Blockley, Bristol, and others, comprised its farm land That the twenty first, twenty-second, twenty-third, and twenty fourth wards, and much of the nineteenth and first, which consist for the most part of farm land and villages, and the twentieth, large portions of which are not built, have a representation, based as aforesaid upon taxable population, which, reckoning all parts of the last mentioned wards namely, the twenty first, twenty second, twenty-third, twenty fourth, nineteenth, first, and twentieth, gives twenty-five members to the Common Council, making five more than are allowed to those wards, namely, the fifth, sixth, seventh, eighth, ninth, and tenth, comprising the territory of the former city That if from these twenty five members any due number were deducted for the probable representation of the built parts of the first, nineteenth, twentieth, and twenty-fourth wards, it would be seen that the villages and farm land of the present city contain a population that bears comparison in point of taxable numbers with that of the entire territory of the late city.

And the said plaintiffs show that by the Act of Assembly, called the Consolidation Act, and the proceedings thereunder, the admistration of all concerns of the said twenty-nine corporations, including their debts, taxes, property, police, and whatever else pertained to municipal office, and also the government of the county itself, were consolidated and absorbed into one. That "all the powers, rights, privileges, and immunities," as declared by the sixth section of the act, "incident to a municipal corporation, and necessary for the proper government of the same, and those of the present corporation, the Mayor Aldermen, and Citizens of Philadelphia," and "all the powers, rights, privileges, and immunities possessed and enjoyed by the following corporations respectively," namely, the other twenty eight corporate bodies aforementioned, which the said act enumerates, each by its name and style which with the old city made up the County of Philadelphia, and also ' the Board of Police of the Police District, the Commissioners of the County of Philadelphia the Treasurer and Auditor thereof, the County Board, the Commissioners of the Sinking Fund, and the Supervisors of the Township," were, by virtue of the process of consolidation, vested in "the City of Philadelphia, as established by this act." That by the thirty seventh section the "right title, and interest of the 'several municipal corporations mentioned in this act of, in and to all the lands, tenements, and hereditaments goods, chattels, moneys, effects and of, in, and to all other property and estate whatsoever and wheresoever, belonging to any or either of them,' are ' vested in the City of Philadelphia,' and all "estates and incomes held in trust by the county, present city, and each of the townships, districts, and other municipal corporations, united by this act," are ' vested in the City of Philadelphia, upon and for the same uses, trusts, limitations, charities, and conditions, as the same are now held by the said corporations respectively."

That by the thirty eighth section, the "net debt of the County of Philadelphia, and the several net debts of the Guardians for the relief and employment of the poor of the City of Philadelphia," and of the Board of Health, 'and of the Controllers of the Public Schools,' and of such, namely, eighteen which are enumerated, of the said twenty nine municipalities, as had contracted debts, were consolidated and formed into one debt, to be called "the debt of the City of Philadelphia, in lieu of the present separate debts so consolidated.'

And the plaintiffs show, that by the terms of the act, and the proceedings thereunder, all the municipal powers, privileges, possessions, and burdens of the said twenty nine municipalities were so as aforesaid transferred to the new city; and that whether the twenty nine corporations are to be regarded as dissolved, and a new corporation erected, or one of the twenty nine, namely, the Mayor, Aldermen, and Citizens of Philadelphia, is to be regarded as having so extended its limits as to include within them the other twenty eight, the plaintiffs are advised, is a consideration immaterial to this their bill. And they show that, in fact, the said consolidation to its final intent and purpose, was carried into full effect; that it was, by the sixth section of the said Act of the 2d February, 1854, provided that the corporators of the new city, having elected a Mayor and members of a Select and Common Council, the said Select and Common Council should direct the said Mayor to appoint a day, not exceeding sixty days after the first Tuesday in July, 1854, when "all the powers, rights, privileges, and immunities possessed and enjoyed" by the various corporations, namely, the districts, boroughs, and townships herein above named, and those also of the said city should "cease and terminate; and that the said Select and Common Councils did accordingly, by resolution passed the 22d June, 1854, direct the said Mayor to "issue his proclamation forthwith dissolving the different corporations superseded by the sixth section of the Act consolidating the City of Philadelphia to take effect on the 30th instant" and that, in obedience thereto, the said Mayor, two days after, by public proclamation, dated the 24th June, 1854 proclaimed that ' all the powers, rights privileges, and immunities possessed and enjoyed" by the now late city and the now late districts, boroughs and townships,—being the above enumerated twenty-nine municipalities of the County of Philadelphia, from the said 30th day of June, 1854, should "cease and terminate ' And the plaintiffs show that from and after the said 30th June, 1854, the said consolidation was complete

And the plaintiffs show that the said late City of Philadelphia was originally laid out by the proper authorities of the Province of Pennsylvania in the year 1683, its boundaries established on the east and west being as afore mentioned,—the River Delaware on the east, and the River Schuylkill on the west and its boundaries on the north and south, as aforementioned, the centres of the said two streets called Vine Street and South Street, the centre of the said street called Vine Street on the north, and the centre of the said street called South Street on the south That the plot or plan of the said city, prepared and made by the Surveyor General of the Province, was duly lodged and now remains in the office of the Surveyor General of the State, where it is registered as and for a muniment of the said city, and of the extent and boundaries of the same, and as such is recognized in all courts of justice, and there and elsewhere is known and admitted to be the original and authentic plot of the said city, its boundaries and limits, and of the sites of the different streets and all local objects and existences pertaining thereto That upon the "inhabitants and settlers" of the city so, in the year 1683, laid out, was afterwards bestowed by the proprietary government of the province, the first charter of the said place, by the name of "the Mayor and Commonalty of the City of Philadelphia,'

D W. S—20

and which dated the 25th of October, 1701. That by the terms of the said charter, the boundaries of the city were declared to be ' the limits or bounds as it is laid out between Delaware and Schuylkill,' namely, the limits and bounds as set forth in the said original survey and plot so deposited in the office of the Surveyor General. That the said charter was, after the Revolution, superseded by another, which, under an act of the General Assembly of the State, dated the 11th March, 1789 was bestowed by the Commonwealth of Pennsylvania on the citizens of the place so in 1683 laid out and in 1701 chartered. That by the terms of the said Act of 1789, the boundaries of the city were declared to be " as the same extends and is laid out between the rivers Delaware and Schuylkill,' namely, the boundaries as laid in the said survey and plot in the office of the Surveyor-General. And the plaintiffs aver that, from the year 1683 to the 30th June, 1854 the said boundaries remained unchanged.

And the plaintiffs to the court here show the said survey and plot of the said city, and the said charter thereof, dated the 25th October, 1701, and the said Act of Incorporation, passed the 11th March 1789 and the said Act of Consolidation, passed the 2d February, 1854, and the said proceedings thereunder to give the same effect; and moreover, the various enactments of the Commonwealth of Pennsylvania, by which were severally incorporated the said twenty nine municipalities, and the supplements to those enactments, from time to time passed by the General Assembly all which the plaintiffs pray may be considered as part of this their bill; and also the various notorious topographical and physical facts proper and necessary to be before the court, regarding the said twenty nine municipalities of the County of Philadelphia, now occupied up to its limits under the said Act of 1854, by the present city which facts they are advised will be judicially noticed, without being at large introduced into this bill

And the plaintiffs having shown to the court what were the last will and testament of Mr Girard, and the devises therein contained, and the Act of Assembly of the 2d February, 1854, commonly called the Consolidation Act and its provisions, and the proceedings thereunder, now proceed to show that the said will of the testator has been set at naught, and the legal consequences thereof. And they are advised that if not technically dissolved, the municipality devised to being now a body not known to the testator, composed of elements foreign to his devises and not capable of carrying them out, is as aforesaid in its new character no longer the devisee of Mr Girard, and the devise in fact is lapsed, and that while it may be in the power of the legislature, in order to continuity of corporate existence to ordain that the name only be deemed changed when actually the corporation is transformed, it is not in their power, nor is it to be supposed to have been, nor was it their design, to reconstruct this testator's will, or divert its legacies to objects not within his purposes.

And they are advised that all uses, even those of a public and general character, and to charitable ends and objects declared by a testator, must be substantially fulfilled by his devisees, and the law is not satisfied by their coming as near them as they can, such a rule of construction not being in force in Pennsylvania and never having been in force anywhere, if it were by the act of the devisees themselves that fulfilment of the terms of the devise became impossible. That no latitude is allowed to defect of compliance which is the voluntary act of the devisee, or a consequence of it, remote or immediate. That if a devisee by his own act could open the way to substitute qualified for substantial fulfilment of testamentary conditions, no devise would go into effect, and the devisee's own inclinations would take the place of the will of the devisor.

And the plaintiffs show that it has become, since the 30th of June, 1854 impossible to carry out the will of Mr Girard, the impediment arises out of the voluntary acts and pro ceedings of his devisees, and the provisions of a new charter duly accepted by them and that, in fact the procurement, as well as the acceptance of the said charter, was the act, and spontaneous act of the citizens of the late City That the vote of the representative being in representative government the vote of the constituent and the recognized exponent of his will and the votes of the representatives of the late City in the General Assembly of the State having been cast unanimously for the erection of the said new municipality, and their most strenuous efforts directed in its favor, the said charter is to be regarded as not merely accepted in a full, lawful, and binding manner, but as having been, as the plaintiffs aver it really was solicited as a boon by the corporators, and as such obtained by them from the authorities of the State

And the plaintiffs show that the entire scheme of consolidation of the City with the surrounding municipalities, in all its details, as seen in the said charter and act of the 2d February, 1854, as well as the said acceptance thereof, and the said proceedings thereunder, was the work of the citizens of the said City That influential persons, having originated and brought it forward, assembled them in public meetings, at which the project of the new charter was regarded in all its bearings, and among the rest, that of its effect on their title to the Girard estates and scrutinized and minutely examined at their said meetings by the said corporators, and by their committees and sub-committees for that purpose appointed, who reported to adjourned meetings plans of consolidation, which after being weighed and approved, by the citizens of the City were finally laid by them before the Legislature of the State, accompanied by petitions earnestly praying their immediate adoption, and the enactment of the said act of the 2d February, 1854 That the public sentiment of the municipality being ascertained, fixed, and expressed, representatives of the City, pledged to the measure of consolidation were, by committees appointed for the purpose, selected from among its citizens, and being elected, took their seats as members of the General Assembly of 1854, instructed to procure its enactment into a law That the chartered authorities of the City, the Select and Common Councils, the measure being laid before them for their approval by the citizens of the City prior to the meeting of the General Assembly deliberated upon and approved it, and concluded to facilitate and did facilitate its becoming a law, and the City members of the General Assembly accordingly were requested by them to procure the consolidation of the City with the said surrounding municipalities That the Legislature of Pennsylvania, having met in the year 1854 the 3d of January, the next day, the 4th of January, the subject was introduced into the Senate, and, on the 6th of that month, into the House, after, in compliance with the pressure of the City upon the authorities of the Commonwealth, especial notice had been called to it by the Governor in his annual message to the two Houses That on the 2d of February, 1854, thirty days after the session had been opened, the consolidation bill, comprising fifty-three sections, drafted and prepared in the City of Philadelphia, by a committee there raised for that purpose by the corporators at their said meetings, and on which sat some of its most prominent citizens, passed both Houses, was signed by the Executive and became a law That in the House of Representatives it received on a call of the yeas and nays, the four votes of the City of Philadelphia, and ten of the eleven votes present from the County there being in the whole House three votes only given against and seventy nine in favor of the bill That in the Senate it received, on a call also of the yeas and nays, all the votes of the Senators of both City and County, namely, the two who represented the City, and three who represented the County, and that of the twenty seven Senators present, not one voted against it That this almost unanimous vote of both Houses of the Legislature was attributable to the united efforts of the corporators of the City of Philadelphia, and those of the twenty-eight municipalities of the County, and the measures, so as aforesaid taken by them, to have their charters consolidated in the manner provided in the said bill. And such was their zeal to accomplish their object at a juncture, when as aforementioned, the opinions of the City authorities coincided on this measure with those of the corporators, that the committee of citizens, so as aforesaid raised for the purpose were not allowed due time for bestowing the requisite attention on the details of the bill; and frequent alterations of the law, since its original enactment, thereby have become necessary. That the Governor, having signed the bill as drafted by the corporators a law, during the same legislative session of 1854, was demanded and passed, entitled "An Act to construe the Act of the 2d of February preceding." That an act, consisting of thirty sections, entitled 'A Supplement to the Act consolidating the City of Philadelphia,' was passed at the session of 1855; an act, consisting of thirty-one sections, entitled "A further Supplement to the Act consolidating the City of Philadelphia," during the session of 1856; five supplements during the session of 1857, namely, one the 28th of April, one the 7th of May, one the 13th of May, and two the 16th of May; at the session of 1858, six supplements more namely, one the 15th of March, one the 30th of March, one the 16th of April, one the 20th of April, one the 21st of April, and one the 22d of April; and at the session of 1859, four supplements, namely, one the 30th March, one the 9th April, one the 11th April and one the 13th April.

And the plaintiffs are advised, that if the devisees be not indeed corporately extinct, but if, by reason of a new municipal position, assumed by them under a new charter, they are disabled to comply with the conditions and fulfil the uses provided for in the will, not only is it, as aforesaid, not the legal effect thereof that they may retain possession of the devised estates, complying as nearly as they can, but that, on the contrary, having sought and obtained the said charter, and accepted for themselves the said position, incompatible with their performance of the said conditions and uses, preferring the advantages arising from their new charter to those pertaining to the possession of the estates so devised them, the said devisees have, to legal intendment thereby disclaimed the said devise. That, as the plaintiffs are advised, their accepting a charter under which they are not able to perform the conditions and uses of the devise is as if they had originally refused to take it.

And the plaintiffs show that, by the section of the Consolidation Act by them above referred to, numbered thirty-seven, in the words of the said section, "all the right, title, and interest" of the various "municipal corporations mentioned in this act of, in and to all the lands, tenements, hereditaments bridges, ferries, railroads, wharves markets stalls, landings, landing places, water-works gas works, buildings, easements and franchises of, in and to all goods, chattels, moneys, effects, debts, dues, demands, amercements, fees, perquisites, rights incomes bonds, obligations, judgments liens actions, and rights of action, books, accounts and vouchers, and of, in and to all other property and estate whatsoever, and wheresoever belonging to any or either of them," were "vested in the City of Philadelphia," namely, these defendants, and that 'all the estates and incomes' "held in trust by the county,' 'city, and each of the townships, districts, and other municipal corporations united by this act,' were declared to be "held by the City of Philadelphia,' namely, these defendants "upon and for the same uses trusts, limitations, charities, and conditions, as the same had been 'held by the said corporations respectively.' And the plaintiffs show, that by the said words of the thirty seventh section of the act together with those of the first section, also above referred to, "that the corporate name of the Mayor, Aldermen and Citizens of Philadelphia shall be changed to the City of Philadelphia, and the boundaries of the said city shall be extended, so as to embrace the whole territory of the County of Philadelphia, and all the powers of the said corporation, as enlarged and modified by this act, shall be exercised and have effect within the said county, and over the inhabitants thereof," the right of these defendants, if any there be, accrues, the property held by the late city in ownership, the property held by them in trust, and their municipal functions, being therein all of them transferred, or attempted to be transferred to the new city. And they are advised, that no larger nor more comprehensive grant could be devised, or enacted, than one which includes all municipal powers, and all property, whether held in trust or ownership.

And being advised, as afore stated, that it is immaterial to these plaintiffs, whether the corporation called the Mayor, Aldermen, and Citizens of Philadelphia, the devisee of Mr Girard, was or was not actually, by the said act of the General Assembly, dissolved, which, however, they are advised it was; but submitting that, in any event, the only party that since the Consolidation Act, can pretend to hold the said estates as against the plaintiffs, is these defendants, the said plaintiffs proceed to show that the said defendants have no right or title thereto. And they show, that under the said act, the said defendants, if entitled to the said estates, must take for one of two purposes, namely, to apply them to the police of the consolidated municipality, the improvement of all its property, and the diminution of its entire burden of consolidated taxes; or to apply them to the police of that part of the city only which was lately governed by the Mayor Aldermen, and Citizens of Philadelphia, and the improvement of the city property and the general appearance of the city, and diminishing the burden of taxation in that particular region, namely, the region of the late city; that is, they are advised they must take either for themselves, or in trust for the late city.

And as regards the said defendants taking in trust for the late city, the plaintiffs are advised that such a trust as one to improve a city and its police, and to diminish its taxation, whether the same were confided to municipal or individual keeping, not being capable of supervision and control by the courts of law, but referable only to the trustee's discretion would be impracticable, and the devise would be void, and the estates comprised in it go to the heirs of the testator. And, if such were indeed the character of the said devise, the plaintiffs ask, at the hands of the court the benefit of their position as heirs at law, the devise being void. But they submit that the testator, in providing for the said municipal uses, did not create, or intend to create, a trust, in the sense of his trusts for the college for orphans, and for poor house and room-keepers; namely, one in which the trust is an interest separate from the beneficial interest and from which the trustee could be removed, but in the sense only in which every gift to a public body is a trust and in which the devises of the testator to the City of New Orleans and the Commonwealth of Pennsylvania are trusts.

That they are advised the fund to maintain the college belongs to the college, and the Mayor Aldermen, and Citizens of Philadelphia were trustees of it only; but that which was devised to municipal uses was their own and belonged to them, with no other qualification than that it should be applied to certain designated improvements and to diminish the burden of taxation.

That if, deeming its burdens greater than its benefits, the Mayor, Aldermen and Citizens of Philadelphia had refused the bequest wherewith to found the college, the courts of law would have supplied some other trustee for it; but if they had refused the legacy to municipal uses, that is the legacy to themselves, the disclaimer would have been effectual. That the fund could not have been forced on them, nor appropriated to their police, taxes or improvements, contrary to the will of the municipality; and that, in the event of disclaimer by the corporation, as in the event of dissolution of it, estates so devised to municipal uses must return to the donor.

That they are advised the courts of justice might lawfully have visited and controlled the administration of the trusts committed to the Mayor, Aldermen, and Citizens of Philadelphia, to maintain and educate poor orphan children, and relieve poor-house and room-keepers, to the same extent, and with the same effect, as they might, had those funds been committed to the hands of individual trustees, the management thereof being not necessarily a municipal function; but that they could have interfered with the city government in the administration of a fund devised to improve its police and its property and diminish the burden of its taxation only as they might have interfered with their administration of a like sum raised for like objects by loan or taxes.

That there is no difference of trust character between the devise to the State of Pennsylvania of three hundred thousand dollars for the purposes of internal improvement by canal navigation, and that to the City of Philadelphia, to improve their police, and their property, and the general appearance of the city, and to diminish the burden of taxation, excepting only that the first is devised to State sovereignty and the latter to municipal. That neither of them is a trust of which the trustee could be changed, with the administration of which the courts could interfere, nor for which it would be so much as in their power, were the trust vacant, to appoint trustees.

That the devise to the corporation of the City of New Orleans is, in the testator's language, denominated "a trust," though bestowed without limitation or restriction, other than that of the broadest discretion of the municipality. That he says, 'I give, devise, and bequeath,' in the nineteenth clause of the will "to the corporation of the City of New Orleans, their successors and assigns, the remaining one undivided third part of the said lands in trust in common with the Mayor, Aldermen and Citizens of Philadelphia,' to sell and dispose of their interest in said lands, gradually, from time to time, and to apply the proceeds of such sale to such uses and purposes as the said corporation may consider most likely to promote the health and general prosperity of the inhabitants of the City of New Orleans,"—the direction to apply it to the health and general prosperity of the place, making a gift, than which, one to the corporation, their successors, and assigns the plaintiffs are advised, would not be in more unqualified ownership, yet declared, by the testator, to be, and being, "in trust."

That the devises to the said two cities were devises in trust but in trust for themselves; the gift to the City of New Orleans to improve its "health and general prosperity" being without qualification and that to the City of Philadelphia to improve their police, their property and the general appearance of the city, and to diminish the burden of taxation, being qualified by its limitation to certain defined uses, and they are advised that to the Mayor, Aldermen, and Citizens of Philadelphia, as well as to the corporation of the City of New Orleans the estates severally devised to them by Mr Girard pertained and belonged in proprietorship, and not in trust in any sense distinct from that of proprietorship

But these plaintiffs are advised that, while it imports them to aver and state, if they are able, the relation whether of conditional trust or conditional ownership, or other, on which the late corporation held the residue so to municipal uses as aforesaid to them bequeathed, the claim of the defendants be it for themselves or for the inhabitants of the late city, must ultimately depend on their being able to establish that the will can be carried out and its conditions performed and satisfied, since the new charter, for the plaintiffs are advised that as the devise, if it were in ownership, must needs remain subject to the conditions imposed by the testator, so if it were in trust, was a trust which must end with the surcease of the objects for which it was created or with the possibility of fulfilling them. And the plaintiffs proceed to set forth that it is now no longer possible Mr Girard's will should be fulfilled, by any means or its uses performed, or conditions complied with by the consolidated city, or any other party, whether such party held for them selves merely, or in trust for the late city, and that the possession by the present corporation of those devised estates being, at the same time, incapable of fulfilling their uses and conditions, is a fraud on the will of the testator

And first, they are advised that the present city being the County of Philadelphia of the day of Mr Girard, and the late city but one of its twenty nine municipalities, and the testator having excluded from participation in the devise all parts other than that to him known as the city, the defendants cannot take and hold these estates for themselves, namely, for the region of the twenty nine late municipalities, twenty eight of which were not devised to That if it were in the power of Mr Girard to bequeath to one geographical district to the exclusion of all else, and he have exercised it, no authority could make over his property to other districts contrary to his will That the plaintiffs are not advised that the capacity of the devisees to take and hold the estates bequeathed to the late city would necessarily be affected by addition to their territory, or even the annexation of another municipality but they are advised that the annexation of twenty-eight municipalities and the addition of sixty-four times more territory, with room for sixty-four times more population, and now nearly four times as much, has such effect

That the late city might have been altered, its franchises extended over more territory, and its capacity and existence moulded at the pleasure of the power that gave them, but not to the alteration of the testamentary uses and conditions declared by Mr Girard That the Mayor, Aldermen, and Citizens of Philadelphia cannot apply a fund bequeathed to make their improvements and diminish their taxes, to other objects because, by reason of an amendment of the charter or dissolution of the corporation, it can no longer be used as devised That the title of the defendants as against the plaintiffs to this property, in their new municipal position under the charter of 1854, is no other than it would be if the consolidation of the city had been with any other places, or any other, however vast, portion of the territory and population of the State, which the legislature might be pleased to incorporate together, no other than if, instead of being centralized in their county, the twenty-nine municipalities had been with all the local governments of the whole Commonwealth drawn to a common centre at the capital of the State. That although the limits and franchises of a municipal corporation be liable to change, its contracts with third persons, or devises from them, are, so far as these persons are concerned, like those of a private corporation or an individual; and the legislature, not being able to impair them, could not, after a testator had bequeathed to pay the taxes and improve the police and property of a certain place, enact a law to extend his bequest to make improvements and pay taxes in other places also.

And the plaintiffs are informed and believe that these defendants have signified their own understanding, that if they can hold these estates, it must be, not for the present but the late city. That the sixth section of the twenty-first clause of the will of the testator having declared that the maintenance and education to be provided at the College for Orphans, should be for the benefit, "first, of 'orphans born in the City of Philadelphia,' and secondly,' for the benefit of "those born in any other part of Pennsylvania," and prior to the Consolidation Act the number of orphans, candidates for admission to the institution, born in the City of Philadelphia, as it then existed being so great that places could not be found in the College for all of them, and those coming from other parts of Pennsylvania being by reason thereof excluded, it became, immediately upon the so called enlargement by the charter of 1854, of the limits of the city, a question for the consideration of the defendants, whether they were to admit as "orphans born in the City of Philadelphia" those born in what the testator denominated 'other parts of Pennsylvania' but not included within the city, or only those born within the limits of that which was the city at the making and proving the will; and the said defendants thereupon did come to, and have acted upon, the conclusion that while the State could, at their pleasure, enlarge the limits of the city, they could not alter the uses of the will, or enlarge the benefits of the college beyond those who were orphans born in the "City of Philadelphia," as it was understood by and known to the testator namely, the late city and not the present city, and accordingly the defendants refused admission to the college to orphans, otherwise qualified, if not born within the boundaries of the old city

And the plaintiffs are informed and believe that since the drafting of this bill, in order to the final ascertaining and settlement of their right to exclude from the said college all orphans born without the said ancient limits of the City of Philadelphia, until those born within the same should have been served, the defendants have made a case presenting the question of such right, and taken the opinion thereon of the Supreme Court of Pennsylvania, and that by the final and solemn judgment and decree of that tribunal it has been ruled that the defendants are not authorized by the will, and have no right in law or otherwise, to admit to the benefits of the college orphans born beyond the ancient city limits, until all those born within the same have been provided for, that is to say it has been so decided that the City of Philadelphia, the devisee of the testator, is the late city and not the present city

And the plaintiffs therefore, assuming that the defendants here set up title, not for themselves, but for the late city, to which the devise was made, and that they pretend to no other not attempting to appropriate the testator's bequest to the consolidated municipalities, as established and bounded under the Act of 1854, proceed to show, that it is contrary to the text of the will, and altogether incompatible with its purposes that the defendants should take for the late city, or take for the citizens of the late city or take in any manner whatever, the property devised by the testator to the Mayor, Aldermen, and Citizens of Philadelphia, to improve their police and their property and diminish the burdens of taxation. That the said devise to the late city was in its nature and character essentially, a devise to municipal power and discretion, a power and a discretion controlled and controllable only by its own proper citizens, and that to disunite the control from the beneficial interest, and give the command of it to those who are not citizens of the city devised to, is to violate the will in its most indispensable feature. That neither is the present city capable of administering, nor are the citizens of the late capable of enjoying at the hands of the present city, or of any but a municipal government of which they are the sole constituency, the uses provided for by the testator.

That they are advised the testator's design to provide for certain municipal uses, to meet which he devised to the municipal power of the place, cannot be carried out or be so much as approached, when the city to which he devised has ceased to have substantive existence and substantive power. That with the extinction of independent condition of the municipality to which the devise was to be applied, and the government which was to apply it, by whatever means affected, whether by dissolving the corporation or merging it in another the whole object of the testator falls, finally, to the ground. That the persons designated by him to be nurtured at his college may receive their bounties which are individual bounties as well since as before the disappearance of the municipality to whose care they were left; but not so the persons composing the municipality devised to, who were to be advanced as a community. That improving the condition of a city and diminishing the burden of its taxes, a communal benefit seemed to the testator to be, and actually was, attainable in no other way than by a devise to the community as a municipal sovereignty. That, in making his devise he devised exclusively and directly to the community which was to be improved and the taxes of which were to be diminished, because, the uses of the gift being their own uses, and the performance of them pertaining to the administration of their government, their performance not only could not be made safe, but could not be attained at all, in any other manner than by giving the fund to the city, to which it was to belong, and whose citizens were the constituency, to protect, use, and enjoy it. That a gift to a municipality to improve its condition and diminish its taxes, presupposes the discretion and power to make those improvements and diminish those taxes, a power and discretion which terminates with its independent existence and into the exercise of which power and discretion enter political functions, which can be supplied from no foreign or other municipality, and by no trustee whatsoever.

That to place the concerns of police, taxes, and improvement of a municipality in the hands of an individual trustee, would not be more inadmissible than to give them to a municipality whose authorities were foreign to or not exclusively the representatives of the citizens for whom they were to be administered. That Mr. Girard's municipal bequests must needs have been a failure had he devised to the Mayor, Aldermen and Citizens of Philadelphia the fund to be applied to the health and prosperity of the City of New Orleans, and to the City of New Orleans the fund for improving the City of Philadelphia. That the municipal office is exercised when the City of New Orleans improves its own police and diminishes its own taxes, but would not be exercised at all when it improved the police or diminished the taxes of the City of Philadelphia.

That this fund was given to political power, self-governing, municipally independent, and measured to the surface to be improved and taxed, but now, since the 30th June, 1854, having no separate existence, no longer independent, but consolidated, absorbed, and lost in surrounding territory and population. That from a municipality which had a basis of territory and population, equal to that to be benefited, they have been taken away and transferred to one with a basis of population, of which the population to be benefited, forms but twenty eighty fifth parts, and a basis of territory of which the territory to be benefited forms less than a sixty-fifth part, the political power to which the uses were devised if it exist at all, and be not extinct, being in presence of another power, between four and sixty five times stronger than itself, a change, which affects the devise to the college to the extent of giving it a new trustee but totally destroys the devise to municipal uses. And the plaintiffs aver that the uses bequeathed to be performed by the Mayor, Aldermen, and Citizens of Philadelphia, would be better served had they been passed over not to the consolidated authorities, but to those of New Orleans, or of New York, for those municipalities would not have, like the present city, an interest immediately opposed to their performance. That the uses under Mr Girard's will, are, by the Act of 1854, provided with a trustee, or superior, unknown to the testator, whose office nominally to care of them, is in fact, to postpone them to its own interests, and take for themselves.

That his purpose is frustrated, as soon as a separation is effected between the municipal power or party that is to perform the uses of improving the police and city property and the general appearance of the city itself, and to diminish the burden of taxation, and those that are to profit by their performance. That when such separation takes place, and a trustee is interposed, as in case of a vacant trust, the municipal power and discretion, to which the testator devised is at an end, and the will cannot be executed. That it was not for the late city to obtain at the hand of the legislature, more than at that of the courts of law, the appointment of a trustee to take their place. That they could not have resigned in favor of the county officers nor have obtained, under the will, authority to transfer the devised estates to the twenty nine unconsolidated municipalities of the county, for the use of the city; nor does the consolidation of those twenty nine municipalities bring them any nearer to the purposes of the testator. That if the old corporation was a trustee capable of being removed from the power to perform these functions and of being replaced with another, so is the new corporation which has succeeded it, and on proof made of infidelity to the municipal uses of the devise, the present city of Philadelphia these defendants, might be removed by the courts of law from the office of employing this fund on the police and city property, and the diminishing of the burden of taxation, and some other corporation or individual, selected by the courts, and appointed in their stead

And the plaintiffs also submit that as the will can be executed only as made by the testator, and not on a rule of expediency, the devise is not to be handed over to these defendants, not being the devisees though really they could administer its uses and could diminish the burden of taxation for the inhabitants of the late city, and could make their improvements. That if the late municipality, without having been, in legal acceptation, dissolved has disappeared or ceased to be capable of holding the bequest of the testator, and the new municipality is unable to take and hold for itself there then remains of the devisee, only territory and population, to which, in the absence of their municipal rights and privileges, the testator did not devise but in the exactly contrary manner. That it is true territory and population entered into the intention of the testator, and were of the essence of the devise but so did municipal franchises, which being taken away or absorbed, there is no longer a devisee. And the plaintiffs are advised that the corporators might have altered the character of their institutions, or procured their alteration, to any extent, without affecting their legal position as legatees of Mr Girard to municipal uses; but that either by the dissolution of their municipality, or by the surrender of its franchises, or by their absorption in those of the surrounding country, municipal identity is lost. That all identity, for the purposes of the will, is obliterated, and no devisee is left to take, when the franchises of the citizens of the city are extended to every citizen of the county, and the constituency of the municipality, for whose benefit the municipal uses were to be performed, is mingled and lost in the constituencies of twenty-eight other municipalities.

And the plaintiffs having submitted that by the mere fact of the extinction of the political independent power to which the said estates were devised, the will of the testator stands without a devisee, now proceed to state that, since the consolidation, it is neither administratively nor arithmetically possible, to apply the income of the Girard estates to the municipal uses of the late city, without, at the same time, applying it to each and every one of the twenty eight late municipalities not devised to, but on the contrary excluded by the testator from all benefit under his will. That it is not possible for the defendants to use the said estates for the late city, or in any other manner than for themselves, and that the most well directed efforts to apply them as bequeathed by the testator would be fruitless. And the plaintiffs are advised that the fact of the consolidation is a perpetual bar to the application of the said estates to any one part more than another of the Consolidated City; that since the 30th June, 1854 there is not a taxation for one part of the municipality which is not for another, but the same burden rests upon all, that the burden of taxation is now the united burdens of the twenty nine late municipalities, and each dollar applied to meet interest or principal of the debt, or to raise revenue, for any part of the year's contingent or current expenses, or to face any municipal want whatsoever, so long as there is a consolidated debt and treasury of the City of Philadelphia, and not two debts and two treasuries, a debt and treasury for the late city and another for the rest of the municipalities, must by arithmetical necessity subserve, in direct violation of the will the purpose of paying the debt and diminishing the burden of taxation in the same ratio for all the twenty nine late districts, townships, boroughs, and city. That the Girard fund, merely applied to diminish a tax laid to meet the interest of the public debt, or any portion of the year's expenses of the present city, must of course be applied to the debt or charges of the entire region of the twenty-nine municipalities, that debt and those charges belonging to all, and that if attempted to be applied to that particular part of the tax paid in the old city, it still would go to diminish the burden of taxation of all parts equally, because the taxes light, watch, pave, and pay debts in the whole consolidated region and the plaintiffs submit that the said taxes can pay for lighting, watching, paving, and all debts in no other way, so long as consolidation exists

And they show that in one event only an event which has not happened, could this be pretended to be otherwise, had the late city brought to the common treasury proportionally small instead of large possessions, and a proportionally large instead of small debt, and a necessity only proportioned to that of the other united municipalities, to level grade, and prepare for opening streets, instead of coming in to the consolidation with all its expensive works made and paid for, it might be pretended that for each dollar of Mr Girard's legacy applied to diminish the burden of taxation for the boroughs, districts, and townships, there was more than a dollar paid in return by the boroughs, districts and townships to diminish the burdens of the city, and thereby that the city was a gainer in other directions to a greater amount than it was a loser in that of the Girard bequest But the plaintiffs show that in the actually existing relations of the members of the new municipality, the old city's property and possessions being great, its debt small, and its wants few, in proportion with those of its neighbors, the result is and ever must be financially inevitable that of each portion of the Girard fund, the region of each of the late municipalities receives its share, which share will be in exact ratio to the extent of its need of aid for itself, and its inability to meet the needs of its neighbors, so that the poorest of the twenty-nine municipalities must receive the largest share of the fund, and the richest, the least

And the plaintiffs aver, that at the period of the consolidation, the taxable basis of the late city, which had wealth and large possessions, was seventy millions of value, or thereabouts, and its public debt less than those of the other municipalities, and that the taxable basis of all the rest together, namely, the other twenty eight municipalities, was thirty seven millions of value, or thereabouts, and their public debts greater than that of the said late city and that their municipal unsupplied wants and necessities so prodigiously exceeded those of the said late city as to make the ratio thereof not capable of estimation

And the plaintiffs show they are further advised that the end is also politically, as well as arithmetically and administratively, unattainable of improving the police, property and general appearance, and diminishing the taxation of one portion and not others of the same municipality. That a legacy may be bequeathed and applied to supply fuel for the inhabitants of any quarter of a city, or educate orphan children within prescribed limits, or to widen one street and no other, but that it is not politically possible to organize and administer a system of police, or of taxation or improvement which is unequal. That police improvement and taxation must be equal. That as long as the municipality of the Mayor, Aldermen, and Citizens of Philadelphia existed separately, the application of the bequest to its separate use was proper and possible but since its absorption and extinction, is neither proper nor possible, and every part of the municipality would be gainers by the omission to attempt the accomplishment of such a purpose as the unequal distribution of government protection among the citizens of the same city. That the city might be richer or poorer, worse or better governed than the adjoining districts, but when brought under the same municipal charter it covers them alike. That between Vine and South Streets the police must not be more "competent" better paid, more vigilant and faithful, "the security of the persons and property of the inhabitants' more cared for, than in the regions of the city north, south, and west of it.

That it would be vain to ask the consolidated authorities to bestow improvements on the region of the old city, to diminish the taxes, better the police, and watch over the security of persons and property there, while other parts of the municipality were more taxed but less improved and guarded. That the late city wards have six votes against eighteen, in the Select Council, and twenty votes against sixty five, in the Common Council: that their relative population entitles them to no more and soon will not entitle them to so much; that it is in the power of a majority already more than three to one, and constantly increasing and the power will be exercised, to take care that the same advantages of government be enjoyed by all citizens alike.

And the plaintiffs submit to the court, that if it were politically and administratively possible, it would not be lawful to diminish the burden of taxation, and improve the police, and the property, and the general appearance of one part of the city, and not the rest, to make distinctions between portions of the population and territory of the same place; and that a devise to uses against, at the same time, the policy of the law, and the policy, drift, and spirit of the institutions of the country, is not to be carried into effect in its courts of justice.

And the plaintiffs proceed now to show that the general policy, also, of the will itself has been violated; that it was the object of Mr. Girard, to improve, finish, and adorn an already well appointed municipality; that his intention was, diminishing at the same time the taxation that went to support it to elevate its standard of municipal comfort. That this design was favored by the circumstances that the late city had no suburbs to exhaust its resources; and by the charter could have none. That the city, as known to Mr. Girard, within its ancient limits, with its primary municipal wants supplied, was ripe for the sort of improvement to contribute to which was his object. That there are in his will devises to remove wooden buildings, that they might be replaced with others more safe, seemly, and commodious devises "to remove or pull down all the buildings, fences and obstructions" which marred the Delaware front of the city. "to completely clean, and keep clean all the docks, 'to pull down platforms carried out' into the stream of the river to make of the wharves a broad and handsome avenue to improve according to a scheme to which he devotes many pages of minute description, the street in which he had lived. That on reference to the copy of the will hereto annexed, it will be seen, that excepting a few legacies, the bequest to the City of New Orleans, and that to the State, the motive for which appears when he directs that it shall not be paid until 'such laws shall have been enacted by the constituted authorities of the said Commonwealth as shall be necessary and amply sufficient to carry into effect, or to enable the constituted authorities of the City of Philadelphia to carry into effect the several improvements above specified, the whole of the testator's estate, including the portion set apart to diminish taxes and improve the city itself and two millions to build the college, which he enjoins upon the municipal authorities to expend with "good taste cautioning them against no ornament that was not 'needless, is devoted by him to the object, studiously and consistently pursued, of improving and adorning the city while he lightened its burdens.

And the plaintiffs show that the said policy is wholly irreconcilable with that of consolidation a policy which assimilates the city with its suburbs. That the burden of taxation, since the 30th June, 1854 has increased largely and improvements, in the testator's sense, have ceased and cannot be resumed until all the area of the city plot shall be at the same point of municipal progress with the late city, a period of time not to be estimated, because additions to the suburbs going on from age to age, the region of the late city must always be engaged in paying to clear the ground for the inhabitants of those suburbs which are, one after another, to come into the close-built portion of the municipality. That the works pertaining to these beginnings of municipal progress must engross the attention and exhaust the resources of the city, until its vacant territory is filled up. That the swamps and hills, to be brought into use by levelling and draining, before improvement or ornament can be thought of, must cost sums and involve debts and taxes enormous in their amount. That to the three hundred and fifty miles of drained, graded and paved streets in the city, as now built, there must be added, to accommodate a population sufficient to cover its yet unbuilt surface, nine thousand miles more; there being at the present day according to official statements of the consolidated authorities, which the plaintiffs are informed and believe to be accurate, more than one hundred and twenty square miles of ground still to be furnished with streets and alleys.

And the plaintiffs, therefore, show and submit to the court that, when the Mayor, Aldermen, and Citizens of Philadelphia consolidated themselves with the said other municipalities, they made it indispensable to postpone Mr. Girard's policy of improving the city and lightening its burdens an indefinite time; the rule being irresistible that a municipality can neither lighten its burdens nor add to its improvements while the work the main source of municipal debt and taxes, that of preparing the surface of the ground for habitation, remains to be accomplished.

And by these and other means, the plaintiffs aver that if substantial compliance with the will of the testator were possible, and not impossible, the acts and proceedings of the devisees have made a change of municipal position so hostile to the performance of the said uses and conditions, as to render the accomplishment of them, to the last degree, uncertain. That by the transfer to the consolidated city of the said devised estates, it has become, not only less certain that the police of the old city will be increased, less certain its property and general appearance will be improved, less certain that the burden of taxation will be diminished, out of the estates bequeathed to those objects by Mr Girard than it was prior to the Act of the 2d February, 1854, and the proceedings thereunder but, as they submit, they are deprived altogether of any certainty whatever. That the legal certainty of performance of the said uses and conditions is wholly gone, and its want of common certainty such, that the corporators of the said city have admitted and do now admit, that no reasonable hope remains that the said devise can be applied according to the will of the testator

And the plaintiffs show, that the corporators of the late city, when they abandoned their place under their former charter, were influenced by motives which induced them to look to the probable inability to perform these uses as a fact of inferior moment the greatness of the result of uniting as a single city the twenty nine municipalities. leading them to the conclusion, to which the plaintiffs, in another part of their bill, have referred, namely that the bequest of Mr Girard ought to be rejected, if it stood in the way of consolidation And that, under the said proceedings of the corporators, it was not to legal intendment only that the said devise was disclaimed; but that it was then actual intent and purpose to disclaim should their continuing to hold it be incompatible with what they deemed, and truly was, an interest, whether to good or ill, so much more important That none of them believed the legacy of Mr Girard, if it might indeed be taken to relieve the burdens of the twenty eight municipalities to which it was not left could sensibly diminish the taxes, or add to the revenues of so great a community as the consolidated city That when Mr Girard bequeathed to improve the late city and diminish the burden of its taxes, he measured his bequest to their revenue and expenditure, but the value of the bequest having disappeared with the separate existence of the city, it became almost indifferent to the twenty-nine united municipalities, whether it have, or have not, the municipal protection under which it was placed by the will, and be applied, or not, to the uses for which it was intended, and whether they hold it by right capable, or not capable, of vindication at law

And the plaintiffs here state, that at another stage of the cause they will have occasion to show what has been the defendants' management of these estates, that lands of immense value produce nothing but are an annual charge, that improved property, from which it is pretended to derive income, is let at rents unaccountably low, and bearing no proportion to those of adjoining property of equal or less worth that expenses are multiplied and waste and disorder prevail in the administration of the bequest of Mr Girard

And the defendants' right to be regarded as claimants to charitable uses, which heretofore, in this bill, the plaintiffs have not controverted they now deny, being advised that a bequest to endow a municipality, to the improvement of its police and property, and the diminishing of the burden of its taxes is not, by the law of Pennsylvania, a charity

And the plaintiffs here show that the bequest of the residue of the said estates to municipal uses is, under the prohibition contained in the twentieth clause of the will of the testator, that any part of the said "real estate in Pennsylvania' "shall ever be sold or alienated," an attempt to create a perpetuity And that, if not originally a successful attempt, it must become so upon the separation of those controlling the said bequest from the beneficiaries, and placing it under a mere trust That as the plaintiffs are advised, a transfer of the said estates to a trustee without right or power to part with them, or make title, namely, these defendants, must bind them in a perpetuity of the closest kind And the said plaintiffs are advised to insist, and do accordingly insist upon their position and rights as heirs at law of the testator, should the court be of opinion that a perpetuity was in fact created, or attempted to be created by the said terms of the said will

And the plaintiffs are advised that their claim as heirs at-law of Mr Girard, upon the disappearance of the late municipality, or its inability to carry out the devise, is not affected by the provision of the will, contained in the twenty fourth clause, namely that in case of breach of certain "conditions," affixed to the bequest to the Mayor, Aldermen and Citizens of Philadelphia, it should go over to the Commonwealth of Pennsylvania, and afterwards to the United States of America, in case of breach of the conditions affixed to the said bequest over to the Commonwealth That, as they are advised, the Commonwealth of Pennsylvania is not to take and hold the estates in case of the inability of the City, nor the United States of America to take and hold them in case of the inability of the Commonwealth, but the titles of the State and United States severally, can accrue only on breach of certain conditions none of which have been broken, or supposed to be broken, the event which has happened, as aforesaid, being not a breach of condition but an extinction or failure of corporate powers And they are advised that such a case is nowhere contemplated by the testator or provided for in his will, and, so far from the consolidation of their franchises making a breach of condition, the Mayor, Aldermen, and Citizens of Philadelphia might have incurred a forfeiture of all their franchises, and lost their charter entire, without breaking one of the conditions of the said devise

And the plaintiffs now proceed to show to the court that on the 15th April, 1842 by decree of the Orphans' Court of the County of Philadelphia the executors of the last will and testament of the said Stephen Girard, were duly discharged from their office as such executors and from all duty and liability under the said will, having first settled their accounts according to law and delivered up to the Mayor, Aldermen, and Citizens of Philadelphia, as the residuary legatees of the testator as aforesaid, all property, assets, and estate whatsoever in their hands or keeping, and having performed and executed all duties upon them under the said will incumbent as in and by the said decree of the said court set forth, and that all the estate, thereupon, of the testator which by the said will should and theretofore had not already come to the hands or possession of the said the Mayor, Aldermen, and citizens of Philadelphia, did forthwith to them pass according to the terms of the said herein before-mentioned devises thereof and that after separating and setting aside from the income of the residuary estates bequeathed by Mr Girard to the Mayor, Aldermen and Citizens of Philadelphia, a sum sufficient to meet annually all the expenses of the College and for its "further improvement and maintenance," as directed to be paid by the twenty-fourth clause of the will, and to meet legacies, taxes, repairs of real estate and all other liabilities and charges, including the five hundred thousand dollars to Delaware Avenue and other objects, and the ten thousand dollars to poor house and room-keepers which go to the debit of the income of the said estates there remains applicable according to the terms of the will, to the aforementioned objects but not applied by these defendants and which they are not capable, for the causes hereinbefore set forth, to apply to the same, namely, "to enable the corporation of the City of Philadelphia to provide more effectually than they now do for the security of the persons and property of the inhabitants of the said City, by a competent police, including a sufficient number of watchmen really suited to the purpose" and 'to enable the said corporation to improve the city property and the general appearance of the city itself, and in effect to diminish the burden of taxation," a very large and annually increasing sum, the proceeds of the now income yielding portion of the said residuary estate, so bequeathed to the Mayor Aldermen, and Citizens of Philadelphia, of which surplus income, together with the capital thereof and other income, capital, estates, and interests hereinafter mentioned the said plaintiffs, as heirs at-law of the testator, here claim their ratable portion

And the plaintiffs show that, at the time of the filing of this bill after the great expenditures in building, fitting and establishing the said College, which they aver is now completely built, fitted, and established, and after the various losses that have been sustained of both personal and real estate of the testator, there remains in the hands and possession of the said defendants, property real and personal as follows namely, of real estate in those parts of the City of Philadelphia which, before the Consolidation Act, were the old city and Liberties one hundred and eighty-two dwelling houses and stores, five vacant lots of ground, and two wharves, and also of real estate in that part of the City of Philadelphia which, before the Consolidation Act was the township of Passyunk, four hundred and thirty seven and three fourths acres, with the improvements thereon also of real estate in that part of the City of Philadelphia which, before the Consolidation Act, was the District of Moyamensing, one hundred and twenty nine acres, with the improvements thereon, which said items of property comprise the real estate late of the testator in the present City of Philadelphia, known to these plaintiffs to be in the hands and possession of the defendants excepting only the said College building and grounds; and also of real estate in the counties of Schuylkill and Columbia, in the State of Pennsylvania twenty nine thousand four hundred and thirty-two acres, being lands containing anthracite coal and of real estate in the County of Erie in the State of Pennsylvania, three thousand and sixty-four acres and of real estate in the State of Kentucky, four thousand seven hundred and seventy five acres and of personal estate consisting chiefly of investments in the public loans of the State of Pennsylvania the City of Philadelphia, the Schuylkill Navigation Company, the Chesapeake and Delaware Canal Company the Philadelphia Exchange Company, the Danville and Pottsville Railroad Company, the Philadelphia County

Public Loan, and the Guardians of the Poor Public Loan, the sum of about one million and one hundred thousand dollars.

And the plaintiffs aver, that there remains also in the hands and possession of the said defendants, of the real and personal estate of the said testator other real and personal estate, to these plaintiffs not known. And the plaintiffs show that the said real estate in the present City of Philadelphia, property selected by Mr. Girard as of the most substantial and available kind, and situate, for the most part in the most eligible parts of the town, and capable of being kept always under leases advantageous to the proprietor, is of an annual value or rental of two hundred and fifty thousand dollars, according to the existing rate of rent of real estate situate and improved as is the aforementioned from which amount of two hundred and fifty thousand dollars, if one fourth or sixty-two thousand five hundred dollars be deducted for the expenses of the year, of every kind, including taxes repairs, and charges of collection and agency,—which is a much larger sum than is therefor expended,—there is left one hundred and eighty seven thousand and five hundred dollars for the net annual income of the said real estate situate in the present City of Philadelphia, and which the plaintiffs aver to be the net income thereof annually.

And the plaintiffs show that the said personal estate, so aforementioned invested yields annually, in dividends on capital stock, and interest on loans, the sum of sixty-two thousand dollars, which the plaintiffs aver to be the income thereof annually; from which is to be deducted thirty thousand dollars, being the interest on the capital of five hundred thousand dollars bequeathed by the testator to the Mayor, Aldermen, and Citizens of Philadelphia, to improve Delaware Avenue and Water Street and pull down and remove wooden buildings, and six hundred dollars being the interest on the capital of ten thousand dollars bequeathed to the Mayor Aldermen, and Citizens of Philadelphia for the use of poor white house and room-keepers and from which sixty two thousand dollars, the income of the said personalty, and one hundred and eighty seven thousand and five hundred dollars the aforesaid net rental of the said real estate situate in the present City of Philadelphia, is to be deducted for the annual expenses of the College, including all charges whatsoever, the sum of seventy three thousand dollars, which the plaintiffs aver covers more than such expenses and charges and which sums of thirty thousand dollars and six hundred dollars and seventy three thousand dollars, include all deductions and abatements of any kind to be made from the income of the said real and personal estate that should precede the application of the same, under the will of the testator, to the said objects of improving the police and the property of the city, and the general appearance of the city itself, and diminishing its burden of taxation and after the making of which deductions, the balance remaining of the said income is applicable to the said objects, and which balance, if the said objects be not, now, since the consolidation attainable, belongs to, and should be of right enjoyed by the heirs at law of the testator

And the said plaintiffs aver, that there has been so payable, on the income of the property in the City of Philadelphia alone, yearly and every year since the 30th June, 1854, to the heirs-at-law of Mr Girard, the sum of one hundred and forty five thousand, nine hundred dollars such being the said balance of the income of personalty and realty situate in the City of Philadelphia, and that there will be so payable, each and every year forever, a like sum out of the income of the said personalty and the realty situate in the present City of Philadelphia, assuming no enhancement to take place in the value of the said dwellings and stores in the late city and liberties, and of the said ground in the late Township of Passyunk and the late District of Moyamensing, the said sums of thirty thousand dollars and six hundred dollars so as above placed to the debit of the said annual income, being according to the will of the testator, sums fixed, and not capable ever to be greater than now they are, and the said seventy-three thousand dollars, so as above placed to the debit of the said income, as the annual outlay for the College, being, as aforesaid, beyond the average sum thereupon annually, during the past five years, expended, including enlargements and additions to the capacity of the College

And the plaintiffs, for greater certainty, here show in figures the facts last above stated, namely

Gross income of personalty			$62,000
Deduct for income of $500,000, at 6 per cent, to provide for the improvements of Delaware Avenue and Water Street, and the pulling down and removal of wooden buildings,	$30,000		
Deduct for income of $10,000, at 6 per cent, to provide fuel for poor house and room keepers,	600		
		30,600	
			$31,400
Gross income of realty in the City of Philadelphia,		$250,000	
Deduct for taxes, repairs, agency, and all other charges,		62,500	
			$187,500
			$218,900
Deduct annually for College,			73,000
Balance of income annually arising from personalty and realty in the City of Philadelphia, after paying all charges against the same,			$145,900

And the said plaintiffs aver that large sums of money, of an amount to them now unknown, but which will appear on the settlement of the account hereinafter prayed between the said defendants and your orators, being the accumulations of the surplus income of the said residuary estates of the testator, beyond the sums applicable and applied to the said College, and improving Delaware Avenue and Water Street, and pulling down and removing wooden buildings, and providing for poor house and room-keepers, and paying for taxes, repairs, agency, and all other lawful charges against the said estate, remain and now actually are in the hands and possession of the said defendants, not by them appropriated, nor have they attempted to appropriate nor can they appropriate, the same, or any portion thereof whatever, for the causes in this bill afore stated, to the said municipal uses of improving the police and property of the city, and its general appearance and to diminish the burdens of taxation, either in the now existing consolidated city, or in that part of the region thereof which was the late city

And the said plaintiffs aver that there has been both by the late corporation, the Mayor, Aldermen, and Citizens of Philadelphia, and by the present corporation, these defendants, unnecessarily and wrongfully expended on the repairs agency, and other expenses of the said estate, real and personal, of the testator, large sums of money, and there have been by them otherwise expended lost, sunk, wasted and misapplied other large sums of money, which the said defendants are not lawfully and equitably entitled to credit for, in settling the account hereafter prayed between the said defendants and your orators

And the plaintiffs, showing that, if, as they aver, the title of the heirs at-law of the testator, as against the parties in possession of the residuary estates, authorizes them to demand, after the wants of the College shall have been met what remains of the said residuary interest which was, before the said consolidation, applicable to the improvement of the police, and of the city property, and of the general appearance of the city itself, and to diminish the burden of taxation, and now, since not capable of being so applied, submit to the court here that the immensity of the value of the said lands in the Counties of Schuylkill and Columbia, and their vast capacity for annual yield and productiveness, which is in proportion, yet more prodigious than their value reckoned in capital are such as to place it beyond doubt that the said lands, if brought into use in any manner, and with however little judgment, whether by sales, or by leases for terms of years, or by working the mines, must give a return, which, after all wants of the College were supplied, including the largest allowance for adding to the buildings, increasing the number of orphans to be maintained and educated, and enlarging in any conceivable lawful way the establishment, would leave very large sums of money to be divided annually or otherwise among the heirs of Mr Girard That the tract of coal lands devised by the testator to the Mayor, Aldermen, and Citizens of Philadelphia, and never mined or used, is fourteen miles in length, containing, in the two Counties of Schuylkill and Columbia, the number, twenty-nine thousand four hundred and thirty-two aforementioned of acres, and is well known to those acquainted with the coal trade and country That it has been repeatedly set down in public reports, works, and documents containing the results of scientific examinations by official persons and explorers, and writers of authority on this region as capable of yielding more abundantly, in point of quantity, coal of a richer, purer, and more unalloyed kind and quality than any other coal-beds that exist. That worked upon the system usual with proprietors of mines, on leases for twenty years, at so much to the landlord at the pit-mouth upon each ton of coal mined and taken out, the revenue from these mines, though not now, by these plaintiffs, in advance of the experiment, suscepible of accurate estimate, and which must in a degreee always depend on the energy and skill with which labor and capital is applied to them, and the amount of force employed, may be counted as many times exceeding in sum all the rest of the income of the Girard possessions together, and as, in fact, making the profits and rents of the other lands and property of the testator comparatively insignificant, and such the plaintiffs are informed and believe and aver to be the actual capacity for production of those lands

And the plaintiffs, further showing that, as heirs at-law of the testator, being entitled to what remains of the said residuary estate, after the liabilities above-mentioned and the uses of the College shall have been satisfied and served and a large surplus remaining, as the plaintiffs have above shown, out of the interest of and dividends upon the personalty aforementioned and the rents of the said houses in the late city and liberties, after the said uses and liabilities have been served and satisfied, and the rest of the said residuary estate which is in addition to and beside the said houses in the late city and liberties and the said personalty namely, the said lands in the late Township of Passyunk and District of Moyamensing, and the said lands in the Counties of Schuylkill and Columbia, and the said lands of the testator in other parts of Pennsylvania and in Kentucky, being property remaining free and clear, and which there is no possibility can be required to serve the said College or meet the aforementioned liabilities under the will, the plaintiffs are advised, and they are not only entitled to receive whatever income the said residuary estate yields, and is capable of yielding, beyond the wants of the College and the aforementioned liabilities of the residuary estate under the will but that they are entitled, moreover, to ask, and they ask accordingly at the hands of this court, that the said lands in the late District of Moyamensing and Township of Passyunk, and in the Counties of Schuylkill and Columbia and in other parts of Pennsylvania, and in Kentucky, be placed, subject always to the order, control, and directions of the court, in the possession, keeping, and management of the said plaintiffs, in order that, subject to such order, control, and directions of the court, they, the said plaintiffs, may by improving, leasing, and cultivating the said lands in the late District of Moyamensing and Township of Passyunk, and by working or leasing the said coal mines, and leasing and cultivating the said lands in the Counties of Schuylkill and Columbia, and in what other lawful manner soever, hold, possess, use, mine, lease, farm, and improve the same, as may be most to the profit and advantage of them the said plaintiffs, provided always, that such possession and use be consistent with the possibility, if the court shall adjudge there be such, that the said lands may be one day required to bear part of the burden of serving the said College, and meeting the aforementioned other liabilities under the will of the testator

But considering that the said two legacies or trusts aforementioned one of five hundred thousand dollars and the other of ten thousand dollars, are both protected by directions of the testator now fully complied with, that the said sums be set aside and securely invested for their proper objects, in order to the application of the income thereof, according to the terms of the will, and that, excepting the uses of the College for orphans, the said two legacies of five hundred thousand dollars and ten thousand dollars, and certain annual payments or annuities, to the amount, as the plaintiffs are informed and believe, of about eleven hundred dollars, which will fall in at the termination of lives now in being, there is no other use, payment, or debt, of any sort to which the said residuary estate is liable the plaintiffs are advised, and here suggest, that the court will, in the exercise of their equitable and just discretion not confine their order and decree to permitting the said plaintiffs to possess, use, and make profit merely of the said lands, but as regards the same or such part of the same as can in no probability, however remote, be needed to meet the liabilities and uses aforementioned remaining to be satisfied and served, will order and adjudge that the said lands or such part of the said lands as cannot so be needed, do pass in such portion as may be due thereof to the said plaintiffs, as certain of the said heirs-at law of the testator, free of reclamation against the same by these defendants for any purpose or under any pretence whatever

And the plaintiffs here show that the investments made

by the late corporation, the Mayor Aldermen, and Citizens of Philadelphia, and now held by the defendants, the present City of Philadelphia, for the purpose of securing, and the plaintiffs aver they do amply secure, to their several objects the said legacies or trusts of five hundred thousand dollars and ten thousand dollars, are as follows namely, to secure the said sum of five hundred thousand dollars in the five per cent loans of the State of Pennsylvania, the sum of fifty-six thousand five hundred and seventy seven dollars and thirty-two cents, in the five per cent loans of the City of Philadelphia, one hundred and forty-nine thousand dollars, in the six per cent City of Philadelphia gas loans, ten thousand dollars, in the capital stock of the Insurance Company of the State of Pennsylvania, four thousand four hundred dollars, in the capital stock of the Union Canal Company of Pennsylvania, five hundred and fifty dollars in the six per cent loan of the Schuylkill Navigation Company, two hundred and fifty five thousand three hundred and twelve dollars and eighty-four cents, in the capital stock of the Philadelphia Mutual Insurance Company two hundred and fifty dollars, and in the Schuylkill Navigation Company loan, thirty-eight thousand three hundred and ninety dollars and seventeen cents and to secure the said sum of ten thousand dollars, in the six per cent loans of the Schuylkill Navigation Company, nine thousand and eighty-nine dollars and thirty seven cents, and the balance of the said sum in cash And the plaintiffs submit that the Mayor, Aldermen, and Citizens of Philadelphia, having according to the directions of the testator separated the said sums of five hundred thousand dollars and ten thousand dollars severally from the rest of the assets of the estate, and invested the same as required by the terms of the will for the said two special objects respectively, have thus fully performed their office so far as concerns first the separation and afterwards the investment of capital for the purposes of the said two legacies, and that if the said investments should at any time now or hereafter be lost, or for any reason prove insufficient to the said objects of securing the said two legacies, no other portion of the assets of the estate could be lawfully taken or resorted to, in aid of the said legacies of five hundred thousand dollars and ten thousand dollars, so that, in fact, they are no longer and have never been, since the said separate and specific respective appropriations and investments were made, an incumbrance upon the rest of the said residuary estate, or a charge or liability which the same could be required to meet.

And the plaintiffs having now shown as above, on the seventh page of this their bill they declared they might and would show that if it be a question whether by the terms of the will of Mr Girard he was to be understood as bequeathing, to be used if necessary in support of the College, the whole remainder of the said residue of his estate or less than the whole of it, namely, the income of his real estate in the now City of Philadelphia and the dividends of his Schuylkill Navigation Company stock and not more, that the solution of the said question could not affect the claim of the said plaintiffs, the estates of the testator being so vast as to leave large amounts of both capital and income coming to these plaintiffs after the College should be served, no matter how liberally, they now also claim that they are entitled to receive at the hands of this Court all of the estates of the testator aforementioned comprised in his said residuary estate not being his "real estate in the City and County of Philadelphia" or his "Schuylkill Navigation Company stock," in present possession free of all future demands thereupon by the defendants or any other party, the same being, as they are advised, in no event applicable to the purposes of the said College, to which only the said income of the real estate in Philadelphia and the dividends of the testator's Schuylkill Navigation Company stock are by the terms of the will applicable in the event of the exhaustion of the said fund of the said two millions of dollars

All which actings, doings, omissions, and refusals, are contrary to equity and good conscience, and tend to the manifest wrong and injury of your orators in the premises. In consideration whereof, and for as much as your orators can only have adequate relief in the premises in a court of equity where matters of this nature are properly cognizable and relievable, to the end, therefore, that the said defendants may, if they can, show why your orators should not have the relief prayed for, and may, upon their several and respective oaths, to the best and utmost of their several and respective knowledge, remembrance, information and belief, full, true, direct and perfect answers make to such of the several interrogatories hereinafter numbered and set forth, as by the note hereunder written they are respectively required to answer, that is to say —

1. Whether the said Stephen Girard did not die, as in the bill stated, resident of Philadelphia, seized and possessed of property of the amount and value as in the bill stated, and whether the plaintiffs are not of kindred with him, as in the bill stated.

2. Whether the said Stephen Girard did not leave a will, proved at Philadelphia the 31st of December, 1831, and whether the exhibit, marked "A," to the plaintiffs' bill annexed, is not a true copy thereof.

3. Whether the municipality, called the Mayor, Aldermen and Citizens of Philadelphia, was not established and chartered with boundaries as stated in the bill; and whether the said municipality was not, by proceedings, as stated in the bill, under the act of the 2d of February, 1854 of the General Assembly of the Commonwealth of Pennsylvania, consolidated with the other twenty-eight municipalities of the County of Philadelphia as one municipality, by the name of the City of Philadelphia. and whether their franchises, debts, taxes, administration, and all other things to them municipally pertaining, were not also then and there, in the manner stated in the bill, consolidated.

4. Whether the consolidation charter was not duly accepted by the corporators of the former City of Philadel

phia, and those of the other twenty eight municipalities of the County, and whether they, the said corporators, did not petition the General Assembly of Philadelphia therefor, and instruct their Senators and Representatives to vote therefor, and whether they did not vote therefor accordingly, and whether the municipal authorities of the former City of Philadelphia did not forbear to oppose the annulling or taking away of their then existing charter purposely, that the General Assembly might, under the pressure upon them of the corporators, annul or take away the same, and consolidate the said former municipality with the twenty-eight other municipalities of the County.

5. Whether the said defendants, as to the property devised by the said testator to the Mayor, Aldermen and Citizens of Philadelphia to improve their police and their property, and the general appearance of the City and, in effect to diminish the burden of taxation, hold the same for themselves the said defendants, or for the late City, or the region or citizens thereof.

6. Whether the defendants have ever applied, and when, any, and what part or portion, and what sum of the said so devised property to the said municipal uses in the last interrogatory mentioned, or to any, and which of those uses.

7. Whether the defendants do not now hold, of the property of the said Stephen Girard, the real estate in the bill mentioned, namely, one hundred and eighty-two dwelling-houses and store-houses, and five vacant lots of ground, and two wharves, or docks, within the bounds of what were, prior to the Consolidation Act, the City and Liberties of Philadelphia, and also four hundred and thirty-seven and three fourths acres of land in what was, before the Consolidation Act, the Township of Passyunk, and also one hundred and twenty-nine acres of land in, what was prior to the Consolidation Act, the District of Moyamensing, and also the said College for orphans, and the land thereto pertaining, and also, in the Counties of Schuylkill and Columbia, twenty nine thousand four hundred and thirty-two acres of

coal land and, in the County of Erie, three thousand and sixty-four acres of land and, in the State of Kentucky, four thousand seven hundred and seventy five acres of land. And whether the said realty, in the old City and Liberties the late Township of Passyunk and late District of Moyamensing, is not of the gross annual value of more than two hundred and fifty thousand dollars ($250,000), and of a clear annual value of more than one hundred and eighty-seven thousand five hundred dollars ($187,500), and whether they hold any, and what other realty, of the estate of the said Stephen Girard, and where situate and of what value

8 Whether the said defendants do not hold of the property of the said Stephen Girard, the personalty in the bill mentioned, amounting to in value, eleven hundred thousand dollars ($1,100,000) or thereabouts, yielding an annual income of sixty two thousand dollars ($62,000), and whether they hold any and what other personalty of the estate of the said Stephen Girard, and of what value

9 Whether the defendants do not hold as set aside by the Mayor, Aldermen and Citizens of Philadelphia and separate and apart from other property or investments the two sums of five hundred thousand dollars ($500,000), to improve Delaware Avenue and Water Street, and to pull down and improve wooden buildings, and ten thousand dollars ($10,000), for the use of poor white house and room-keepers

10 Whether if from the said $62,000, the said income of the said personalty, and the said $187,500, the said income of the said realty, situate in the present City of Philadelphia, beyond that so set apart, there be deducted the said sum of seventy three thousand dollars ($73,000) for the expenses annually of the said College, there is any other and what deduction or abatement that ought to be made from the income of the said real and personal estate, which should precede the application of the said income, under the will of the testator, to the said objects of improving the police and the property of the city, and the general appearance of the city itself, and diminishing the burden of taxation and

which, if the said objects be not since the consolidation, lawfully attainable belongs to and should of right be enjoyed by, the heirs at law of the testator

11. Whether there has not been payable, out of the said income of the said personalty and the said realty in the City of Philadelphia, alone, yearly and every year, since the 2d February, 1854, to the said heirs at law of the testator, the sum of one hundred and forty-five thousand nine hundred dollars ($145,900), and whether there will not be hereafter annually payable to them therefrom a like sum even supposing no enhancement to take place in the value of the said real estate in the said city

12. Whether now there are not large sums of money, and to what exact amount remaining in the hands of these defendants, being the accumulations of the surplus income of the said residuary estates of the testator, beyond the amounts applicable, and which have been applied to the said college, and to improving Delaware Avenue and Water Street, and pulling down and removing wooden buildings, and providing for poor house and room keepers, and for paying taxes, repairs, agency and all other lawful charges against the said estates, and which surplus the defendants do not appropriate and have not appropriated, and have not attempted to nor can appropriate to the said municipal uses of improving the police and property of the city, and its general appearance, and to diminish the burden of taxation, either within the bounds of the present or late city

13. Whether, if the coal mines of the said lands in the Counties of Schuylkill and Columbia were worked and made, in proportion to their capacity, reasonably productive, the income of the estates of the testator would not be so immensely increased, as to very far exceed any amount capable of being expended by the defendants, under the will, unless applied to the said municipal uses of improving the police and property, and general appearance of the city, and diminishing the burden of taxation?

14. Whether, beside the liabilities severally and specially

aforementioned the estates and income of the testator are liable to any other by the terms of the said will or otherwise, excepting only certain annuities, amounting to about the sum of eleven hundred dollars ($1100), and whether those are not from time to time falling in with the lives of those to whom they are now due and payable. And the defendants are required to append to their answer to these interrogatories full and accurate copies of all accounts and writings showing what from year to year have been, and now are the annual receipts of and from the said estates and what they might be increased to by bringing into activity those portions of the same now idle and unproductive, and likewise of the annual charges and liabilities thereof so that it may appear to the Court what the surplus income thereof now is and what such surplus income would be were the said estates all brought into use and rendered productive.

15. What the amount was of personal estate received by the Mayor, Aldermen and Citizens of Philadelphia under the residuary bequest contained in the said will and in what manner was so much of the said personal estate invested as came to their hands invested by the testator. And in what manner was so much of the said personal estate invested by themselves as came to their hands in cash? And what amount thereof was received by the said devisees in cash? And what was the whole amount paid by them to other devisees under the will and to creditors? And if there was filed in the office of the Register of Wills an inventory and appraisement and one or more supplementary inventories and appraisements of the personalty of the testator the defendants are required to annex copies of the same to this interrogatory, and they are also required to say whether any other personalty was left by the testator than that which appears by the said inventory or inventories. They are also required to annex hereto copies of the accounts as settled with the Mayor, Aldermen and Citizens of Philadelphia by the executors of Mr Girard, and by the trustees or assignees of the said banking house, going to show the debits and

credits against and in favor of the said Mayor, Aldermen and Citizens of Philadelphia, as allowed in the settlement of the estate of the testator whether said settlements were settlements made with the said the Mayor, Aldermen and Citizens of Philadelphia, or otherwise, in due course of law and administration of the estate of the testator. And the defendants are further required to set forth what amounts were received, and when by the said Mayor, Aldermen and Citizens of Philadelphia, from that part of the testator's estate comprised in his bank and the business of his bank whether as assets thereof, capital, credits, or otherwise.

16. What was the amount expended in building the said College, and what was the amount, after the said building was finished, that was expended in fitting and furnishing the same, before it was opened for the reception of the youths nurtured and educated there?

17. What amounts, and whence derived other than from the said two millions of dollars, and from income of the real estate of the testator in the city and county of Philadelphia and from dividends of his Schuylkill Navigation stock, have been applied to the purposes of the said college for orphans?

18. What was the amount received by the Mayor, Aldermen and Citizens of Philadelphia, as their portion of the purchase money, under proceedings in partition of certain four thousand acres of land in the counties of Schuylkill and Columbia, or one of those counties, and where was it received, and how invested, or on what objects, and when expended? The defendants are required to append to their answer to this interrogatory, copies of so much of the Docket Entries of the said proceedings in partition as will serve to show the names of the parties to the said partition, the name of the counsel who therein appeared, the term and number of the action or actions, and the court or courts wherein the same was or were brought.

19. What amounts were received, and at what time or times, by the said residuary legatees, as the proceeds of sales

of the said lands of the testator situated in Kentucky, and how have such amounts been invested or appropriated?

20. What entries, not of the dates of 7th January, 1854, and of 19th January, 1854, are contained in the journals of the Select and Common Councils of the Mayor, Aldermen and Citizens of Philadelphia, of and concerning the proposal to consolidate into one the various municipal bodies of the county of Philadelphia? The defendants are required to annex copies of such entries to their answer to this interrogatory.

21. When, and to what amount, and in what manner has income of the testator's estate been at any time invested by the Mayor, Aldermen and Citizens of Philadelphia, or by these defendants, and of such investments what are there which now exist?

22. What investments in public stocks, loans, mortgages, or otherwise, have been made since the death of the testator, of the income or capital of the said estate?

23. What was the sum of income and what the sum of capital expended upon the buildings erected since the testator's death upon the testator's lot or square of ground lying between Market street and Chestnut street, and Eleventh street and Twelfth street, in the city of Philadelphia? And at what dates and in what amounts severally and respectively were such sums of capital and income so applied and expended?

24. What sum or sums, and at what dates since the testator's death have been appropriated to buildings (the college for orphans and the buildings mentioned in the last preceding interrogatory not included) which have been erected upon the testator's real estate, and what sum or sums have been appropriated, and at what dates, to improvements of buildings already thereon erected at the time of his death?

25. What was the total amount expended by the defendants upon the said college during the last year, including every expense whatever? The defendants are required to annex to their answer to this interrogatory an account containing items in full, with dates and all particulars necessary

to the understanding of such expenditure, both in the general and the detail, and the merits thereof.

26. Did the Mayor, Aldermen and Citizens of Philadelphia set apart, and when, and always keep so set apart, certain cash and public loans, stocks and other securities, to the amount of two millions of dollars, for the purpose of erecting and maintaining the said college? The defendants are required to append to their answer to this interrogatory a list or account showing each item of cash or securities so set aside, and the amount thereof. And if the said cash and securities did not suffice, out of the capital and income thereof to meet the annual charges incurred in building or otherwise, the defendants are required to set forth what additional items of securities have been set apart to the use of the college from time to time.

27. What sum or sums portion of the residuary estate of Mr. Girard and at what dates, have been expended, omitting those expended on the college by the Mayor, Aldermen and Citizens of Philadelphia, and by these defendants on improvements of real estate or other property outside of the corporate limits which was of the Mayor, Aldermen and Citizens of Philadelphia; and what sum or sums, portion of the said residuary estate and at what dates have been expended, omitting those expended on the college by the Mayor, Aldermen and Citizens of Philadelphia, and by these defendants on improvements of real estate or other property not part of the said residuary estate, outside of the corporate limits which were of the Mayor, Aldermen and Citizens of Philadelphia?

28. To what uses are put, for profit or revenue, the said five hundred and sixty-seven acres of farm land in the late districts of Passyunk and Moyamensing, and what annual profit and revenue is thence derived?

29. Whether any alteration or alterations of the charter of the said Mayor, Aldermen and Citizens of Philadelphia or of the said City of Philadelphia, from the time when the said first mentioned corporation was established to this day,

has or have been made, against the remonstrance of the said corporations? And if, in answer to this interrogatory it be said that alterations of the said charter have been so made against the remonstrance of the said corporations the said defendants are further required to state in what instance or instances and at what date or dates and what such alterations were, and to append to this interrogatory copies of such remonstrances or remonstrance and to show in what manner the will of the said corporations to the such alterations of such charter was manifested

And that the said defendants and their confederates when discovered may answer the premises and that they may produce and leave in the hands of such person as the court shall direct, all deeds and writings in their custody or power or in the custody or power of any person or persons for their use pertaining to the title and estate of the said Stephen Girard in the said messuages, lands, and chattels And that an account may be taken by and under the direction and decree of the court, of the lands, tenements, and personalty and of all the estate and effects of the said Stephen Girard, now or heretofore possessed by the said defendants, or come to their hands or to the hands of any other person or persons, by their order or for their use

And that the court will order and decree an inquiry by the master, or such other person as they may think proper, to ascertain after the wants are supplied, and all allowances made and provided for enlarging and increasing the establishment of the said college, and for all its necessities whatever and after setting aside the said sum of five hundred thousand dollars, in order to provide thirty thousand dollars a year for the improvement of Delaware Avenue and Water Street, and pulling down and removing wooden buildings and ten thousand dollars in order to provide six hundred dollars a year to buy fuel for poor house and room keepers and after the cost of repairs, agency, and taxes of real estate, and all other charges whatsoever against the entire estate, real and personal, of the testator, applicable to the said college, has been allowed and provided for, whether there does not remain out of the annual income of the estate of the testator, and which is payable, and ought to be and to have been paid to your orators as heirs at law of the testator, a large sum of money. And that the court, such inquiry having been made, will order and decree the surplus beyond the wants of the college, and the proceeds of the said two several investments of five hundred thousand dollars and ten thousand dollars, and the cost of keeping the said real and personal estate and agency and other lawful charges attending the same, to be paid annually to your orators.

And that the court, if necessary to the due and equitable division of the proceeds of the said present income of the said estate applicable to the said college between the defendants and your orators, and to your orators' receiving their due surplus thereof, as aforementioned will order and decree that the said estates do pass into the possession and keeping of a receiver, to be appointed for the purpose.

And that the court will order and decree an inquiry by the master, or such other person as they may think proper, into the gross value and also the present capacity for annual yield of the said lands of the testator, in the City of Philadelphia and elsewhere, not now yielding income or profit and especially the said twenty-nine thousand four hundred and thirty-two acres of land in the Counties of Schuylkill and Columbia, containing mines of anthracite coal and should it be the result of such inquiry that the gross value and capacity for annual yield of the said lands is such as to show and prove the capacity of the said estate for affording income beside and beyond the said wants of the College, and the cost of keeping of the said real and personal estate, and the agency and other lawful charges attending the same, to immensely exceed the wants of the College, and the annual expenses of the said real and personal estate, that the court in that case, if they should be of the opinion that the whole residuary estate is applicable to the said College, will direct, order and decree to be transferred to your orators of the realty in fee simple and of personalty absolutely, such surplus so found to exist beyond and beside all possible and lawful wants of the said College and the amount properly applicable to the expenses attending the keeping and management of that part of the said real and personal estate of the testator which may be ordered and decreed to remain in the hands of these defendants. And that the court will order and decree, if they should not be of opinion the whole residuary estate is applicable to the said College that of all such estates, real and personal, not applicable to the said College the plaintiffs ratable shares as heirs at law of the testator be to them presently conveyed and duly made over free of all claim thereto by these defendants.

And that the court will order and decree by the master, or such other authority as they think proper, an inquiry into the expenditures hitherto made, and expenses incurred of whatever kind, by the Mayor, Aldermen, and Citizens of Philadelphia, and by these defendants in the improvements, repairs, agencies, taxes paid, and other costs and expenses, and debits generally of the real estate, and also of the sums charged to the debit of personalty, in order to the ascertainment and settling of the due portion of the said realty and personalty to be set off in the manner aforementioned to your orators.

And that the court would be pleased to ascertain the respective rights of the parties plaintiffs and defendants in the premises, and make such orders and decrees therein as to the court may seem meet and that the court would be pleased to grant to your orators such further and other relief in the premises as may seem meet and proper, and their writ of subpœna directed to the said defendants, commanding them, by a certain day and on a certain pain, to be and appear before this court, and then and there to answer all and singular the premises, and further to stand to, perform and abide such further order, direction, and decree therein as to the court shall seem most meet; and also their writ of injunction to be directed to the said defendants

And your orators will ever pray, etc

C INGERSOLL, for the complainants.

Note —The defendants are required to answer, severally, interrogatories 1, 2, 3, 4, 5, 6, 7, 8, 9, 10, 11, 12, 13, 14

C. INGERSOLL,
for the Complainants

Will of Stephen Girard

I, STEPHEN GIRARD, of the City of Philadelphia, in the Commonwealth of Pennsylvania, Mariner and Merchant being of sound mind, memory and understanding, do make and publish this my last Will and Testament, in manner following that is to say—

I. I give and bequeath unto "The Contributors to the Pennsylvania Hospital," of which Corporation I am a member, the sum of *Thirty Thousand Dollars*, upon the following conditions, namely, that the said sum shall be added to their Capital, and shall remain a part thereof forever, to be placed at interest, and the interest thereof to be applied, *in the first place*, to pay to my black woman Hannah (to whom I hereby give her freedom) the sum of two hundred dollars per year in quarterly payments of fifty dollars each in advance, during all the term of her life; and, *in the second place*, the said interest to be applied to the use and accommodation of the sick in the said Hospital, and for providing, and at all times having, competent mations, and a sufficient number of nurses and assistant nurses, in order not only to promote the purposes of the said Hospital, but to increase this last class of useful persons, much wanted in our city.

II. I give and bequeath to "The Pennsylvania Institution for the Deaf and Dumb," the sum of *Twenty Thousand Dollars*, for the use of that Institution.

III. I give and bequeath to "The Orphan Asylum of Philadelphia," the sum of *Ten Thousand Dollars*, for the use of that Institution.

IV. I give and bequeath to "The Comptrollers of the Public Schools for the City and County of Philadelphia" the sum of *Ten Thousand Dollars*, for the use of the Schools upon the Lancaster system, in the first section of the first school district of Pennsylvania.

V. I give and bequeath to "The Mayor, Aldermen and Citizens of Philadelphia," the sum of *Ten Thousand Dollars*, in trust safely to invest the same in some productive fund, and with the interest and dividends arising therefrom to purchase fuel, between the months of March and August in every year forever, and in the month of January in every year forever, distribute the same amongst poor white house keepers and room keepers, of good character, residing in the City of Philadelphia.

VI. I give and bequeath to the Society for the relief of poor and distressed Masters of Ships, their Widows and Children, (of which Society I am a member,) the sum of *Ten Thousand Dollars*, to be added to their Capital stock for the uses and purposes of said Society.

VII. I give and bequeath to the gentlemen who shall be Trustees of the Masonic Loan, at the time of my decease, the sum of *Twenty Thousand Dollars*, including therein ten thousand and nine hundred dollars due to me, part of the Masonic Loan, and any interest that may be due thereon at the time of my decease, in trust for the use and benefit of "The Grand Lodge of Pennsylvania, and Masonic Jurisdiction thereto belonging," and to be paid over by the said Trustees to the said Grand Lodge, for the purpose of being invested in some safe stock or funds, or other good security, and the dividends and interest arising therefrom to be again so invested and added to the Capital, without applying any part thereof to any other purpose until the whole Capital shall amount to thirty thousand dollars, when the same shall forever after remain a permanent fund or Capital, of the said amount of thirty thousand dollars, the interest whereof shall be applied from time to time to the relief of poor and respectable brethren, and in order that the real and benevolent purposes of masonic institutions may be attained, I recommend to the several lodges not to admit to membership, or to receive members from other lodges, unless the applicants shall absolutely be men of sound and good morals.

VIII. I give and bequeath unto Philip Peltz, John Lentz,

Francis Hesley Jacob Baker and Adam Young of Passyunk township, in the County of Philadelphia, the sum of *Six Thousand Dollars*, in trust, that they or the survivors or survivor of them shall purchase a suitable piece of ground, as near as may be in the centre of said township, and thereon erect a substantial brick building, sufficiently large for a school-house, and the residence of a school-master, one part thereof for poor male white children, and the other part for poor female white children of said township; and as soon as the said school-house shall have been built that the said trustees, or the survivors or survivor of them, shall convey the said piece of ground and house thereon erected, and shall pay over such balance of said sum as may remain unexpended to any board of directors and their successors in trust, which may at the time exist or be by law constituted consisting of at least twelve discreet inhabitants of the said township, and to be annually chosen by the inhabitants thereof, the said piece of ground and house to be carefully maintained by said directors and their successors solely for the purposes of a school as aforesaid, forever, and the said balance to be securely invested as a permanent fund, the interest thereof to be applied from time to time towards the education in the said school of any number of such poor white children of said township; and I do hereby recommend to the citizens of said township to make additions to the fund whereof I have laid the foundation.

IX. I give and devise my house, and lot of ground thereto belonging, situate in rue Ramouet aux Chartrons, near the city of Bordeaux, in France, and the rents, issues, and profits thereof, to my brother, Etienne Guard, and my niece Victoire Fenellon, (daughter of my late sister Sophia Guard Capayron,) (both residing in France,) in equal moieties for the life of my said brother, and, on his decease, one moiety of the said house and lot to my said niece Victoire, and her heirs forever, and the other moiety to the six children of my said brother, namely John Fabricius, Marguerite, Ann Henriette Jean August, Marie, and Madelaine Henriette, share and share alike, (the issue of any deceased child, if more than one, to take amongst them the parent's share,) and their heirs forever

X. I give and bequeath to my said brother, Etienne Girard, the sum of *Five Thousand Dollars*, and the like sum of *Five Thousand Dollars* to each of his six children above named. If any of the said children shall die prior to the receipt of his or her legacy of five thousand dollars, the said sum shall be paid, and I give and bequeath the same to any issue of such deceased child, if more than one, share and share alike.

XI. I give and bequeath to my said niece, Victoire Fenellon, the sum of *Five Thousand Dollars*.

XII. I give and bequeath absolutely to my niece, Antoinetta, now married to Mr. Hemphill, the sum of *Ten Thousand Dollars*, and I also give and bequeath to her the sum of *Fifty Thousand Dollars*, to be paid over to a trustee or trustees to be appointed by my executors, which trustee or trustees shall place and continue the said sum of fifty thousand dollars upon good security, and pay the interest and dividends thereof, as they shall from time to time accrue, to my said niece for her separate use, during the term of her life, and from and immediately after her decease, to pay and distribute the capital to and among such of her children and the issue of deceased children, and in such parts and shares as she the said Antoinetta, by any instrument under her hand and seal, executed in the presence of at least two credible witnesses, shall direct and appoint, and for default of such appointment, then to and among the said children and issue of deceased children in equal shares, such issue of deceased children, if more than one, to take only the share which their deceased parent would have taken if living.

XIII. I give and bequeath unto my niece Carolina, now married to Mr. Haslam, the sum of *Ten Thousand Dollars*, to be paid over to a trustee or trustees to be appointed by my executors, which trustee or trustees shall place and continue the said money upon good security, and pay the interest and dividends thereof from time to time as they shall accrue, to my said niece, for her separate use, during the term of her life and from and immediately after her decease, to pay and distribute the capital to and among such of her children, and issue of deceased children, and in such parts and shares, as she the said Carolina, by any instrument under her hand and seal, executed in the presence of at least two credible witnesses, shall direct and appoint, and for default of such appointment, then to and among the said children, and issue of deceased children, in equal shares, such issue of deceased children, if more than one, to take only the share which the deceased parent would have taken if living; but if my said niece Carolina shall leave no issue, then the said trustee or trustees, on her decease, shall pay the said capital, and any interest accrued thereon, to and among Caroline Lallemand, (niece of the said Carolina,) and the children of the aforesaid Antoinetta Hemphill, share and share alike.

XIV. I give and bequeath to my niece Henrietta, now married to Dr Clark, the sum of *Ten Thousand Dollars*, and I give and bequeath to her daughter Caroline, (in the last clause above named,) the sum of *Twenty Thousand Dollars*—the interest of the said sum of twenty thousand dollars, or so much thereof as may be necessary, to be applied to the maintenance and education of the said Caroline during her minority, and the principal, with any accumulated interest, to be paid to the said Caroline, on her arrival at the age of twenty-one years.

XV. Unto each of the Captains who shall be in my employment at the time of my decease, either in port, or at sea, having charge of one of my ships or vessels, and having performed at least two voyages in my service, I give and bequeath the sum of *Fifteen Hundred Dollars*—provided he shall have brought safely into the port of Philadelphia, or if at sea at the time of my decease, shall bring safely into that port, my ship or vessel last entrusted to him, and also that his conduct during the last voyage shall have been in every respect conformable to my instructions to him.

XVI All persons, who, at the time of my decease, shall be bound to me by indenture, as apprentices or servants, and who shall then be under age, I direct my executors to assign to suitable masters immediately after my decease, for the remainder of their respective terms, on conditions as favorable as they can in regard to education, clothing and freedom dues, to each of the said persons in my service, and under age at the time of my decease, I give and bequeath the sum of *Five Hundred Dollars*, which sums respectively I direct my executors safely to invest in public stock, to apply the interest and dividends thereof towards the education of the several apprentices or servants, for whom the capital is given respectively, and at the termination of the apprenticeship or service of each, to pay to him or her the said sum of five hundred dollars, and any interest accrued thereon, if any such interest shall remain unexpended in assigning any indenture, preference shall be given to the mother, father, or next relation, as assignee, should such mother, father, or relative desire it and be at the same time respectable and competent

XVII I give and bequeath to Francis Hesley (son of Mrs S Hesley, who is mother of Marianne Hesley,) the sum of *One Thousand Dollars*, over and above such sum as may be due to him at my decease

XVIII I charge my real estate in the State of Pennsylvania with the payment of the several annuities or sums following, (the said annuities to be paid by the Treasurer or other proper officers of the City of Philadelphia, appointed by the Corporation thereof for the purpose, out of the rents and profits of said real estate hereinafter directed to be kept constantly rented) namely —

1st I give and bequeath to Mrs Elizabeth Ingersoll, Widow of Jared Ingersoll, Esq, late of the City of Philadelphia, Counsellor at law, an annuity, or yearly sum of *One Thousand Dollars*, to be paid in half-yearly payments, in advance, of five hundred dollars each, during her life

2d I give and bequeath to Mrs Catharine Girard, now

widow of Mr. J. B. Hoskins, who died in the Isle of France, an annuity, or yearly sum of *Four Hundred Dollars*, to be paid in half yearly payments, in advance, of two hundred dollars each, during her life.

3d. I give and bequeath to Mrs. Jane Taylor, my present housekeeper, (the widow of the late Captain Alexander Taylor, who was master of my ship Helvetius, and died in my employment,) an annuity, or yearly sum of *Five Hundred Dollars*, to be paid in half-yearly payments, in advance, of two hundred and fifty dollars each, during her life.

4th. I give and bequeath to Mrs. S. Hesley, my house keeper at my place in Passyunk Township an annuity, or yearly sum of *Five Hundred Dollars*, to be paid in half-yearly payments, in advance, of two hundred and fifty dollars each during her life.

5th. I give and bequeath to Marianne Hesley, daughter of Mrs. S. Hesley, an annuity, or yearly sum of *Three Hundred Dollars*, to be paid to her mother, for her use, in half-yearly payments, in advance, of one hundred and fifty dollars each until the said Marianne shall have attained the age of twenty one years, when the said annuity shall cease, and the said Marianne will receive the five hundred dollars given to her and other indented persons, according to clause XVI of this Will.

6th. I give and bequeath to my late housekeeper, Mary Kenton, an annuity, or yearly sum of *Three Hundred Dollars* to be paid in half-yearly payments, in advance, of one hundred and fifty dollars each, during her life.

7th. I give and bequeath to Mrs. Deborah Scott, sister of Mary Kenton, and wife of Mr. Edwin T. Scott, an annuity or yearly sum of *Three Hundred Dollars*, to be paid in half-yearly payments, in advance, of one hundred and fifty dollars each, during her life.

8th. I give and bequeath to Mrs. Catharine M'Laren, sister of Mary Kenton, and wife of Mr. M'Laren, an annuity, or yearly sum of *Three Hundred Dollars*, to be paid in half-yearly payments, in advance, of one hundred and fifty dollars each, during her life.

9th. I give and bequeath to Mrs Amelia G. Taylor, wife of Mr. Richard M. Taylor, an annuity, or yearly sum of *Three Hundred Dollars*, to be paid in half-yearly payments, in advance, of one hundred and fifty dollars each, during her life.

XIX. All that part of my real and personal estate, near Washita, in the State of Louisiana, the said real estate consisting of upwards of two hundred and eight thousand arpens, or acres of land, and including therein the settlement hereinafter mentioned, I give, devise, and bequeath, as follows, namely: 1. I give, devise and bequeath to the Corporation of the City of New Orleans, their successors and assigns, all that part of my real estate, constituting the settlement formed on my behalf by my particular friend, Judge Henry Bree, of Washita, consisting of upwards of one thousand arpens, or acres of land, with the appurtenances and improvements thereon, and also all the personal estate thereto belonging, and thereon remaining, including upwards of thirty slaves now on said settlement, and their increase, in trust, however, and subject to the following reservations.

I desire, that no part of the said estate or property, or the slaves thereon, or their increase, shall be disposed of or sold for the term of twenty years from and after my decease, should the said Judge Henry Bree survive me and live so long, but that the said settlement shall be kept up by the said Judge Henry Bree, for and during said term of twenty years, as if it was his own: that is, it shall remain under his sole care and control, he shall improve the same by raising such produce as he may deem most advisable, and, after paying taxes, and all expenses in keeping up the settlement, by clothing the slaves and otherwise, he shall have and enjoy for his own use all the nett profits of said settlement. Provided, however, and I desire that the said Judge Henry Bree shall render annually, to the Corporation of the City of New Orleans, a report of the state of the settlement, the income and expenditure thereof, the number and increase of the slaves, and the nett result of the whole. I desire that, at the expiration of the said term of twenty years or on the decease of the said Judge Henry Bree, should he not live so long, the land and improvements forming said settlement, the slaves thereon or thereto belonging, and all other appurtenant personal property, shall be sold, as soon as the said Corporation shall deem it advisable to do so, and the proceeds of the said sale or sales shall be applied by the said Corporation to such uses and purposes as they shall consider most likely to promote the health and general prosperity of the inhabitants of the City of New Orleans. But, until the said sale shall be made, the said Corporation shall pay all taxes, prevent waste or intrusion, and so manage the said settlement and the slaves, and their increase thereon as to derive an income, and the said income shall be applied from time to time, to the same uses and purposes for the health and general prosperity of the said inhabitants.

2. I give, devise and bequeath to the Mayor Aldermen and Citizens of Philadelphia, their successors and assigns, two undivided third parts of all the rest and residue of my said real estate, being the lands unimproved near Washita, in the said State of Louisiana, in trust, that, in common with the Corporation of the City of New Orleans, they shall pay the taxes on the said lands, and preserve them from waste or intrusion, for the term of ten years from and after my decease, and, at the end of the said term, when they shall deem it advisable to do so, shall sell and dispose of their interest in said lands gradually from time to time, and apply the proceeds of such sales to the same uses and purposes hereinafter declared and directed, of and concerning the residue of my personal estate.

3. And I give, devise and bequeath to the Corporation of the City of New Orleans, their successors and assigns, the remaining one undivided third part of the said lands, in trust, in common with the Mayor, Aldermen and Citizens of Philadelphia, to pay the taxes on the said lands, and pre-

serve them from waste and intrusion, for the term of ten years from and after my decease, and, at the end of the said term, when they shall deem it advisable to do so, to sell and dispose of their interest in said lands gradually from time to time, and to apply the proceeds of such sale to such uses and purposes as the said Corporation may consider most likely to promote the health and general prosperity of the inhabitants of the City of New Orleans.

XX And, whereas, I have been for a long time impressed with the importance of educating the poor, and of placing them, by the early cultivation of their minds and the development of their moral principles, above the many temptations, to which, through poverty and ignorance, they are exposed, and I am particularly desirous to provide for such a number of poor male white orphan children, as can be trained in one institution, a better education, as well as a more comfortable maintenance than they usually receive from the application of the public funds and whereas, together with the object just adverted to I have sincerely at heart the welfare of the city of Philadelphia, and as a part of it, am desirous to improve the neighbourhood of the river Delaware, so that the health of the citizens may be promoted and preserved, and that the eastern part of the city may be made to correspond better with the interior Now, I do give, devise and bequeath *all the residue and remainder of my real and personal estate* of every sort and kind wheresoever situate, (the real estate in Pennsylvania charged as aforesaid,) unto ' the Mayor, Aldermen and Citizens of Philadelphia," their successors and assigns, in trust, to and for the several uses intents and purposes hereinafter mentioned and declared of and concerning the same, that is to say so far as regards my real estate in Pennsylvania, in trust, that no part thereof shall ever be sold or alienated by the said Mayor, Aldermen and Citizens of Philadelphia, or their successors, but the same shall forever thereafter be let from time to time, to good tenants, at yearly or other rents, and upon leases in possession not exceeding five years from the commencement thereof, and that the rents, issues and profits arising therefrom shall be applied towards keeping that part of the said real estate situate in the City and Liberties of Philadelphia constantly in good repair, (parts elsewhere situate to be kept in repair by the tenants thereof respectively,) and towards improving the same, whenever necessary by erecting new buildings, and that the nett residue (after paying the several annuities hereinbefore provided for) be applied to the same uses and purposes as are herein declared of and concerning the residue of my personal estate and so far as regards my real estate in Kentucky, now under the care of Messrs Triplett & Brumley, in trust, to sell and dispose of the same, whenever it may be expedient to do so, and to apply the proceeds of such sale to the same uses and purposes as are herein declared of and concerning the residue of my personal estate

XXI And so far as regards the residue of my personal estate, in trust, as to *two millions of dollars*, part thereof, to apply and expend so much of that sum as may be necessary, in erecting, as soon as practicably may be, in the centre of my square of ground between High and Chestnut streets, and Eleventh and Twelfth streets, in the city of Philadelphia, (which square of ground I hereby devote for the purposes hereinafter stated, and for no other, forever,) a permanent college, with suitable out-buildings, sufficiently spacious for the residence and accommodation of at least three hundred scholars, and the requisite teachers and other persons necessary in such an institution as I direct to be established, and in supplying the said college and out-buildings with decent and suitable furniture, as well as books and all things needful to carry into effect my general design

The said college shall be constructed with the most durable materials, and in the most permanent manner, avoiding needless ornament, and attending chiefly to the strength, convenience, and neatness of the whole. It shall be at least one hundred and ten feet east and west, and one hundred and sixty feet north and south, and shall be built on lines parallel with High and Chestnut streets, and Eleventh and Twelfth streets, provided those lines shall constitute at their junction right angles. It shall be three stories in height, each story at least fifteen feet high in the clear from the floor to the cornice. It shall be fire proof inside and outside. The floors and the roof to be formed of solid materials, on arches turned on proper centres, so that no wood may be used, except for doors, windows and shutters. Cellars shall be made under the whole building, solely for the purposes of the institution; the doors to them from the outside shall be on the east and west of the building, and access to them from the inside shall be had by steps, descending to the cellar floor from each of the entries or halls hereinafter mentioned, and the inside cellar doors to open under the stairs on the north east and north west corners of the northern entry, and under the stairs on the south-east and south west corners of the southern entry. there shall be a cellar window under and in a line with each window in the first story—they shall be built one-half below, the other half above the surface of the ground, and the ground outside each window shall be supported by stout walls; the sashes should open inside, on hinges, like doors and there should be strong iron bars outside each window. the windows inside and outside should not be less than four feet wide in the clear. There shall be in each story four rooms, each room not less than fifty feet square in the clear, the four rooms on each floor to occupy the whole space east and west on such floor or story, and the middle of the building north and south; so that in the north of the building, and in the south thereof, there may remain a space of equal dimensions, for an entry or hall in each, for stairs and landings. In the north-east and in the north-west corners of the northern entry or hall on the first floor, stairs shall be made so as to form a double stair case, which shall be carried up through the several stories; and, in like manner, in the south-east and south-west corners of the southern entry or hall, stairs shall be made, on the first floor, so as to form a double stair-case, to be carried up through the several stories;

the steps of the stairs to be made of smooth white marble, with plain square edges, each step not to exceed nine inches in the rise, nor to be less than ten inches in the tread; the outside and inside foundation walls shall be at least ten feet high in the clear from the ground to the ceiling, the first floor shall be at least three feet above the level of the ground around the building, after that ground shall have been so regulated as that there shall be a gradual descent from the centre to the side of the square formed by High and Chestnut and Eleventh and Twelfth streets; all the outside foundation walls, forming the cellars, shall be three feet six inches thick up to the first floor, or as high as may be necessary to fix the centres for the first floor; and the inside foundation wall, running north and south, and the three inside foundation walls running east and west, (intended to receive the interior walls for the four rooms, each not less than fifty feet square in the clear, above mentioned,) shall be three feet thick up to the first floor, or as high as may be necessary to fix the centres for the first floor; when carried so far up, the outside walls shall be reduced to two feet in thickness, leaving a recess outside of one foot, and inside of six inches—and when carried so far up, the inside foundation walls shall also be reduced, six inches on each side, to the thickness of two feet; centres shall then be fixed on the various recesses of six inches throughout, left for the purpose, the proper arches shall be turned, and the first floor laid; the outside and the inside walls shall then be carried up to the thickness of two feet throughout, as high as may be necessary to begin the recess intended to fix the centres of the second floor, that is, the floor of the four rooms, each not less than fifty feet square in the clear, and for the landings in the north, and the landings in the south of the building, where the stairs are to go up—at this stage of the work, a chain, composed of bars of inch square iron, each bar about ten feet long, and linked together by hooks formed of the ends of the bars, shall be laid straightly and horizontally along the several walls, and shall be as tightly as possible worked into the centre of them throughout, and shall be secured wherever necessary, especially at all the angles, by iron clamps solidly fastened, so as to prevent cracking or swerving in any part, centres shall then be laid, the proper arches turned for the second floor and landings, and the second floor and landings shall be laid, the outside and the inside walls shall then be carried up of the same thickness of two feet throughout as high as may be necessary to begin in the recess intended to fix the centres for the third floor and landings, and, when so far carried up, another chain, similar in all respects to that used at the second story, shall be in like manner worked into the walls throughout, as tightly as possible and clamped in the same way with equal care centres shall be formed, the proper arches turned, and the third floor and landings shall be laid the outside and the inside walls shall then be carried up, of the same thickness of two feet throughout, as high as may be necessary to begin the recess intended to fix the centres for the roof and, when so carried up, a third chain, in all respects like those used at the second and third stories, shall in the manner before described be worked as tightly as possible into the walls throughout, and shall be clamped with equal care, centres shall now be fixed in the manner best adapted for the roof, which is to form the ceiling for the third story, the proper arches shall be turned, and the roof shall be laid as nearly horizontally as may be, consistently with the easy passage of water to the eaves, the outside walls still of the thickness of two feet throughout, shall then be carried up about two feet above the level of the platform, and shall have marble capping, with a strong and neat iron railing thereon The outside walls shall be faced with slabs or blocks of marble or granite, not less than two feet thick, and fastened together with clamps securely sunk therein,—they shall be carried up flush from the recess of one foot formed at the first floor where the foundation outside wall is reduced to two feet The floors and landings, as well as the roof, shall be covered with marble slabs, securely laid in mortar, the slabs on the roof to be twice as thick as those on the floors. In constructing the walls as well as in turning the arches, and laying the floors, landings and roof, good and strong mortar and grout shall be used, so that no cavity whatever may anywhere remain. A furnace or furnaces for the generation of heated air shall be placed in the cellar, and the heated air shall be introduced in adequate quantity, wherever wanted, by means of pipes and flues inserted and made for the purpose in the walls and as those walls shall be constructed. In case it shall be found expedient for the purposes of a library, or otherwise, to increase the number of rooms by dividing any of those directed to be not less than fifty feet square in the clear, into parts, the partition walls to be of solid materials. A room most suitable for the purpose, shall be set apart for the reception and preservation of my books and papers, and I direct that they shall be placed there by my executors, and carefully preserved therein. There shall be two principal doors of entrance into the college, one into the entry or hall on the first floor, in the north of the building, and in the centre between the east and west walls; the other into the entry or hall in the south of the building, and in the centre between the east and west walls; the dimensions to be determined by a due regard to the size of the entire building, to that of the entry, and to the purpose of the doors. The necessity for, as well as the position and size of other doors internal or external, and also the position and size of the windows, to be in like manner, decided on by a consideration of the uses to which the building is to be applied, the size of the building itself, and of the several rooms, and of the advantages of light and air; there should in each instance be double doors, those opening into the rooms to be what are termed glass doors, so as to increase the quantity of light for each room, and those opening outward to be of substantial woodwork well lined and secured. The windows of the second and third stories I recommend to be made in the style of those in the first and second stories of my present dwelling house, North Water Street, on the eastern front thereof and outside each window I recommend that a substantial and neat iron balcony be placed, sufficiently wide to admit the opening of the shutters against the walls, the windows of the lower story to be in the same style, except that they are not to descend to the floor, but so far as the surbase, up to which the wall is to be carried, as is the case in the lower story of my house at my place in Passyunk Township. In minute particulars, not here noticed, utility and good taste should determine. There should be at least four out buildings, detached from the main edifice and from each other, and in such positions as shall at once answer the purposes of the institution and be consistent with the symmetry of the whole establishment; each building should be, as far as practicable, devoted to a distinct purpose; in that one or more of those buildings, in which they may be most useful, I direct my executors to place my plate and furniture of every sort.

The entire square, formed by High and Chestnut streets, and Eleventh and Twelfth streets, shall be enclosed with a solid wall, at least fourteen inches thick, and ten feet high, capped with marble and guarded with irons on the top, so as to prevent persons from getting over; there shall be two places of entrance into the square, one in the centre of the wall facing High street, and the other in the centre of the wall facing Chestnut street; at each place of entrance there shall be two gates, one opening inward, and the other outward; those opening inward to be of iron, and in the style of the gates north and south of my Banking house; and those opening outward to be of substantial wood work, well lined and secured on the faces thereof with sheet iron. The messuages now erected on the south-east corner of High and Twelfth streets, and on Twelfth street, to be taken down and removed as soon as the college and out buildings shall have been erected, so that the establishment may be rendered secure and private.

When the college and appurtenances shall have been constructed, and supplied with plain and suitable furniture and books philosophical and experimental instruments and apparatus, and all other matters needful to carry my general design into execution the income, issues and profits of so much of the said sum of two millions of dollars as shall remain unexpended, shall be applied to maintain the said college according to my directions

1 The institution shall be organized as soon as practicable, and to accomplish the purpose more effectually, due public notice of the intended opening of the college shall be given—so that there may be an opportunity to make selections of competent instructors, and other agents and those who may have the charge of orphans may be aware of the provisions intended for them

2 A competent number of instructors, teachers assistants, and other necessary agents shall be selected, and when needful their places from time to time, supplied, they shall receive adequate compensation for their services but no person shall be employed, who shall not be of tried skill in his or her proper department, of established moral character and in all cases persons shall be chosen on account of their merit, and not through favor or intrigue

3 As many poor <u>white</u> male orphans, between the age of six and ten years, as the said income shall be adequate to maintain, shall be introduced into the college as soon as possible, and from time to time, as there may be vacancies, or as increased ability from income may warrant, others shall be introduced

4 On the application for admission, an accurate statement should be taken, in a book prepared for the purpose, of the name birth-place, age, health condition as to relatives, and other particulars useful to be known of each orphan

5 No orphan should be admitted until the guardians or directors of the poor, or a proper guardian or other competent authority, shall have given, by indenture, relinquishment, or otherwise, adequate power to the Mayor, Aldermen and Citizens of Philadelphia, or to directors or others by them appointed to enforce, in relation to each orphan, every

proper restraint, and to prevent relatives or others from interfering with or withdrawing such orphan from the institution

6. Those orphans, for whose admission application shall first be made, shall be first introduced, all other things concurring—and at all future times, priority of application shall entitle the applicant to preference in admission, all other things concurring; but if there shall be, at any time, more applicants than vacancies, and the applying orphans shall have been born in different places, a preference shall be given—*first*, to orphans born in the city of Philadelphia; *secondly*, to those born in any other part of Pennsylvania; *thirdly*, to those born in the city of New York (that being the first port on the continent of North America at which I arrived) and *lastly*, to those born in the city of New Orleans, being the first port on the said continent at which I first traded, in the first instance as first officer, and subsequently as master and part owner of a vessel and cargo

7. The orphans admitted into the college shall be there fed with plain but wholesome food, clothed with plain but decent apparel, (no distinctive dress ever to be worn,) and lodged in a plain but safe manner. Due regard shall be paid to their health, and to this end their persons and clothes shall be kept clean, and they shall have suitable and rational exercise and recreation. They shall be instructed in the various branches of a sound education, comprehending reading, writing, grammar, arithmetic, geography, navigation, surveying, practical mathematics, astronomy, natural, chemical, and experimental philosophy, the French and Spanish languages, (I do not forbid, but I do not recommend the Greek and Latin languages.)—and such other learning and science as the capacities of the several scholars may merit or warrant. I would have them taught facts and things, rather than words or signs; and especially, I desire, that by every proper means a pure attachment to our republican institutions and to the sacred rights of conscience, as guar-

anteed by our happy constitutions shall be formed and fostered in the minds of the scholars

8. Should it unfortunately happen, that any of the orphans admitted into the college shall, from malconduct, have become unfit companions for the rest and mild means of reformation prove abortive, they should no longer remain therein

9. Those scholars, who shall merit it, shall remain in the college until they shall respectively arrive at between fourteen and eighteen years of age, they shall then be bound out by the Mayor, Aldermen and Citizens of Philadelphia or under their direction to suitable occupations, as those of agriculture, navigation, arts, mechanical trades, and manufactures, according to the capacities and acquirements of the scholars respectively, consulting as far as prudence shall justify it, the inclinations of the several scholars, as to the occupation, art or trade to be learned

In relation to the organization of the college and its appendages, I leave, necessarily, many details to the Mayor, Aldermen and Citizens of Philadelphia and their successors, and I do so with the more confidence, as, from the nature of my bequests, and the benefit to result from them, I trust that my fellow-citizens of Philadelphia will observe and evince especial care and anxiety in selecting members for their City Councils, and other agents

There are, however some restrictions, which I consider it my duty to prescribe, and to be, amongst others conditions on which my bequest for said college is made, and to be enjoyed, namely. *First* I enjoin and require that if, at the close of any year, the income of the fund devoted to the purposes of the said college shall be more than sufficient for the maintenance of the institution during that year, then the balance of the said income, after defraying such maintenance, shall be forthwith invested in good securities, thereafter to be and remain a part of the capital; but, in no event, shall any part of the said capital be sold, disposed of or pledged, to meet the current expenses of the said institution, to which

I devote the interest income, and dividends thereof, exclusively. *Secondly,* I enjoin and require that *no ecclesiastic, missionary, or minister of any sect whatsoever, shall ever hold or exercise any station or duty whatever in the said college, nor shall any such person ever be admitted for any purpose, or as a visitor, within the premises appropriated to the purposes of the said college.*—In making this restriction, I do not mean to cast any reflection upon any sect or person whatsoever; but, as there is such a multitude of sects, and such a diversity of opinion amongst them, I desire to keep the tender minds of the orphans who are to derive advantage from this bequest free from the excitement which clashing doctrines and sectarian controversy are so apt to produce. my desire is, that all the instructors and teachers in the college shall take pains to instil into the minds of the scholars *the purest principles of morality,* so that, on their entrance into active life they may, *from inclination and habit,* evince *benevolence towards their fellow creatures,* and *a love of truth sobriety, and industry,* adopting at the same time such religious tenets as their *matured reason* may enable them to prefer. If the income, arising from that part of the said sum of two millions of dollars remaining after the construction and furnishing of the college and out buildings, shall, owing to the increase of the number of orphans applying for admission, or other cause, be inadequate to the construction of new buildings, or the maintenance and education of as many orphans as may apply for admission, then such further sum as may be necessary for the construction of new buildings, and the maintenance and education of such further number of orphans as can be maintained and instructed within such buildings as the said square of ground shall be adequate to, shall be taken from the final residuary fund hereinafter expressly referred to for the purpose, comprehending the income of my real estate in the city and county of Philadelphia, and the dividends of my stock in the Schuylkill Navigation Company—my design and desire being, that the benefits of said institution shall be extended to as great a number of orphans as the limits of the said square and buildings therein can accommodate

XXII. And as to the further sum of *Five Hundred Thousand Dollars*, part of the residue of my personal estate, in trust, to invest the same securely and to keep the same so invested, and to apply the income thereof exclusively to the following purposes that is to say—

1. To lay out, regulate, curb, light and pave a passage or street, on the east part of the city of Philadelphia, fronting the river Delaware, not less than twenty-one feet wide and to be called *Delaware Avenue*, extending from Vine to Cedar street, all along the east part of Water street squares and the west side of the logs, which form the heads of the docks or thereabouts, and to this intent to obtain such Acts of Assembly, and to make such purchases or agreements, as will enable the Mayor, Aldermen and Citizens of Philadelphia to remove or pull down all the buildings, fences and obstructions which may be in the way, and to prohibit all buildings, fences, or erections of any kind, to the eastward of said Avenue, to fill up the heads of such of the docks as may not afford sufficient room for the said street, to compel the owners of wharves to keep them clean, and covered completely with gravel or other hard materials, and to be so levelled that water will not remain thereon after a shower of rain, to completely clean and keep clean all the docks within the limits of the city, fronting on the Delaware and to pull down all platforms carried out, from the east part of the city over the river Delaware, on piles or pillars

2. To pull down and remove all wooden buildings, as well those made of wood and other combustible materials, as those called brick-paned, or frame buildings filled in with bricks, that are erected within the limits of the city of Philadelphia, and also to prohibit the erection of any such building, within the said city's limits, at any future time

3. To regulate, widen, pave and curb Water street, and to distribute the Schuylkill water therein upon the following plan, that is to say—that Water street be widened east and

west, from Vine street all the way to South street, in like manner as it is from the front of my dwelling to the front of my stores on the west side of Water street, and the regulation of the curbstones continued at the same distance from one another as they are at present opposite to the said dwelling and stores, so that the regulation of the said street be not less than thirty nine feet wide, and afford a large and convenient footway, clear of obstructions and incumbrances of every nature, and the cellar doors on which, if any shall be permitted, not to extend from the buildings on to the footway more than four feet, the said width to be increased gradually, as the fund shall permit, and as the capacity to remove impediments shall increase, until there shall be a correct and permanent regulation of Water street, on the principles above stated, so that it may run north and south as straight as possible. That the ten feet middle alley, belonging to the public, and running from the centre of the east squares to Front street, all the way down across Water street to the river Delaware, to be kept open and cleansed as city property, all the way from Vine to South street; that such part of each centre or middle alley as runs from Front to Water street, be arched over with bricks or stone, in so strong a manner as to facilitate the building of plain and permanent stone steps and platforms, so that they may be washed and kept constantly clean; and that the continuance of the said alleys, from the east side of Water street, be curbed all the way to the river Delaware, and kept open forever. (I understand that those middle or centre alleys were left open in the first plan of the lots, on the east front of the city, which were granted from the east side of Front street to the river Delaware, and that each lot on said east front has contributed to make those alleys, by giving a part of their ground in proportion to the size of each lot; those alleys were in the first instance, and still are, considered public property, intended for the convenience of the inhabitants residing in Front street, to go down to the river for water and other purposes; but, owing to neglect or to some other cause, on the part of those who have had the care of the city property, several encroachments have been made on them by individuals, by wholly occupying or building over them, or otherwise, and in that way the inhabitants more particularly those who reside in the neighborhood, are deprived of the benefit of that wholesome air, which their opening and cleansing throughout would afford) That the iron pipes in Water street, which, by being of smaller size than those in the other streets, and too near the surface of the ground, cause constant leaks, particularly in the winter season, which in many places render the street impassable, be taken up and replaced by pipes of the same size, quality and dimensions in every respect, and laid down as deeply from the surface of the ground, as the iron pipes which are laid in the main streets of the city and as it respects pumps for Schuylkill water and fire-plugs in Water street that one of each be fixed at the south west corner of Vine and Water streets, and so running southward, one of each near the steps of the centre alley, going up to Front street one of each at the south west corner of Sassafras and Water streets, one of each near the steps of the centre alley going up to Front street, and so on at every south west corner of all the main streets and Water street, and of the centre alleys of every square, as far as South or Cedar street and when the same shall have been completed, that all Water street shall be repaved by the best workmen, in the most complete manner, with the best paving water stones, after the height of the curb-stones shall have been regulated throughout as well as the ascent and descent of the street, in such manner as to conduct the water through the main streets and the centre alleys to the river Delaware, as far as practicable, and whenever any part of the street shall want to be raised, to use nothing but good paving gravel for that purpose so as to make the paving as permanent as possible By all which improvements, it is my intention to place and maintain the section of the city above referred to in a condition which will correspond better with the general cleanliness and appearance of the whole city, and be more consistent with the safety, health, and comfort of the citizens. And my mind and will are, that all the income, interest and dividends of the said capital sum of five hundred thousand dollars, shall be yearly, and every year, expended upon the said objects, in the order in which I have stated them, as closely as possible, and upon no other objects until those enumerated shall have been attained; and, when those objects shall have been accomplished, I authorize and direct the said, the Mayor, Aldermen and Citizens, to apply such part of the income of the said capital sum of five hundred thousand dollars, as they may think proper, to the further improvement, from time to time, of the eastern or Delaware front of the city.

XXIII. I give and bequeath to the Commonwealth of Pennsylvania, the sum of *Three Hundred Thousand Dollars*, for the purpose of internal improvements by canal navigation, to be paid into the State treasury by my executors, as soon as such laws shall have been enacted by the constituted authorities of the said Commonwealth as shall be necessary and amply sufficient to carry into effect, or to enable the constituted authorities of the city of Philadelphia to carry into effect, the several improvements above specified namely,—1 *Laws*, to cause Delaware Avenue, as above described, to be made, paved, curbed and lighted; to cause the buildings, fences, and other obstructions now existing, to be abated and removed; and to prohibit the creation of any such obstructions to the eastward of said Delaware Avenue. 2 *Laws* to cause all wooden buildings, as above described, to be removed, and to prohibit their future erection within the limits of the city of Philadelphia. 3 *Laws*, providing for the gradual widening, regulating, paving and curbing Water street, as hereinbefore described, and also for the repairing the middle alleys, and introducing the Schuylkill water, and pumps, as before specified;—all which objects may, I persuade myself, be accomplished on principles at once just in relation to individuals, and highly beneficial to the public: the said sum, however, not to be paid, unless said laws be passed within one year after my decease.

XXIV. And as it regards *the remainder of said residue* of my personal estate, in trust, to invest the same in good securities, and in like manner to invest the interest and income thereof, from time to time, so that the whole shall form a permanent fund, and to apply the income of the said fund,

1st. To the further improvement and maintenance of the aforesaid College, as directed in the last paragraph of the XXIst clause of this Will.

2d. To enable the Corporation of the city of Philadelphia to provide more effectually than they now do for the security of the persons and property of the inhabitants of the said city, by a competent police including a sufficient number of watchmen, really suited to the purpose: and to this end, I recommend a division of the city into watch districts or four parts, each under a proper head and that at least two watchmen shall, in each round or station, patrole together.

3d. To enable the said Corporation to improve the city property, and the general appearance of the city itself, and, in effect, to diminish the burden of taxation, now most oppressive, especially on those who are the least able to bear it.—

To all which objects, the prosperity of the city, and the health and comfort of its inhabitants, I devote the said fund as aforesaid, and direct the income thereof to be applied yearly, and every year forever, after providing for the College as hereinbefore directed, as my primary object. But if the said City shall knowingly and wilfully violate any of the conditions hereinbefore and hereinafter mentioned, then I give and bequeath the said remainder and accumulations to the Commonwealth of Pennsylvania, for the purpose of internal navigation, excepting however, the rents, issues and profits of my real estate in the city and county of Philadelphia, which shall forever be reserved and applied to maintain the aforesaid College in the manner specified in the last paragraph of the XXIst clause of this Will. And if the Commonwealth of Pennsylvania shall fail to apply this or the preceding bequest to the purposes before mentioned, or shall apply any part thereof to any other use, or shall for the term of one year from the time of my decease, fail or omit to pass the laws hereinbefore specified for promoting the improvement of the city of Philadelphia, then I give devise and bequeath the said remainder and accumulations (the rents aforesaid always excepted and reserved for the College as aforesaid) to the United States of America, for the purposes of internal navigation, and no other.

Provided, nevertheless, and I do hereby declare, that all the preceding bequests and devices of the residue of my estate to the Mayor, Aldermen and Citizens of Philadelphia, are made upon the following express conditions that is to say:—*First*, That none of the monies principal, interest, dividends or rents, arising from the said residuary devise and bequest, shall at any time be applied to any other purpose or purposes whatever than those herein mentioned and appointed. *Second*, That separate accounts distinct from the other accounts of the Corporation, shall be kept by the said Corporation, concerning the said devise, bequest, college, and funds, and of the investment and application thereof, and that a separate account or accounts of the same shall be kept in bank, not blended with any other account, so that it may at all times appear, on examination by a committee of the Legislature, as hereinafter mentioned, that my intentions had been fully complied with. *Third*, That the said Corporation render a detailed account annually, in duplicate, to the Legislature of the Commonwealth of Pennsylvania, at the commencement of the session, one copy for the Senate and the other for the House of Representatives, concerning the said devised and bequeathed estate, and the investment and application of the same, and also a report in like manner of the state of the said college, and shall submit all their books, papers, and accounts touching the same, to a committee or committees of the Legislature for examination, when the same shall be required.

Fourth, The said Corporation shall also cause to be published in the month of January, annually, in two or more newspapers, printed in the city of Philadelphia, a concise but plain account of the state of the trusts, devises and bequests herein declared and made, comprehending the condition of the said college, the number of scholars, and other particulars needful to be publicly known for the year next preceding the said month of January annually.

XXV. And whereas, I have executed an assignment in trust, of my banking establishment, to take effect the day before my decease, to the intent that all the concerns thereof may be closed by themselves without being blended with the concerns of my general estate, and the balance remaining to be paid over to my executors. Now, I do hereby direct my executors hereinafter mentioned, not to interfere with the said trust in any way except to see that the same is faithfully executed, and to aid the execution thereof by all such acts and deeds as may be necessary and expedient to effectuate the same, so that it may be speedily closed, and the balance paid over to my executors, to go as in my Will, into the residue of my estate. And I do hereby authorize, direct, and empower the said trustees, from time to time, as the capital of the said bank shall be received, and shall not be wanted for the discharge of the debts due thereat, to invest the same in good securities, in the names of my executors, and to hand over the same to them to be disposed of according to this my Will.

XXVI. Lastly, I do hereby nominate and appoint Timothy Paxson, Thomas P. Cope, Joseph Roberts, William J. Duane, and John A. Barclay, executors of this my last Will and Testament. I recommend to them to close the concerns of my estate as expeditiously as possible, and to see that my intentions in respect to the residue of my estate are and shall be strictly complied with. And I do hereby revoke all other Wills by me heretofore made.

In witness, I, the said Stephen Girard, have to this my last Will and Testament, contained in thirty-five pages, set my hand at the bottom of each page, and my hand and seal at the bottom of this page, the said Will executed, from motives of prudence, in duplicate, this sixteenth day of February, in the year one thousand eight hundred and thirty

      STEPHEN GIRARD [SEAL]

Signed, sealed, published, and declared by the said Stephen Girard, as and for his last Will and Testament, in the presence of us, who have at his request hereunto subscribed our names as witnesses thereto, in the presence of the said Testator, and of each other, Feb 16, 1830

      JOHN H IRWIN
      SAMUEL ARTHUR,
      S H CARPENTER

WHEREAS, I, STEPHEN GIRARD, the Testator named in the foregoing Will and Testament, dated the sixteenth day of February, eighteen hundred and thirty, have since the execution thereof, purchased several parcels and pieces of real estate, and have built sundry Messuages, all which, as well as any real estate that I may hereafter purchase, it is my wish and intention to pass by the said Will. Now, I do hereby republish the foregoing last Will and Testament, dated February 16, 1830, and do confirm the same in all particulars. In witness, I, the said Stephen Girard, set my hand and seal hereunto, the twenty-fifth day of December, eighteen hundred and thirty

      STEPHEN GIRARD. [SEAL]

Signed, sealed, published, and declared by the said Stephen Girard, as and for a republication of his last Will and Testament, in the presence of us, who, at his request, have hereunto subscribed our names as witnesses thereto, in the presence of the said Testator and of each other, December 25th, 1830

      JOHN H IRWIN,
      SAMUEL ARTHUR,
      JNO THOMSON

WHEREAS, I, STEPHEN GIRARD, the Testator named in the foregoing Will and Testament, dated February 16, 1830, have, since the execution thereof, purchased several parcels and pieces of land and real estate, and have built sundry

Messuages, all which, as well as any real estate that I may hereafter purchase, it is my intention to pass by said Will. And whereas, in particular, I have recently purchased from Mr. William Parker, the Mansion House, out-buildings, and forty five acres and some perches of land, called Peel Hall, on the Ridge Road, in Penn Township. Now, I declare it to be my intention, and I direct, that the Orphan establishment, provided for in my said Will, instead of being built as therein directed upon my square of ground between High and Chestnut and Eleventh and Twelfth streets, in the city of Philadelphia, shall be built upon the estate so purchased from Mr. W. Parker, and I hereby devote the said estate to that purpose, exclusively, in the same manner as I had devoted the said square, hereby directing that all the improvements and arrangements for the said Orphan establishment, prescribed by my said Will as to said square, shall be made and executed upon the said estate, just as if I had in my Will devoted the said estate to said purpose—consequently the said square of ground is to constitute, and I declare it to be a part of the residue and remainder of my real and personal estate, and given and devised for the same uses and purposes as are declared in section twenty of my Will, it being my intention that the said square of ground shall be built upon and improved in such a manner as to secure a safe and permanent income for the purposes stated in said twentieth section. In witness whereof, I, the said Stephen Girard set my hand and seal hereunto, the twentieth day of June, eighteen hundred and thirty one.

      STEPHEN GIRARD [SEAL]

Signed, sealed, published, and declared by the said Stephen Girard, as and for a republication of his last Will and Testament, and a further direction in relation to the real estate therein mentioned, in the presence of us, who, at his request have hereunto subscribed our names as witnesses thereto, in the presence of the said Testator, and of each other, June 20, 1831.

      S. H. CARPENTER,
      L. BARDIN,
      SAMUEL ARTHUR

GIRARD, ET AL *vs* THE CITY OF PHILADELPHIA	October Sessions, 1859 No 3

To the Judges of the Circuit Court of the United States for the Eastern District of Pennsylvania Sitting in Equity

The undersigned, appointed Examiner the 20th July, 1860, respectfully reports

That having given notice to the respective solicitors, he was attended at his office, the inst , by Charles Ingersoll, Esquire solicitor for the plaintiffs, and Edward Olmsted, Esquire, solicitor for the defendants, when, after conference between them, it was thought not necessary to call witnesses on either side to the proofs about to be laid before the Court, which it was said consisted of facts appearing by records, documents, and proceedings of a public character, and further, that to lay such records, documents and proceedings entire before the Court, parts of them only being pertinent, would be unnecessary and cumbersome to the case and inconvenient to the Court It was agreed, by the said solicitors for the plaintiffs and defendants respectively, in manner and form following That the undersigned should report at the request of the said complainants, that the following are true copies of entries in the Journal of the Senate of Pennsylvania, and shall be used as given in evidence

"Tuesday, January 3, 1854

"This being the day appointed by the Constitution for "the meeting of the General Assembly, a number of mem- "bers of the Senate, and other gentlemen elected to supply "vacancies, assembled in the Senate chamber

"The Secretary of the Commonwealth being introduced, "stated that in obedience to the directions of the eighty- "seventh section of the Act of July 2, 1839, entitled 'An "'Act relating to the elections of this Commonwealth,' he "presented to the Senate the returns of the elections of "Senators for the last year

"On motion, the said returns were then read, by which it "appeared that the following persons were duly elected viz

"First District, composed of the city of Philadelphia Eli "K Price

"Second District, composed of the county of Philadelphia, "Levi Foulkrod"

That the following is truly copied from page 3 of the Journal of the Senate of Pennsylvania, for the year 1854, and shall be used as given in evidence

"Number of the districts and names of the members of "the Senate, with the date of the expiration of their respec- "tive terms of service, arranged agreeably to the provisions "of the Apportionment Bill of May 15th, 1850

"I District, composed of the city of Philadelphia, Wil- "liam A Crabb, 1854, Eli K Price, 1856

"II District, composed of the county of Philadelphia, "Samuel G Hamilton 1854 William Goodwin, 1855 Levi "Foulkrod, 1856"

That the following are true copies of entries in the Journal of the House of Representatives of Pennsylvania, and shall be used as given in evidence

' Tuesday, January 3, 1854

* * * * * *

"The said returns were read, by which it appeared that "the following gentlemen were returned as Representatives "of the city of Philadelphia and the several counties of this "Commonwealth, for the present year, viz

"City of Philadelphia

' William C Patterson,   "George H Hart,
"M W Baldwin,   "Henry K Strong

"County of Philadelphia

"Thomas Manderfield, "Isaac W Moore,
"Robert M Carlisle, "Richardson L Wright,
"George W Hillier, "Erastus Pulson,
"John J Boyd, "James H Hurtt,
"Robert B Knight, "Benjamin R Miller,
  "Joshua S Fletcher."

That the following are true copies of entries in the Journal of the Senate of Pennsylvania, and shall be used as given in evidence

"Wednesday, January 18th, 1854"

* * * * * *

"Agreeably to order, the Senate resumed the considera-"tion of bill No 4, entitled, 'A further Supplement to an "Act entitled An Act to incorporate the City of Philadel-"phia,' and,

* * * * * *

"The question recurring, Shall the bill pass?

"The yeas and nays were required by Mr Crabb and Mr "Goodwin, and are as follows, viz

"*Yeas.*—Messrs Barnes, Crabb, Cresswell, Darlington, "Darsie, Evans, Ferguson, Foulkrod, Goodwin, Hamilton, "Byron D Hamlin, Ephraim W Hamlin, Hendricks, Hies-"ter, Jamison, Kinzer, McClintock, McFarlan, Mellinger, 'Pratt, Price, Quiggle, Sager, Skinner, Slifer, Wherry, and "McClaslin, *Speaker*—27.

"*Nays*—None

"So the question was determined in the affirmative "Ordered, that the Clerk present the same to the House of "Representatives for concurrence"

That the following are true copies of entries in the Journal of the House of Representatives of Pennsylvania, and shall be used as given in evidence

"Monday, 30 January, 1854"

* * * * * *

"Bill from the Senate (No 101), entitled 'A further Sup-

"plement to an Act entitled An Act to incorporate the City "of Philadelphia'"

* * * * * *

"And on the question Shall the same pass?

"The yeas and nays were required by Mr Moore and Mr "Patterson, and are as follows, viz

"*Yeas*—Messrs Abraham, Adams, Atherton, Baldwin, "Ball, Beans, Beck, Beyer, Bigham, Boyd, Bush, Byerly, "Caldwell, Calvin, Carlisle, Chamberlin, Cook, Cummings, "Daugherty, Davis, Deegan, De France, Dunning, Edinger, "Eldred, Ellis, Fletcher, Foster, Fry, Gallentine, Gilmore, "Groom, Gwin, Hamilton, Hart, Hillier, Hills, Hipple, Hum-"mel, Hunsecker, Hunter, Hurtt, Jackman, Kilgore, Knight "Lawry (Lehigh), Linn, Magee, Maguire, Manderfield, Mc-"Kee, Miller, Montgomery, Moser Muse, Palmer, Parke, "Parmlee, Passmore, Patterson, Pulson, Putney Rawlins "Roberts, Sallade, Scott, Shenk, Sidle, Smith (Berks), Smith "(Crawford), Stewart, Stockdale, Strong, Struthers, Wheeler, "Wicklein, Wright, Ziegler, and Chase, *Speaker*—79

"*Nays*—Messrs Barton, Horn, and Moore—3.

"So the question was determined in the affirmative And "ordered, that the Clerk return the same to the Senate, and "request its concurrence in the amendments made thereto "by this House."

That the following are true copies of entries in the Journal of the Senate of Pennsylvania, and shall be used as given in evidence

"Tuesday, January 31, 1854"

* * * * * *

"On motion of Mr Price and Mr Crabb, the amendments "made by the House of Representatives to bill No 4, enti-"tled 'A further Supplement to an Act to incorporate the "City of Philadelphia,' were twice read and considered.

"The amendments embraced in the second, fourth, sixth, "tenth, twelfth, fifteenth, sixteenth, seventeenth, eighteenth, "twentieth, twenty-second, twenty-seventh, thirty-first, thir-

"ty-sixth, thirty seventh, thirty eighth, thirty-ninth, forty-
second forty-eighth, fifty first, fifty second sections, were
concurred in

"On the question, Will the Senate concur in the amendment embraced in the fifty-third section?

* * * * * *

"On the question, Will the Senate concur in the first
'division?

"It was determined in the affirmative

"On the question, Will the Senate concur in the second
'division?

* * * * * *

'So the question was determined in the affirmative"

"Wednesday, February 1, 1854"

* * * * * *

"Mr Foulkrod, from the committee appointed to compare
"bills, and present them to the Governor for his approbation, made a report, which was read as follows, viz

"That in conjunction with a similar committee from the
House of Representatives, they have compared, and on
'January thirty first, presented to the Governor for his
'approbation, the bill entitled as follows, to wit, 'A further
"Supplement to an Act entitled An Act to incorporate the
'City of Philadelphia'

'Saturday, February 11, 1854"

* * * * * *

"The Deputy Secretary of the Commonwealth being
'introduced, presented a message from the Governor which
was read as follows viz

"Executive Department,
"Harrisburg, Feb 11, 1854

"To the Senate and House of Representatives of the
Commonwealth of Pennsylvania Gentlemen,—I have
'approved and signed the following Acts of the General
"Assembly, viz On the 25th ult

* * * * * *

"On the 2d inst, 'A further Supplement to an Act enti-"tled An Act to incorporate the City of Philadelphia'"

That the following are true copies of entries in the Journal of the Select Council of the City of Philadelphia, and shall be used as given in evidence

"Thursday, June 22, 1854'

* * * * * *

"Mr Cornman offered the following, to wit

"*Resolved*, That the Hon. Robert T Conrad, Mayor of the 'City of Philadelphia, be requested to issue the Proclama 'tion as provided in the 6th section of the Act of Consoli-'dation, on the 5th day of July next, and that he fix the "time for the dissolution of the various local Boards of "Commissioners, &c, at forty days thereafter

"Which was read

"And being under consideration,
"Mr Miller moved to amend"

* * * * * *

"So the amendment was agreed to
"The resolution, as amended, was agreed to'

That the following are true copies of entries in the Journal of the Common Council of the City of Philadelphia, and shall be used as given in evidence

'Thursday, June 22, 1854"

* * * * * *

"Message from Select Council informing this Council that "they had passed the following resolution

'*Resolved*, That the Hon Robert T Conrad, Mayor of the "City of Philadelphia, be requested to issue his proclama-'tion forthwith, dissolving the different corporations super-"ceded by the 6th section of the Act consolidating the City "of Philadelphia, to take effect on the thirtieth inst"

* * * * * *

"So Common Council concurred"

That the following are true copies of entries in the Journal of the Select Council of the City of Philadelphia, and shall be used as given in evidence

"Thursday, June 29, 1854."

* * * * * *

"A message from the Mayor was received, stating that he "had approved and signed the resolution of Councils direct-'ing him to issue his proclamation fixing a period for the "termination of the various municipalities in the county of "Philadelphia, and that he had issued his proclamation"

That all Acts of the Provincial and State Legislatures of Pennsylvania shall be used as given in evidence

That all inventories, accounts, and other papers and proceedings, of record in the offices of the Register for the County of Philadelphia, and the Clerk of the Orphans' Court of the County of Philadelphia, and the Prothonotary of the Court of Common Pleas of the County of Philadelphia, in the matter of the estate of the late Stephen Girard, shall be used as given in evidence

That the maps called "Barnes' new map of the consolidated city of Philadelphia," published in 1855, and the map called "A map of the County of Philad., from actual survey, by Chas Ellet, in accordance with the Act of Assembly passed June 30, 1839," shall be used as given in evidence

That in the various municipalities, prior to the 2d February, 1854, within the county of Philadelphia, by the laws and usages regulating the same, when new roads or streets were to be acquired and opened for public use, the acquisition of the ground was an expense paid by the county, and the grading, draining, paving, and all other charges, were an expense paid in some of the municipalities by the owners of the adjacent soil, and in others by the public

That the following is truly copied from the annual report of the Comptroller of the City of Philadelphia to the Select and Common Councils, dated the 17th January, 1857, and shall be used as given in evidence:

'*Taxes of* 1856.

"John M Coleman and Peter Armbruster

	ASSESSED			ASSESSED
1st Ward,	$76,287 27	13th Ward,		100,786 07
2d "	60,263 52	14th "		95,598 21
3d "	46,587 22	15th "		109,323 38
4th "	53,748 93	16th "		56,714 43
5th "	263,333 50	17th "		36,238 51
6th "	408,238 94	18th "		50,852 83
7th "	135,978 07	19th "		95,890 38
8th "	254,445 60	20th "		94,931 51
9th "	211,681 69	21st "		54,306 79
10th "	156,824 61	22d "		59,771 54
11th "	83,620 65	23d "		64,883 01
12th "	77,783 60	24th "		97,525 75

$2,745,016 01

That, of the twenty-four Wards mentioned in the said Comptroller's report, those called the 5th, 6th, 7th 8th, 9th and 10th are the Wards which composed the late corporation called the Mayor, Aldermen and Citizens of Philadelphia.

That the following is a true copy of a memorial to the Legislature of Pennsylvania, presented in January, 1854, and shall be used as given in evidence

And which was accompanied by a draft of a proposed bill for consolidating the municipalities of the county of Philadelphia, of which the following is a true copy, and shall be used as given in evidence.

To the Honorable the Senate and House of Representatives of the Commonwealth of Pennsylvania

The memorial of the Executive Committee, appointed by the citizens of the City and County of Philadelphia, to present to your honorable bodies the subject of consolidating the various civil subdivisions of the city and county into one municipal corporation, respectfully represents·

That the measure of uniting into one the small governments into which Philadelphia is now unhappily divided, has been attracting the attention of the people for many years, and has finally enlisted in its support the organic declarations of all political parties, and the approbation of the mass of the inhabitants. Believing, as your memorialists do, that this beneficial union can no longer be delayed without enduring injury to the people of Philadelphia, and satisfied that your honorable bodies will cheerfully yield to an early consideration of the subject, your memorialists have, with much care, prepared a bill to present to the Legislature at an early day of the session, not, however, with any desire to insist upon details, but to demonstrate that the measure itself, with all its vast ramifications, is susceptible of being reduced into a simple and plain system, free of all legal, constitutional or practical difficulty.

It is necessary to a correct understanding of this important subject, that your honorable bodies should be possessed of a view of the various municipalities into which the actual city of Philadelphia is now cut up, as well as of the other public corporations to which the people of the city and county are subjected; and, with this object, your memorialists will proceed to submit a correct statement thereof.

It will be seen, that that part of Philadelphia which bears the corporate title of the City is but a small portion of the actual city—the suburbs having become part of the city itself, and given place to suburbs more remote.

In 1853, the taxables of the city and suburbs are as follows.

The Corporate City,	22,024
Northern Liberties,	9,130
Spring Garden,	12,813
Kensington,	11,563
Southwark,	8,193
Moyamensing,	6,153
Penn,	2,658
North Penn,	701

West Philadelphia,	1,438
Germantown,	2,203
Richmond,	1,873
Frankford Borough,	1,270
Belmont, estimated,	300
Aramingo,	300
	80,624

The balance of the county, which is composed of rural districts, except the borough of Manayunk, which contains 1,530 taxables, and the borough of Whitehall, has the following number of taxables, viz

Passyunk,	335
Kingsessing,	500
Blockley,	504
Roxborough,	716
Bristol,	501
Unincorporated Northern Liberties,	311
Bridesburg,	259
Oxford,	492
Lower Dublin,	1017
Byberry,	239
Moreland,	115
	4,730

TOTAL

City and suburbs,	80,624
Manayunk borough,	1,330
Bridesburg "	259
Rural districts,	4,730
	86,943 taxables

Philadelphia was laid out by William Penn, on a neck of land between the rivers "Delaware and Schuylkill, having two fronts on the water, each a mile, and two from river to river," and by his charter, dated the 25th October, 1701, he

D W S—31

erected the said town of Philadelphia into a city. The powers of the city corporation were very limited, and, by subsequent acts of Assembly, the regulation of the nightly watch, and the "enlightening' the streets, lanes and alleys, and watering them, were vested in six Wardens, elected by the inhabitants, whilst the pitching, paving, and cleaning the streets, and regulating the water courses and common sewers, were vested in six Commissioners, elected in the same manner

The municipal duties of pitching, paving, cleaning, lighting, watching and watering the streets, were thus entrusted to two separate boards, with full taxing powers, but entirely irresponsible to the corporation of the city, which exercised no taxing powers whatever

By the Revolution, the corporation of the city was dissolved, and the Justices of the Peace were substituted for the Mayor, Recorder and Aldermen, in performing any duties or services required by the existing laws, and also for the Mayor's Court The effect of these changes was, that, in 1789, the municipal government of the city was parcelled out between the Wardens of the City of Philadelphia and the Commissioners for paving and cleaning the streets, who formed separate boards, and had entirely separate powers of taxing and the City Court, which was held by the Justices of the Peace of the city, who, in their individual capacities, also exercised certain authorities in connection with one or other of the above bodies of local police

The citizens, however, desired a popular restoration of the old form of city government, which should unite the various branches of the police, then subsisting in different and necessarily discordant hands, under one legislative and executive head, and with these views the Act of the 11th March, 1789, to incorporate the city of Philadelphia, was passed

Upwards of twenty Acts of Assembly have been since passed, altering this original law, and all these form together what is popularly called the charter of the city The Mayor is elected by the people, and is the nominal executive head, whilst the whole of the legislative power is vested in the Select and Common Councils, consisting of thirty-two members, who are elected in separate districts

The powers of the city corporation are very extensive, and reach nearly every branch of municipal police. They have dammed the Schuylkill at Fairmount, and erected water works and gas-works, built colleges, hospitals, markets, stores, tobacco warehouses, culverts, wharves, landings, bridges, railroads, and ice boats, paved streets, laid water-pipes and gas-pipes, ornamented squares, and purchased grounds for the summer resort of their citizens

The City Debt is as follows

Gas loans,	$1,272,000 00
Other loans, to 1st January, 1853,	6,237,200 00
" " since 1st January, 1853, including $100,000 to Hempfield Railroad,	173,000 00
	$7,682,200 00

Per Contra

Gas sinking fund,	$482,582 89	
Do contingent fund,	293,249 59	
City sinking fund,	606,336 36	
Increase, do., 1853,	30,000 00	
Penna. R. R. stock,	4,000,000 00	
Hempfield do.,	100,000 00	
Gas Works,	1,409,940 03	
City Railroad, income, $10,000,	100,000 00	
		7,022,108 87

Apparent balance against the city, $660,091 83

But the following income is to be taken into account

		PER ANNUM
Water rents, .	$158,000	
Deduct permanent expense of Water works,	28,500	
		129,500 00
Market rents, . . .		35,000 00
Rents of city property, .		34,000 00
" tobacco warehouses,		9,000 00
		207,500 00
Representing a capital of		$3,458,333 83

There are, besides these, the unproductive landings at the ends of the streets on the Schuylkill, the four public squares, Independence Square, and Pratt's Garden, which would make a beautiful summer resort for our fellow citizens

These grounds, the Fairmount works, and the Girard College, are all beyond the present city limits, and to the north of it, whilst the city, as the trustee of the Girard estate, owns property in the city proper, and north and south of it.

The area is 1402½ acres, divided into seventeen wards, all of which are subdivided into precincts. The taxables are 22,024 and the assessed value of real estate, $66,497,465; occupations, $646,625; furniture, $1,622,500; money at interest, stocks and debts, $18,311,241.

SOUTHWARK.

The District of Southwark was originally laid out under an act of the 26th of March, 1762, and public landings were purchased under acts of 15th April and 20th September, 1782, and, under an act of the 29th September, 1787, and a supplement thereto, a plan for the streets in said district, and for certain roads in the townships of Moyamensing and Passyunk, was reported to the Supreme Executive Council, and adopted by them (with the exception of Mead alley) on the 5th of January, 1790. By these acts, various police powers are exercised by the Assessors, Surveyors or Regulators of Streets and the Supervisors of the Highways, which last were, for special purposes, erected into a body politic and corporate.

The Legislature, however, finally, on the 18th April, 1794, created the inhabitants of Southwark a corporation, by the name of "The Commissioners and Inhabitants of the District of Southwark," and invested them with the usual municipal powers.

The funded debt of the District is

Five per cents,	$158,350
Six per cents,	256,550
	$414,900

The value of the corporate property is $178,417. The income from it is $8,000. The floating unfunded debt of the District is about $20,000. The area is 508½ acres, divided into six wards. The taxables are 8,193, and the assessed value of real estate, $6,036,047.

The executive and legislative power is vested in a single Board of Commissioners, of eighteen members, one-third elected annually in the different wards, at the constables' election, in March. The representation in this body is of wards, each ward electing one commissioner every year.

NORTHERN LIBERTIES.

On the 9th March, 1771, Regulators were appointed in the Northern Liberties, and, under subsequent acts, surveys or plans were made of the streets north and south of the Cohocksink creek: and on the 28th March, 1803, an act was passed to incorporate that part of the township of the Northern Liberties lying between Sixth street and the Delaware, and Vine street and the Cohocksink, which was repealed and supplied by the act of the 16th March, 1819.

The area is 320 acres, divided into seven wards, which are subdivided into election precincts; taxables, 9,130, and the assessed value of real estate, $9,637,466.

The funded debt of the District is

Six per cents,	$307,900
Five per cents,	37,840
Pennsylvania Railroad loan,	500,000
	$845,700
The property of the District consists of Pennsylvania Railroad stock,	500,000
	$345,700
Also, their interest in Schuylkill Water Works, gross income,	35,000
Market houses, gross income,	10,000
Public landings, income,	12,000
Real estate, income,	400
	$57,400

Besides that used by the corporation

The executive and legislative power is vested in a single Board of Commissioners, of twenty-one members, one-third elected annually by general ticket, with a nominal head to the corporation, under the title of Mayor, also elected annually.

Spring Garden

On the 22d March, 1813, the inhabitants of Penn Township, between the middle of Sixth and Broad, and Vine street and Hickory lane, or Coates street, were incorporated by the name of "The Commissioners of the District of Spring Garden," and by a supplement, passed 2d March, 1829, the bounds were extended to the Schuylkill, and 200 feet north of Poplar lane

The area is 1100 acres, divided into seven wards. The taxables, 12,813, and the assessed value of real estate, $15,128,817.

The funded debt of the District is

Six per cents,	$1,673,500 00
Five per cents,	148,500 00
	$1,822,000 00

The corporate property is

Pennsylvania Railroad stock,	$500,000 00	
Gas Works, cost,	334,967 19	
Market Houses, cost,	39,821 83	
Hall, lot west of Hall, and sundry other property, cost,	241,303 44	
Water Works, cost,	124,270 09	
		1,240,362 55
Besides registered taxes, claims and debts,	.	240,119 17
The gross income for 1853, from gas, was	.	71,441 41
Do do from market rents,		7,896 00
Do. do from public land'gs,		287 50
Do do from water rents,		47,935 40

The legislative and executive power is vested in a single Board of Commissioners, of twenty one members, one third elected annually by separate ticket

KENSINGTON.

Kensington was incorporated on the 6th March, 1820, and by the addition of the Fair Hill district, contains 1288 acres, divided into eight wards

The taxables were, in 1853, 11,563, and the assessed value of real estate, $7,148,502

The funded debt consisted, in January, 1853—

Of 5 per cent. loans, .	$65,716 17
Of 6 " "	269,022 52
Of 6 " Water-works loan, .	259,441 35
	$591,180 04

The corporate property is:

Water Works,	$274,566 32	
Real estate,	41,443 80	
		316,010 12

The income from market houses is $2,005.15, representing a capital of $33,419 17, and the income from public landings is $362, being 6 per cent. interest on $6,033 33.

The legislative and executive power is vested in a Board of Commissioners of twenty-four members, one-third annually elected by general ticket.

MOYAMENSING

Moyamensing was incorporated by an act of the 24th of March, 1812, which has been supplied by the act of 24th of March, 1842, and has been changed by the act of the 5th of April, 1848, to "The Commissioners and Inhabitants of the District of Moyamensing."

The area is 1,486 acres, divided into five wards. The taxables are 6,153, and the assessed value of real estate, $3,838,791.

The funded debt of the District is:

5 per cents,		$62,493 15
5½ "		9,000 00
6 "		46,850 00
		$118,343 15

The corporate property of the District consists of Hall, real estate, value $41,500.

The legislative and executive power is vested in a single Board of Commissioners of fifteen members, one-third elected annually by general ticket.

PENN.

The District of Penn was incorporated on the 28th of February, 1844. It has taxables, 2,658, and the assessed value of real estate is $3,522,652.

The funded debt of the District is

Six per cents,	$237,000

The corporate property consists of—

Hall and lot, 10th and Thompson streets,	4,000
Lot, Schuylkill 5th and Master streets	23,000
Market houses, cost,	20,000
The unfunded debt is	6,000

The executive and legislative power of the District is vested in a Board of Commissioners, one-third elected annually at the constables' election in March

RICHMOND

The District of Richmond was incorporated on the 27th February, 1847, and has 1,873 taxables, and the assessed value of real estate is $2,756,995

The funded debt of the District is

Six per cent loan,	$220,000
The corporate property consists of landings, market houses, docks and hall, valued at	$100,000
Debts for paving, &c.,	24,500
Registered taxes,	3,500
	$128,000

The executive and legislative powers of the District is vested in a single Board of Commissioners, one third elected annually by general ticket

WEST PHILADELPHIA

The Borough of West Philadelphia was incorporated by an act of Assembly of the 17th February, 1844, and, by act of 3d April, 1851, was changed into a District, with the title of 'The District of West Philadelphia.' It has 1,436 taxables, and the assessed value of real estate is $2,052,195

The funded debt is

Ordinary loan, 6 per cent.,	$112,000
Gas loan, do	35,000
Water loan, do	120,000
	$267,000

The corporate property is

Lot at Water Works,	$8,000
Lot for Stand Pipe,	6,000
Hall and lot,	25,000
Gas Works,	35,000
Water Works (at cost),	108,000
Water pipe included in loan of $120,000, to be paid for by owners of property,	30,000
District liens, &c.,	7,000
	$219,000

The income upon the corporate estate cannot be stated until the water-works are completed. The gas works yielded, last year, eight per centum on the cost. The corporation tax, 55 cents, yielded, in 1853, $11,000. In 1854 it is estimated at $14,000. The value of assessed property is increasing so rapidly in the District, that the corporation tax, at the same rate, will soon produce double the amount. The area of the District is nearly twice the surface of the city proper.

The executive and legislative power of the District is vested in a President of the Board, with the powers of Burgess, and twelve Commissioners, elected separately in wards, four to each ward, for two years.

ARAMINGO.

The Borough of Aramingo (formerly Doverville) was incorporated on the 11th of April, 1850, with all the municipal powers of a District. It is governed by a Board of Commissioners, and authorized to levy a loan on real estate, not exceeding three mills on the dollar, for borough purposes

Belmont

The District of Belmont was incorporated April 14, 1853, with the corporate title of "The Commissioners and Inhabitants of the District of Belmont." It is governed by a Board of Commissioners, who are authorized to levy a tax on real estate not exceeding one-half of one per cent. The District owes no funded debt.

The Boroughs of Manayunk, Germantown, Frankford, Whitehall, and Bridesburg, are governed by Town Councils, with authority to levy taxes on real estate.

The funded debt of the Borough of Frankford is $20,000. The value of the corporate property of the borough is $16,000; the income derived from the parts rented is $200. The borough is about erecting Gas works and laying gas pipes, for the purpose of supplying Frankford and Aramingo with gas; the cost of which will be about $25,000.

The funded debt of the Borough of Bridesburg is $2,500; the corporate property is about equal in value to the debt.

The remaining portions of the county are townships, and are, with little variation, regulated by the general township laws.

These make eleven distinct municipal corporations within a portion only of the proposed limits, the earliest beginning as far back as 1701, and the last created in 1853; to which are to be added five boroughs, all invested with the power to tax; making thus far sixteen governments.

But besides all these municipal corporations, there is another corporation called "The Guardians for the Relief and Employment of the Poor of the City of Philadelphia, the District of Southwark, and the Townships of Northern Liberties and Penn," which has taxing powers uncontrolled by any other body, with a large and valuable real estate under its charge.

The Poor Tax raised in the city and districts included in the present jurisdiction of the Guardians of the Poor, for 1853, are assessed (on real estate) at 20 cents on $100, and amounted to $251,829 94   The corporation property of the Board of Guardians is

Blockley Farm, cost,	$51,761 81
Cost of Almshouse,	859,743 84
Ground rents State loan and Schl. Navigation and Lehigh stock,	23,520 47
Seventh street estate cost subject to ground rent,	2,000 00
	$937,026 12
The loan due by the Guardians is	$642,904 04

The Board of Guardians is composed of eighteen members

The Board of Health consists, by the present law of eighteen members. It owes no funded or other debt. Their property principally consists of real estate, used for public sanitary purposes, and not productive. The income of the corporation is fluctuating, depending mainly on fees, on vessels and passengers, permits for removing nuisances, and the like. From these resources, the Board pay the expenses of keeping up their establishment, including the salaries of officers appointed under existing acts of Assembly.

The Board of County Commissioners (three in number), controlled by a County Board consisting of the Senators and Representatives of the city and county for the time being, exercise powers of a local government, and among other powers that of taxing real and personal property and persons. Their debt is large, owing to the operation of the law awarding damages for the opening of streets, out of the county treasury, and that portion of the public debt always will be on the increase until the law of New York is adopted, which lays these damages upon the owners of land who are benefitted by the new highway.

The funded debt of the County, July 1st, 1853, was

Five per cents,	$1,195,900 09
Six per cents,	934,533 33
One per cents,	74 60
	$2,130,508 02
The County Sinking Fund is	$272,552 91

By adding these debts together, we obtain the aggregate amount of the consolidated debt of the new City of Philadelphia. This consolidated city debt will be $14,961,735 25 as follows, viz:

Funded Debts of City and Districts, &c.

City,	$7,682,200 00
County,	2,130,508 02
Southwark,	414,900 00
Northern Liberties,	845,700 00
Spring Garden,	1,822,000 00
Kensington,	591,180 04
Moyamensing,	118,343 15
Penn,	247,000 00
Richmond,	220,000 00
West Philadelphia,	257,000 00
Guardians of the Poor,	642,904 04
Frankford,	20,000 00
Bridesburg,	2,500 00
Total,	$11,984,235 25

This total is large, but it should be remembered that the sinking fund and contingent fund of the City Gas Works, and the sinking fund of the City and of the County is $1,684,721 71

Railroad stock of the City and Northern Liberties,	4,600,000 00
Gas Works of the City,	1,409,940 03
The Water Works of the City, Northern Liberties, Spring Garden and Kensington produce an income of about $230,000, being an interest at 6 per cent of our $3,500,000 cost about	2,500,000 00
Spring Garden Gas Works and Railroad stock,	834,967 19
	$11,029,628 93

Besides all the other corporate property hereinbefore mentioned.

Any apprehension, therefore, on the part of the outer or any other districts, that the interest on the public debt will require severe taxation to meet it, is groundless, for it must be obvious to any observer, that a capitalist who would take upon himself the public debt and public property would be enriched by the operation, and it is one of the prominent intentions of the bill that the corporation incomes shall be appropriated to the interest

The Board of Comptrollers of the Public Schools own a large real estate—value, at cost, $932,290—which is used for the purpose of instruction, and is of course unproductive By an act of Assembly passed April 8th, 1853, the Board is authorized ' to report to the County Commissioners annually on or before the first day of May, the amount of money which *they may deem necessary* to defray the expenses of the district for the current year '

And the County Commissioners " *shall* ascertain the percentum upon the amount of the county assessment, which will produce the sum required by the Comptrollers," and deliver duplicates to the collectors of taxes The collectors are required to pay the tax so ordered by the Comptrollers to the County Treasurer, who shall keep the same distinct from the county funds, and pay out the same on the orders of the Comptrollers By this act, which has taken the public by surprise, the Board of Comptrollers possess the right to tax property at their discretion

On the 29th April, 1853, the Board informed the County Commissioners that they required for the support of the public schools the sum of $414,260
Commissions for collection, and allowance in anticipation of payment, . 35,640
$449,900

Thereupon the County Commissioners, as required by the act, assessed a school tax of 30 cents on the $100, on real estate and personal property, . $451,260
The aggregate assessed value of real and personal estate in the School District being . $150,420,821

This interesting branch of the public government is in a prosperous condition. The following statement comparing its condition for the year ending June 30th, 1852, and June 30th, 1853 will exhibit a satisfactory increase of usefulness.

	SCHOOLS							TEACHERS			SCHOLARS		
	High	Normal	Grammar	Secondary	Primary	Unclassified	Total	Male	Female	Total	Male	Female	Total
1852	1		51	54	34	149	40	279	83	741	824	26,034	23,601	49,635
1853	1	1	55	35	152	42	286	80	760	840	25,836	24,249	50,085

	1852	1853
Number of Directors,	231	237
Number of Comptrollers	24	24

The increase of schools is 7, of teachers, 16 of scholars, 450. Total scholars 50,085. Amount of tax, including commission and allowances $451,260, making an average of about $9 per year for each scholar, excluding interest on cost of school houses.

The cost of supporting the High School, with 512 pupils, is $17,449 52, or $32 97 for each pupil.

The cost of supporting the Normal School and School of Practice, with 519 pupils, is $5,796 72, or $10 98 for each pupil.

The assessed value of real and personal property in the city and county of Philadelphia is as follows:

Real estate,	$128,218,658
Occupations,	2,240,871
Furniture,	1,919,590
Money at interest, stock, loans & debts,	21,955,269
Emoluments of office,	130,825
Horses and cows,	500,581
Carriages,	194,868
Watches,	6,288
Total,	$155,260,662

The total amount of taxes assessed in the city and county, for 1853, for State, county, corporation, borough and township purposes, was $2,469,760

It was difficult to state with precision the amount of commissions paid to tax collectors. By the last report of the County Commissioners, page 42, it appears that on the county tax of 1852, of $973,827 12, the commissions paid to the tax collectors were $42,717 03. Assuming this as a fair average, a proximate result, very near the truth may be arrived at by stating that the commissions on the total of $2,469,760, for 1853, will average $4\frac{1}{10}$ per cent, amounting to $101,260 16. The taxes levied on real and personal estate in the city and county, for 1853, were as follows. In the city, the county tax is 40 cents in $100 of the assessed value, State tax, 30 cents; school, 30 cents; poor, 20 cents, corporation, 58 cents. The same rate of county, state, school and poor tax is collected in the Northern Liberties, Spring Garden, Kensington, Southwark, Moyamensing, Penn, North Penn, West Philadelphia, Richmond, Bridesburg and Unincorporated Northern Liberties, and the same county and State tax in the rest of the county. In the Northern Liberties, the corporation tax was 31 cents on real estate only; in Spring Garden, 50 cents; in Kensington, 60 cents, and eight cents per year per foot for gas pipes; in Southwark on real estate only, 85 cents; in Moyamensing, 95 cents; in Penn District 50 cents, and 20 cents watch and lamp tax; in West Philadelphia, 55 cents; Richmond, 60 cents; Belmont, 30 cents; Aramingo, 15 cents. In Passyunk, road tax, 48 cents; poor, 20 cents. In Kingsessing, road tax, 30 cents; poor, 20 cents. In Blockley, road tax, 23 cents; poor, 13 cents. In North Penn, road tax, 18 cents; poor, 15 cents. In Roxborough, poor tax, 15 cents; road tax, 10 cents. In Manayunk, borough tax, 35 cents; poor tax, 20 cents. In Germantown, borough tax, 40 cents; poor, 18 cents. In Bristol, poor tax, 18 cents. In Unincorporated Northern Liberties, road tax, 25 cents. In Bridesburg, borough tax, 30 cents; poor, 20 cents. In Frankford, borough tax, 85 cents, poor, 7 cents. In Oxford, road tax, 17 cents poor, 7 cents. In Lower Dublin, poor tax, 7 cents, road tax, 12 cents. In Byberry, road and poor tax 20 cents each in Whitehall, 15 cents in Moreland, road and poor tax 20 cents each

The Borough of Germantown owns, in real estate, the Poor House property, value $20,000, and a lot of ground 300 feet by 100, not productive

Lower Dublin, Frankford and Oxford own, in real estate the Almshouse property, value $15,000. The only real estate of the Borough of Manayunk is the Poor House and farm, value over the mortgage, $7,000. Roxborough owns the Poor House and farm attached to it, valued at $5,000, and mortgaged for $3,000

It will be seen from the preceding data, that the city of Philadelphia is cut up into eleven municipalities, and that there must be added to this deplorable catalogue of jurisdictions five suburban boroughs, exercising municipal powers independent of control, together with the three supplemental corporate bodies which impose upon the citizens the poor the county and the school tax

Instead of one municipal body or corporation governing as it ought, the whole of the metropolis of Eastern Pennsylvania, it is separated, by imaginary lines, into eleven distinct jurisdictions, of various powers, of discordant and different laws governed by dissimilar bodies, elected at different periods, and varying in size and population from 4,186 acres and 125,020 inhabitants, down to 150 acres and 1500 souls

This cannot be just or expedient. The same population with the same interests, on the same plot of ground, and forming to the eye of the stranger the second great city in America, ought unquestionably to have the same government, the same laws, and the same police. This is the clear right of its citizens, and the Legislature, for their sake, and for the general interests of the State at large, should at once place all its inhabitants under the charge of one municipal corporation, obliterating, by a single act of its power, those artificial distinctions which have produced all the evils of conflicting jurisdictions and prejudices, and at one period led to the shedding of blood, and the practical imposition of a voluntary martial law

All these forms of legislative action cannot be equally good. Either the two separate bodies, like a Senate and House of Representatives, or the single body of Commissioners or Town Council, like the old discarded Assembly of the Constitution of 1776, must be the best fitted for municipal rule. So, as to the executive power, either it should be reposed in one man, called a Mayor, or it should be united with the legislative authority in a single body, varying in number from five to twenty-four. Whichever form is the best should be applied to all. Now it is clear, that the single body of Commissioners, clothed with both legislative and executive authority, has always been considered as an imperfect form of city government, adapted only to small districts, and for an incipient state only. It is not suited to a great city, requiring a vigorous and united government, where the energies of a large population should be directed to the peace, safety and happiness of all.

It appears, therefore, that sound policy dictates that the whole of Philadelphia should be united under one municipal government, with an executive head to be called a Mayor, whilst the legislative power should be vested in a Select and Common Council, elected by the respective wards, and not by a general ticket, so that all parties may be represented according to their numbers.

At present, including the County, the Guardians of the Poor, the Comptrollers of Public Schools, and five suburban Boroughs, there are nineteen distinct corporations, with that number of distinct sets of taxes, collected by distinct sets of tax collectors, and with at least twelve distinct debts. Ten of these corporations have, in their legislative management, one hundred and seventy-seven persons, consisting of Select and Common Councilmen, Town Council, Commissioners, and members of the County Board, all of which will be dispensed with on the plan of consolidation, and be replaced by two bodies of citizens, chosen by, and amenable to, the electors of the different wards

This change will secure only one set of ordinances for the government and regulation of the good people of Philadelphia, easily learned and known by all, instead of distinct codes of municipal laws, varying according to the prejudices and passions of each municipality, and really inaccessible to the citizen.

The same corporate unity dispenses with a multitude of treasurers, solicitors, clerks, superintendents, or their equivalents, besides hosts of subordinates It dispenses with one hundred and sixty-eight tax collectors, and will cause a saving in this item alone of one hundred thousand dollars per year.

It creates, instead of numerous different sets of debts of varying value and uncertain credit, one consolidated city debt of the same value and undoubted credit, and replaces at least twelve different sets of books by one set kept in the simplest form

Your memorialists will not enter into an analysis or explanation of the provisions of the bill herewith submitted They speak for themselves It is believed that they comprehend every subject necessary to be considered by the Legislature in providing for consolidation

The bill does not contemplate the contingency of a popular vote on the main question of consolidation, and this for reasons that will doubtless be as satisfying to your honorable bodies as they are to your memorialists If a single doubt rested upon the question, such a provision would be wise, but so general and unmistakeable have been the evidences of the popular will in favor of the measure, that a vote of the people is entirely unnecessary to decide a point which has been already conclusively settled beyond all reasonable doubt, while the fruitless appeal would burden the County Treasury with the expense of a special election of over $20,000

Each and every one of the three political parties, into which the people of Philadelphia are divided, have, by their organized conventions, over and over again declared in favor of consolidation. It would, therefore, be but a prolongation of the evils which the proposed law is intended to remedy, to postpone this great and beneficial measure for that or any other reason whatever. With a view to shed light upon the subject embraced in the second section of the bill, your memorialists annex a detailed statement of the taxables in the city and county.

Your memorialists, with abiding faith in the wisdom, necessity and importance of consolidation, submit it to you for your final action.

       MORTON McMICHAEL,
            Chairman

GEORGE NORTHROP, *Secretary*

Enumeration of Taxable Inhabitants for the year 1853, in Wards, Districts, Townships, &c., in the City and County of Philadelphia.

City.

North Mulberry Ward,	2210
South Mulberry Ward,	1734
North Ward,	2351
South Ward,	1210
Locust Ward,	1861
Middle Ward	1478
Lombard Ward,	1138
Spruce Ward,	819
Cedar Ward,	2054
New Market Ward,	1253
Pine Ward,	922
Dock Ward,	1055
Walnut Ward,	398
Chestnut Ward,	476
High Street Ward,	656
Lower Delaware Ward,	1121
Upper Delaware Ward,	1288
	—— 22,024

Northern Liberties

First Ward,	758
Second Ward,	816
Third Ward,	1128
Fourth Ward,	968
Fifth Ward,	1539
Sixth Ward,	1590
Seventh Ward,	2331
	9,130

Spring Garden.

First Ward,	1250
Second Ward,	1477
Third Ward,	2917
Fourth Ward,	1181
Fifth Ward,	2066
Sixth Ward,	2168
Seventh Ward,	1804
	12,813

Kensington

First Ward,	1076
Second Ward,	1151
Third Ward,	2447
Fourth Ward,	1170
Fifth Ward,	1850
Sixth Ward,	1892
Seventh Ward,	1357
Eighth Ward,	620
	11,563

Southwark

First Ward,	1674
Second Ward,	1414
Third Ward,	1044
Fourth Ward,	1473
Fifth Ward,	1302
Sixth Ward,	1286
	8,193

Moyamensing

First Ward,	1120
Second Ward,	1563
Third Ward,	1501
Fourth Ward,	1036
Fifth Ward,	1033
	6,153

District of Penn.

First Ward,	1270
Second Ward,	943
Third Ward,	445
	2,658

West Philadelphia

First Ward,	699
Second Ward,	468
Third Ward,	271
	1,438

Townships and Boroughs

Passyunk,	335
Kingsessing,	500
Blockley,*	804
North Penn,	701
Roxborough,	716
Manayunk, Upper Ward,	687
Do Lower Ward,	643
Germantown Borough,	1679
Upper Ward, Germantown,	529
Bristol,	501
Unincorporated Northern Liberties,†	611
Bridesburg,	259
Frankford Borough,	1270
Oxford,	492
Lower Dublin,‡	1017
Byberry,	239
Moreland,	115
Richmond,	1873
	12,971

* Including Belmont † Including Aramingo. ‡ Including Delaware

Recapitulation.

City,	22,024
Northern Liberties,	9,130
Spring Garden,	12,813
Kensington,	11,563
Southwark,	8,193
Moyamensing,	6,153
District of Penn,	2,658
West Philadelphia,	1,438
Townships and Boroughs,	12,971
Total,	86,943

That the debt of the city of Philadelphia, being the aggregated debts of the several municipalities consolidated by the act of the 2d February, 1854, amounted at the period of the consolidation thereof, in the year 1854 to the sum of sixteen million five hundred and thirteen thousand six hundred and fourteen dollars and seventy-seven cents ($16,513,614 77)

That the debt of the city of Philadelphia amounted, in the year 1859, to the sum of twenty-one millions ten thousand three hundred and seventy six dollars and fifty six cents ($21,010,376 56)

That at the period of the said consolidation of the said several municipalities, in the year 1854, certain assets of the nominal value of ten millions twenty-three thousand three hundred and thirty six dollars ($10,023 336), of which the actual value is not known, were held by the said various municipalities, and upon the consolidation thereof became held by the said city of Philadelphia, which assets have since, by the said city of Philadelphia, been made part of a sinking fund for the liquidation of the city debt, and that, in the said sinking fund, and part thereof, are also assets which amount to the sum of six hundred and five thousand four hundred and seven dollars and seventy cents ($605,407 70), of which assets, part were property of the said various municipalities at the period of their consolidation, and part are the proceeds of taxes since laid by the said city of Philadelphia

That, of the debt incurred between 1854 and 1859, one million seven hundred and twenty five thousand dollars was on account of subscriptions made to the Northwestern Railroad Company and the Sunbury and Erie Railroad Company by the Mayor, Aldermen and Citizens of Philadelphia, before 2d February, 1854

That the statement aforegoing of the debt of the city of Philadelphia does not include gas loans

That the various ordinances of the Mayor, Aldermen and Citizens of Philadelphia, and of the City of Philadelphia, touching the said gas loans, shall be used as given in evidence

And further, it was agreed by the solicitors for the said plaintiffs and defendants respectively, in manner and form following, that the undersigned should report, at the request of the said defendants

That the records of the following suits be used as given in evidence

Record of suit in the Circuit Court of the United States, to October Sessions, 1852, No —, in which Madelaine Henrietta Girard, et al, are plaintiffs, and the Mayor, Aldermen and Citizens of Philadelphia defendants

Records of suits in the Supreme Court of Pennsylvania, to December Term, 1852, Nos 79, 80 81, 83, in which Madelaine Henrietta Girard, and others, are plaintiffs, and the Mayor, Aldermen and Citizens of Philadelphia defendants

Record of suit in the Court of Common Pleas of Schuylkill County, to September Term, 1859, No 703, in which Madelaine Henrietta Girard, et al, are plaintiffs, and the City of Philadelphia are defendants

Record of suit in the Circuit Court of the United States to October Sessions, 1836, No 1, in which Vidal, et al, are plaintiffs, and the Mayor, Aldermen and Citizens of Philadelphia are defendants

That the following are true copies from the journals of the Select and Common Councils of the Mayor, Aldermen and Citizens of Philadelphia, and be used as given in evidence

The Common Council of the said corporation, at their meeting held January 7, 1854, by a majority of votes, passed the following preamble and resolutions, to wit "Whereas, a movement has been made in the House of Representatives to consolidate the city of Philadelphia, incorporated districts, boroughs and townships of the county of Philadelphia, into one municipal corporation, and the measure contemplated being one generally desired by the citizens of the city of Philadelphia, they believing that the consolidation contemplated would be productive of increased prosperity to all included within its action Therefore,

"*Resolved*, That the Senators and members of the House of Representatives from the city of Philadelphia be and they are hereby requested to endeavor to secure the passage of an act to consolidate the city, incorporated districts, boroughs and townships into one municipality

"*Resolved*, That the clerks of Select and Common Councils be and they are hereby directed to transmit to the Senators and members of the House of Representatives from the city of Philadelphia copies of the foregoing preamble and resolutions'

"Select Council January 7, 1854 These resolutions were ordered to be printed for the use of the members, and at a meeting held January 19, it was

"*Resolved*, That a joint special committee of three members from each chamber be appointed to examine a bill now pending before the Legislature, for consolidating the city and districts into one corporation, for the purpose of endeavoring to have the provisions of said bill placed upon such a basis as will best protect the interests and trusts of the city "

That Etienne Girard, in the bill mentioned as the father of the plaintiffs, on the 2d January, 1833, by his attorney, John F Girard, received from the executors of Stephen

Girard his legacy, mentioned in the will of the said Stephen Girard, for the sum of five thousand dollars.

That Margaret P. Lardy, one of the complainants, on the 2d January, 1833, received from the said executors her legacy, five thousand dollars, under the will.

That Madelaine H. Girard, one of the complainants, by her guardian, on the 24th January, 1833, received from the said executors her legacy of five thousand dollars, under the will.

That Anna H. Girard, mother of F. D. Dumaine and Margaret P. Dumaine, two of the complainants, on the 2d January, 1833, received by her attorney, John F. Girard, her legacy of five thousand dollars, under the will.

That an ordinance of the Councils of the City of Philadelphia, approved February 11, 1859, entitled "An ordinance to levy and fix the rate of taxes for the year 1859," be used as if given in evidence.

That the following is a copy of one of the blanks kept in the office of the Receiver of Taxes, and used in the making up the bills presented to the tax payers, and shall be used as given in evidence.

OFFICE OF RECEIVER OF TAXES,
Philadelphia, 1860

M   Dr. for Taxes for 1860

Page	Description of Property in Twentieth Ward.	Valuation	City Tax Rate, $1 75	State Tax Rate 2½ cents	Dollars	Cts

Ice Boat &c., 4
Highways, 22
Police, 22
Loan, 75
Lighting city, 9
School, 28
Poor, 15
—
$1 75

Discount of 12 per cent per annum from the date of payment to the 1st of January, 1861, off City Tax. Discount off State Tax 5 per cent, if paid before 25th July, 1860.
State tax on pleasure carriages, 1 per ct.
"   "   emoluments of office, 2 "
Received payment for Wm. P. Hamm, Receiver of Taxes.

Clerk.

☞ See that no property is omitted. Bills furnished when called for at this office.

Whereupon, the undersigned hereby reports to the Court the various matters afore stated, as evidence taken in the cause, and that no further evidence was offered by the said parties, complainants and defendants

All of which is respectfully submitted by

AUBREY H. SMITH,
Examiner

ANSWER.

To the Honorable the Judges of the Circuit Court of the United States, in and for the Eastern District of Pennsylvania

The answer of the City of Philadelphia to the bill of complaint of MADELEINE HENRIETTE GIRARD, MARGUERITE P. LARDY, ANNE STEPHANIE DE LENTILHAC, and ALFRED DE LENTILHAC, her husband, FRABRICIUS DEVARS DUMAINE, a minor, and MARGUERITE PALMIRE, a minor, by her next friend, John Devars Dumaine, aliens

These respondents, saving and reserving to themselves, now and at all times hereafter, all and all manner of exception to the various errors, imperfections, and uncertainties in the said bill of complaint contained, for answer thereunto or unto so much thereof as they are advised that it is material for them to answer, they answer and say, that the plaintiffs in the said bill, together with John Devars Dumaine, in right of his wife, Ann Henriette Girard, John Auguste Girard, Marie C. Guard Deroux, and Louis Deroux, her husband, and Francois Constance Fenelon Vidal, on the 24th day of December, 1852, caused a writ of summons in ejectment to issue out of this Court to October Sessions, 1852, No 12 against the defendants in their corporate name of the Mayor, Alderman, and Citizens of Philadelphia, which said writ was duly served, and the suit thereby instituted is yet pending and undetermined That in the said suit the parties therein, plaintiffs sought to recover from the defendants the same lands in Schuylkill and Columbia counties, which the plaintiffs, in the bill filed, pray may be transferred to them

That the said plantiffs, in the said bill, together with John Devars Dumaine, in right of his wife Ann Henriette Girard, Marie C Girard Deroux, and Louis Deroux her husband, Francois C Fenelon Vidal, Marie Antoinette Hemphill, Harriet Girard Clark, and John Y Clark, her husband, and Caroline E Girard Peale, and Franklin Peale, her husband, on the 22d day of December, 1852, caused certain writs of summons in ejectment to issue out of the Supreme Court of the Commonwealth of Pennsylvania, to December Term Nos 79, 80, 81, and 83, against the defendants in their said corporate name of The Mayor, Aldermen, and Citizens of Philadelphia, which writs were duly served, and the suits thereby instituted are yet pending and undetermined, and in the said suits the plaintiffs therein sought to recover from the defendants the houses and lands in the City of Philadelphia, mentioned in the said bill

And the said plaintiffs, in the said bill together with John F Girard, John Fabricius Girard, Louis F Deroux, and Marie his wife, Francois C Vidal, John Y Clark and Harriet his wife, Marie A Hemphill, Franklin Peale, and Caroline E his wife have since the filing of the said bill, namely, on the 3d day of September, 1859, caused a writ of summons in ejectment to issue out of the Court of Common Pleas for Schuylkill County, in the Commonwealth of Pennsylvania, to September Term, 1859, No 703, against the defendants, which writ was duly served, and the suit thereby instituted is yet pending and undetermined. In the said suit the parties therein plaintiffs seek to recover from the defendants one of the tracts of land in Schuylkill County, containing about four hundred acres which the plaintiffs in the bill filed pray may be transferred to them. And the defendants claim the same benefit as if they had pleaded in form the matters above stated, coupled with an answer, setting forth the facts herein above mentioned. And if the Court should determine that none of the facts above set forth are sufficient to abate or bar the plaintiffs' bill, then the defendants pray that the plaintiffs may be required to elect between the said proceedings at law and the present suit in equity.

And the defendants, without waving the matters herein before stated, as an answer in lieu of a plea, further answering, say, that it is true, as therein stated, that the late Stephen Girard died at his domicil, in the city of Philadelphia, in December, in the year 1831, unmarried without issue, leaving neither father or mother, but leaving a brother, Etienne Girard, and the heirs and representatives of another brother, John Girard, then deceased, and the heirs and representatives of a sister, Sophia Girard, also then deceased. But whether or not the said Etienne Girard is now deceased, and whether the parties mentioned in the said bill were his children, living at the time of his alleged death, is not known to these respondents, though they have no reason to believe to the contrary, and are content that the same may be held and taken to be as in the bill alleged.

That the said Stephen Girard died possessed of a large real and personal estate. But the amount and value of the same is greatly overstated in the said bill, as will hereafter be particularly shown and set forth.

That the said Stephen Girard, in his lifetime, on or about

the 16th February, 1830, duly made and published his last will in writing, and also, did on the 25th of December, 1830, and on the 20th June, 1831, make and publish codicils thereto. Which said will and codicils were duly proved before the register of wills for the City and County of Philadelphia, and letters testamentary thereon issued to the parties therein appointed to be the executors thereof.

That by the said last will and testament the said testator, after making certain bequests to trustees or corporations for charitable purposes, and bequests to his relatives and friends, made the following bequests and devises to the respondents by their then corporate name of "The Mayor, Aldermen, and Citizens of Philadelphia," namely:

(1) The sum of ten thousand dollars, in trust to invest the same, and with the income, yearly, to purchase fuel and distribute the same amongst the poor white house and room-keepers, residing in the City of Philadelphia.

(2) All the residue and remainder of his real and personal estate, in trust (1) as to the sum of two millions of dollars, out of his personal estate, to apply and expand so much as might be necessary in erecting, in a prescribed location, a permanent college, with suitable outbuildings, sufficiently spacious for the residence and accommodation of at least three hundred scholars, poor white male orphans of the City of Philadelphia, between the ages of six and ten years, to remain until they shall arrive at between fourteen and eighteen, and the requisite teachers and other persons necessary to the institution, and in supplying furniture, books, and all things needful for the same, and in further trust, to apply the income of so much of the $2,000,000 as should remain, after erecting and furnishing the said College, to maintain the same, (2) as to the sum of $500,000 out of the personal estate, in trust, to invest the same, and apply the income, annually, (*a*) to lay out, pave, and light a street

or passage fronting the river Delaware, to be called Delaware Avenue, extending from Vine to Cedar street, (*b*) to pull down and remove all wooden or other buildings constructed of combustible materials, within the limits of the City of Philadelphia, and to prohibit the future erection of any such, and (*c*) to widen, regulate, pave, and curb Water street in the said city, and to distribute the Schuylkill water therein upon a plan set forth by the said testator, and (*d*) when the said objects should have been accomplished, to apply the said income from time to time to the further improvement of the Delaware front of the city. (3) And as to the remainder, to apply the income including therein as well the rents and income of his real estate in Pennsylvania, and the income of the proceeds of real estate elsewhere situate directed to be sold, as well as of his personal property, in trust,

(1) To the further improvement and maintenance of said College.

(2) To enable the said corporation to provide more effectually than then existed for the security of persons and property of the City by a competent police.

(3) To enable "the said corporation to improve the city property and the general appearance of the City itself, and, in effect, to diminish the burden of taxation, now most oppressive, especially on those who are the least able to bear it."

But the said last mentioned bequest and devise was upon this further trust, that if the income arising from that part of the two millions of dollars remaining, after the construction and furnishing of the College and out buildings, should, owing to the number of orphans applying for admission, or other cause, be inadequate to the construction of new buildings, or the maintenance and education of as many orphans as might apply for admission, that such further sum as might be necessary for the construction of new buildings and the maintenance and education of such further number of orphans, as could be maintained and instructed within such buildings, as the place appropriated for the erection of the said same, (containing about forty acres of ground,) should be adequate to, should be taken from the income of the said residuary estate.

And of the residuary estate, the testator declares the trusts to be the said improvement of the city, after providing for his said College, as his primary object.

And the respondents submit, that the income of the whole of the testator's residuary estate is to be applied to the maintenance and enlargement of the said College, if the same is needed for such purposes. And that the said city corporation is not entitled to apply any part of the said income for the municipal purposes mentioned by the testator, until the College is fully and adequately provided for. And that so much of said income as is not needed and used for such purposes, the defendants are entitled to use for such municipal purposes as are indicated in the said will.

And for a further answer to so much of the bill as alleges that the testator did not bequeath the whole ' remainder of the said residue" of his estate for the support and maintenance of the said College, but only the income of his real estate in the City and County of Philadelphia, and the dividends of his stock in the Schuylkill Navigation Company, they say that, on the contrary, they allege and insist, and submit, that the testator bequeathed and devised all the residue and remainder of his real and personal estate to the respondents, in trust, among other things, so far as regarded his real estate in Pennsylvania, to apply the net income to the same uses and purposes as were declared of and concerning the residue of his personal estate, and of the said personal estate he declared the uses and purposes to be—

(1) As to $2,000,000, to erect the College aforesaid;

(2) As to $500,000, to improve the eastern front of the city, and

(3) As to the remainder, to apply the same

> (a) To the further improvement and maintenance of the said College, if the income of what remained of the sum of $2,000 000 would not suffice for its enlarged maintenance,
> (b) For the improvement of the police
> (c) For municipal purposes,

Which declaration of said uses and purposes, they say, requires and authorizes them to apply the whole of the net income of the remaining real and personal estate of the testator, to maintain the said College, and that until all the demands of the same are supplied, they will not be allowed to expend the said income for other purposes

That the legislature of the Commonwealth of Pennsylvania, by an Act approved March 24th, 1832 entitled 'An Act to enable The Mayor, Aldermen, and Citizens of Philadelphia to carry into effect certain improvements and to execute certain trusts," authorized the respondents to open the said Delaware avenue, widen the said Water street, and to provide for the removal of wooden buildings, and forbid their future construction in the said city and in § 24 thereof, provided as follows. "That it shall be lawful for The Mayor, Aldermen, and Citizens of Philadelphia to exercise all such jurisdiction, enact all such ordinances, and do and execute all such acts and things whatsoever, as may be necessary and convenient for the full and entire acceptance, execution, and prosecution of any and all the devises and bequests, trusts, and provisions contained in the said will," (of Mr Girard,) "which are the subjects of the preceding parts of this Act and to enable the constituted authorities of the City of Philadelphia to carry which into effect, the said Stephen Girard has desired the legislature to enact the necessary laws'

And by a supplement to the said Act, approved April 4, 1832, the said corporation, through their Select and Common Councils, were authorized to provide, by ordinance or otherwise, for the election or appointment of such officers and agents as they might deem essential to the duties and trusts enjoined and created by the said will, which said acts of assembly the respondents pray may be taken as part of this their answer, as if the same were herein at large set forth.

That the executors of the said will handed over delivered, assigned, and paid in the months of January, April, and May, 1833, and subsequently, to the defendants, then known by the corporate name of The Mayor, Aldermen, and Citizens of Philadelphia, as the residuary legatees of the said testator, certain certificates of stock and loans and other evidences of debt, in which the personal estate of the testator had been invested by him or by the said executors.

The corporation, under the advice of counsel, set apart, from the said personal estate, certificates of stock or loans of the market value of $10,000 as an appropriation of so much thereof to fulfil the trust of the testator, to purchase fuel, and distribute the same among poor white house and room keepers of the said city; and in like manner they set apart certificates of stocks or loans, of the market value of $500,000, as an appropriation of so much of the said personal estate to fulfil the trust for the opening of Delaware avenue &c. And they further set apart from the said personal estate, like certificates of the market value of 2,000,000 dollars as an appropriation of so much thereof for the purpose of building, furnishing, and maintaining the said college. The balance of the said personal estate the said corporation considered and treated as part of the residue of the testator's estate, to be applied, together with the income of his real estate, to the municipal purposes directed by the testator, and they accordingly applied the net income to the municipal purposes indicated by the testator, until the same was required for the college, as will be hereinafter mentioned.

The said corporation, upon the death of the testator,

entered upon all the real estate in the State of Pennsylvania, devised by the said will, and held, and now hold the same, except such thereof as has been taken from them, as will be hereafter mentioned for the purpose and uses, and in the manner directed by the testator in his said will.

The income of the said fund, or appropriation of ten thousand and five hundred thousand dollars, has been appropriated respectively to the purchase and distribution of fuel, and the opening of the Delaware avenue and the widening of Water street, as directed by the testator.

The construction of the said college buildings was commenced in the year 1833, and finished in the year 1847. For a time the income alone of the said two millions of dollars was used for this purpose but, from time to time, as the necessity of a speedy prosecution of the work required more than the annual income would supply, parts of the capital were sold. At one time this was rendered imperative by the failure of some of the corporations, in whose stocks or loans the capital was invested, to pay dividends or interest. Finally, upon the completion of the college buildings, the whole of the two millions had been absorbed. Then the contingency provided for by the testator arrived, namely there was no remaining part of the $2,000,000 with which to maintain the college—and, as the testator had directed, recourse was had to the income of the residuary for that purpose. From that time to the present the whole of the net income from the residuary estate, including therein all the net income of the real estate held by the defendants, has been appropriated to the maintenance and endowment of the said college, and used for that purpose.

The real estate owned, or supposed to be owned, by Mr Girard, at the time of his decease, and which he devised or supposed he had devised, to the said corporation, consisted besides houses and unoccupied lots of ground in the city and county of Philadelphia of fifty-four tracts of unseated land in Schuylkill and Columbia counties, containing about twenty two thousand eight hundred acres, of an undivided three-fourth parts in thirteen tracts of unseated land in Schuylkill county, containing about four thousand acres, of fifteen tracts of land, containing about eight thousand three hundred and eighty acres, in Erie county, in the State of Pennsylvania, of two undivided third parts of about two hundred and seven thousand acres of land near Washita, in the State of Louisiana, and of   acres of land in the State of Kentucky.

The co-tenants of the said thirteen tracts of land in Schuylkill county, instituted proceedings for a partition of the same among the owners, which proceedings were so carried on, in due course of law, as to terminate in a sale of the lands sometime in the year 1851, and the said corporation's share of the proceeds was duly received, and applied to certain improvements of a portion of the real estate devised to them, situate in the City of Philadelphia.

The next of kin of Mr. Girard, or some of them, in the year 1850, brought an action of ejectment against the said corporation to recover possession of eleven of the said fifty-four tracts of land in Schuylkill and Columbia counties, (containing about four thousand four hundred acres,) on the ground, as they alleged, that the testator had no title thereto at the date of his will. In 1853, the case was heard by a jury, who returned a verdict for the plaintiffs, which verdict after argument, upon a motion for a new trial refused to set aside, or order a new trial. A writ of habere facias possessionem was subsequently issued, and the plaintiffs were put into possession of the said eleven tracts by the marshal for the Eastern District of Pennsylvania.

The title to a number of the remaining tracts in Schuylkill and Columbia counties, is claimed by various parties, and in some cases ejectments have been brought and are now pending. In all these cases of adverse titles, the claims are of title paramount to Mr. Girard's.

The lands in Erie county were claimed by the heirs of John B. Wallace, Esq., who brought their suit in the Court of Common Pleas, of Erie County, to May term, 1853. In this case a verdict, after trial by a jury, was rendered for the plaintiffs, which was affirmed by the Supreme Court of Pennsylvania, upon a writ of error sued out by the defendants, in the year 1855

The lands in Louisiana were claimed by the United States An Act of Congress having been passed to enable the defendants and certain parties claiming to be the owners of land in Louisiana, similarly situated, to proceed in equity to establish their title, they availed themselves, in conjunction with their co-devisee, the corporation of the City of New Orleans, of the privilege so given, and instituted the proper proceedings in the District Court of the United States for the District of Louisiana In this proceeding in the District Court, a decree was made in favor of the plaintiffs From this the United States appealed, and after hearing and argument, the Supreme Court of the United States reversed the decree, and decided and decreed the title to be in the United States

The lands in Kentucky were allowed to remain in the charge of the agent employed by Mr Guard for sale The greater part of them have been sold at prices averaging less than two dollars per acre, the proceeds have been regularly accounted for, and invested as part of the residue of the testator's estate For that portion of the lands unsold, the price of one dollar per acre cannot be obtained, and the lands are still waiting purchasers

Of the real estate out of the City and County of Philadelphia, there remains in the possession of the defendants, the balance of the lands in Kentucky and forty three tracts, containing about seventeen thousand acres, in Schuylkill and Columbia counties About one third of this land contains coal the balance is only valuable for its timber, or for agricultural purposes

The defendants admit that at the time of the death of Mr Guard, the territorial boundaries of the corporation of The Mayor, Aldermen, and Citizens of Philadelphia were the north side of Vine street, the south side of South street and the rivers Delaware and Schuylkill. These boundaries were established originally by the provincial charter of 1701, and until the year 1854 had never been changed or altered. The legislative power of this corporation at the time of the said death, was vested in two bodies called the Select and Common Councils; one-third of the members of the former and all of the latter were annually elected. The powers and the constitution of these legislative bodies had been from time to time variously enlarged, curtailed and modified by the authority of the legislature.

The City of Philadelphia, thus bounded, formed a part of the territory of the County of Philadelphia. The legislature, from time to time, commencing in the year 1794, set apart certain of the territory of the county for the boundaries of municipal corporations, and incorporated the inhabitants therein into bodies politic. The corporations thus formed, were named respectively: "The Commissioners and Inhabitants of the District of Southwark," "The Commissioners of the District of the Northern Liberties," "The Commissioners of the District of Spring Garden," "The Commissioners of the District of Kensington," "The Commissioners and Inhabitants of the District of Moyamensing," "The Commissioners of the District of Penn," "The Commissioners and Inhabitants of the District of Richmond," "The District of West Philadelphia," "The Borough of Aramingo," "The District of Belmont," "The Borough of Manayunk," "The Borough of Germantown," "The Borough of Frankford," "The Borough of Whitehall," and "The Borough of Bridesburg." All these corporations had certain legislative powers exercised by Boards of Commissioners, or Town Councils.

The other corporations mentioned in the complainants' bill were township organizations, without any legislative powers.

The corporation of the Mayor, Aldermen, and Citizens of Philadelphia, were empowered to levy taxes to enable it to perform its corporate duties. Among these corporate duties were not those of providing for the support of the administration of justice, the care of the poor, the regulation of the port, the maintenance of a system of public education the opening of streets, &c. These were exercised by the county authorities. The County of Philadelphia, of which the city formed a part, had, among other county officers, three commissioners, one of whom was annually elected by the people of the county. These commissioners were vested with the power to levy and collect the taxes for county purposes, among which were those which have just been enumerated except the poor, and over the exercise of their discretion in the laying of these taxes the corporation of the city, as such, had no control. The care of the poor was separately provided for. A corporation for that purpose was in existence which exercised the right to assess and levy the taxes necessary in their opinion for such purpose. Thus the taxes for county and poor always exceeded those of the city for her own municipal purposes. To instance one year for an example. In the year 1853, the tax of the city, for her municipal purposes, was fifty eight cents on the one hundred dollars of the assessed value of the property while the county tax was for county, school, and poor purposes ninety cents on one hundred dollars. The improvement of the city and the consequent increased value of property therein always increased the amount of taxes, since the county rate was uniform, and assessed upon the value of the property.

This government of the City and County of Philadelphia and its consequences and results were well known to Mr Girard. He was an inhabitant of the city for nearly fifty years, and was for several years a member of her Councils.

The project of uniting parts or the whole of the county of Philadelphia into one local government, was for some years previous to 1854 much discussed, and in the latter or previous year its friends had so favorably impressed the community with its practicability and advantages, that a volunteer committee of citizens met publicly for the purpose of arranging the details and submitting them to the legislature of the Commonwealth for their adoption into a law. The fruits of all this is to be seen in the Act referred to in the plaintiffs' bill, and called the Consolidation Act. The Select and Common Councils of the corporation of The Mayor, Aldermen, and Citizens of Philadelphia, had not an opportunity of being heard on this subject by the legislature.

The Common Council of the said corporation at their meeting held January 7, 1854, by a majority of votes, passed the following preamble and resolutions, to wit:

'WHEREAS, A movement has been made in the House of Representatives to consolidate the City of Philadelphia, incorporated districts, boroughs, and townships of the county of Philadelphia into one municipal corporation, and the measure contemplated, being one generally desired by citizens of the City of Philadelphia, they believing that the consolidation contemplated would be productive of increased prosperity to all included within its action; therefore,

'*Resolved*, That the Senators and Members of the House of Representatives from the City of Philadelphia, be, and they are hereby requested to endeavor to secure the passage of an act to consolidate the city, incorporated districts, boroughs, and townships, into one municipality.

Resolved, That the clerks of Select and Common Councils be and they are hereby directed to transmit to the Senators and members of the House of Representatives from the City of Philadelphia, copies of the foregoing preamble and resolutions.'

According to the course of proceeding, these resolutions were sent to the Select Councils for concurrence. In this body, at their meeting on January 7, 1854, these resolutions were ordered to be printed for the use of the members, and at a meeting held January 19, it was

'*Resolved*, That a joint special committee of three members from each chamber be appointed to examine a bill now pending before the legislature, for consolidating the city and districts into one corporation, for the purpose of endeavoring to have the provisions of said bill placed upon such a basis as will best protect the interests and trusts of the city."

In this resolution the Common Council concurred. Both bodies appointed their respective members of the committee. Before the committee could report upon the subject referred to them, the bill was passed into a law.

The defendants submit that their acquiescence or dissent in or to the proposed measure of consolidating the said corporations could not have been effective to prevent or consummate that purpose. The said city corporation was the creature of the legislature, to be destroyed or perpetuated at its pleasure. The said corporation neither accepted or repudiated its new or altered charter; it had no choice offered to it but to obey the will of the legislature.

The defendants allege and submit that the Act of Assembly of February 2, 1854, entitled, "A further supplement to an Act entitled, 'An Act to incorporate the City of Philadelphia,'" did not destroy or abrogate the corporation of "The Mayor, Aldermen, and Citizens of Philadelphia." It enlarged the territorial boundaries of the latter corporation and changed its name to that of "The City of Philadelphia."

The first section of the said Act provided that the powers of the corporation of The Mayor, Aldermen and Citizens of Philadelphia, as enlarged and modified by the said Act, should be exercised and have effect over all the territory for the first time included within its corporate limits, and over all the inhabitants therein; and in the sixth section that the said corporation should be vested with all the powers, rights, privileges, and immunities of the corporation of The Mayor, Aldermen, and Citizens of Philadelphia.

And the defendants deny that it was provided in the said Act, that upon the election of a Mayor or Councils, as provided therein, the powers, rights, privileges, and immunities possessed and enjoyed by the said corporation of The Mayor, Aldermen, and Citizens of Philadelphia, should cease and terminate, or that the same ceased or terminated upon the issue of any proclamation, or otherwise howsoever; but they allege and say that the powers, rights, privileges, and immunities of the said last named corporation were expressly continued in full force, vigor, and effect.

The defendants further show, that it is provided in the said Act that all estates and incomes, at the passage thereof, held by any of the corporations united by the said Act, shall be held by the City of Philadelphia, upon and for the same uses, trusts, limitations, charities, and conditions, as the same were held at that time; and the defendants pray that the said Act and all the supplements thereto may be taken as part of this, their answer, as if the same were herein at large set forth.

And the defendants, in answer to so much of the complainants' bill as professes to show that they are incapable and unable to carry into effect so much of the devise and bequest of the said testator as applies to the appropriation of such part of the income of the residue of his estate as shall remain annually, after the necessities of the said college are provided for, to municipal purposes, say that they deny that they are incapable or unable to make and apply such appropriation, as they now proceed to show.

The defendants submit to the Court, whether the bequests and devise aforesaid to The Mayor, Aldermen, and Citizens of Philadelphia was a gift to them absolutely, or whether the same was a devise and bequest in trust for the municipal purposes set forth.

If the Court should be of opinion that the said bequest was an absolute gift, then the defendants submit that the plaintiffs have no right or title to call upon them to account therefor, or to question their title thereto.

But if the Court should be of opinion that the said bequest was in trust for municipal purposes, they say that they claim to hold the same in trust to apply the said income for municipal purposes affecting and relating to the property and inhabitants situate and residing within that part of their corporation limits which is bounded by Vine and South streets, and the rivers Delaware and Schuylkill.

The said trust of the remainder of the residue of the testator's estate is for the following objects

1. To the further improvement and maintenance of the said college

2. To enable the city to provide more effectually for the security of person and property by a competent police

3. To enable the corporation to improve the city property and the general appearance of the city itself, and, in effect, to diminish the burden of taxation

In respect to the execution of the said trusts, the defendants say, that they are in no wise hindered or interfered with by the provisions or consequences or effects of the said Act of February 2, 1854, and they do not admit, nor have they admitted, that they cannot apply the said trust according to the will of the testator By the said Act of February 2, 1854, the councils of the said city are authorized and required to fix the rate and levy all the taxes authorized by law, within its corporate limits, (except the State tax,) and direct the amount to be applied and paid for health, school, poor, city, and other purposes according to law, and they are required to vote the said taxes so as to show how much is raised for the said objects respectively And they say, then in voting said taxes they specify in their ordinance for such purpose, how much of the taxes is assessed and levied for each object of taxation Thus, in such ordinance assessing and levying the taxes for the year 1859, it is set forth as follows

For the relief and employment of the poor, 15 cents in the $100 of the assessed value of said property

For public schools, 28 cents in the $100 of the assessed value of said property.

For lighting the city, 9 cents in the $100 of the assessed value of said property.

For the loan tax, 75 cents in the $100 of the assessed value of said property

For expenses of police, 22 cents in the $100 of the assessed value of said property

For the care of public highways, 22 cents in the $100 of the assessed value of said property

For city department and ice boat, other than those mentioned, 4 cents in the $100 of the assessed value of said property.

And they also require that the receiver of taxes shall print on the bills furnished to the tax payers the rate of taxes voted, and the objects

And the defendants say, that whenever the income from the said residuary fund will suffice for the necessities of the said college, and leave a surplus, applicable to the other trusts declared concerning the income of the said residue, that they can apply such overplus to the cost of maintaining the police in that part of the said city, between Vine and South streets and the rivers Delaware and Schuylkill, and reduce the rate of taxation for the support of the police on the property situate within the said limits, to the difference between the sum applicable from the said residuary for that purpose, and the sum assessed on property outside of the said limits, and if the sum applicable from the said residuary for the expenses of the police will amount to the whole sum necessary for such expenses within the said limits, they may levy no tax upon property within the said limits for such expenses And if such surplus will exceed the amount needed for the police expenses within the said limits, they will be enabled to improve the corporate property within the said limits, or apply it to improve the appearance of that portion of the city without resort to taxation for that purpose And if it will be within the terms of the trust to disregard the specific objects mentioned, then they may and can pay such surplus, beyond that which is needed for the necessities of the college directly into the city treasury in aid of the tax fund, and levy and assess upon the property within the said limits a sum less the amount so paid in aid of the tax fund

The defendants instance the foregoing as some of the modes in which they may administer the aforesaid trusts; and the said act, called the Consolidation Act, having provided that the property or estates held by any of the corporations thereby united or consolidated, upon any trusts, should be held by the consolidated corporation upon the same trusts, limitations, charities, and conditions, expressly confers upon them the power and authority to carry out and execute the trusts in the said will, in the manner they have designated This administration of the trust, they submit, is in no wise contrary to public policy, and that no rule of public policy is violated by accepting and administering a gift to improve one portion of the city and not the rest, and that an example of such is to be found in that part of the will of Mr Girard, which bequeaths the income of the sum of $500,000 to open one and widen another street in one portion of the city, and when these objects are accomplished to apply the income "to the further improvement of the eastern or Delaware front of the city"

And the defendants, referring to that part of the bill which alleges that since the passage of the said Act of February 2d, 1854, there has been called into existence an interest in the said corporation, opposed to the performance of said trust, say, that the aid of a Court of Chancery can as readily be moved to interfere under the constitution of the corporation as made by the said Act, as under that which existed previously, and that when the defendants refuse or decline to execute the said trusts on the ground of their inability to perform their accepted duty therein, the interposition of Chancery may be invoked, but they submit that they ought not to be deprived of their property on an imagination of difficulties that have not yet, at least, an existence

And the defendants say, that the said bequest is for a charitable use, because it is for public purposes, and that the condition annexed by the testator, that no part of his real estate in Pennsylvania "shall ever be sold or alienated" does not create a perpetuity forbidden by law, but that if any part of the said bequest is void, it is the condition and not the bequest

And the defendants further answering say, that they never doubted that the said college was to be so administered, that orphans born in the City of Philadelphia were to be admitted therein in preference to those born elsewhere, but that it was questioned whether the testator meant by the City of Philadelphia, the territorial limits of the corporation of the Mayor, Aldermen, and Citizens of Philadelphia, or what was commonly and popularly known as the City of Philadelphia, namely, the built part of the County of Philadelphia, and it was also questioned what was an orphan within the meaning of the said will, whether a child who was without a father living was an orphan, or whether a parentless child alone was such orphan. The case mentioned in the plaintiff's bill was submitted to the Supreme Court of Pennsylvania for decision upon the said questions, and not for any other purpose. And they say, in this connection, that such case was not made and submitted by the defendants, as is therein alleged, but a bill was filed by a party who represented a child, whose admission into the college was refused because its mother was living, and that the suit was to them an invitum.

And the defendants further answering say, that at the present time there is in their hands, possession, or control, the following property, real and personal, (exclusive of $10,000 and $500,000, set apart for furnishing the poor with fuel and for the improvement of Delaware avenue front, &c.,) devised or bequeathed to them by the aforesaid testator, or the proceeds of the same, and no more or other, namely, in the City of Philadelphia 152 dwelling houses or stores, 3 vacant lots of ground, 2 wharves, 567 acres of farm land, with the buildings thereon, in that part of the said city which formerly was the Borough of Passyunk and the District of Moyamensing, beside the Girard College and the lot appurtenant thereto. In Schuylkill and Columbia county, in the State of Pennsylvania, 43 tracts, containing about 17,000 acres of land, about one third of which is believed to contain anthracite coal, and in the State of Kentucky about   acres of unimproved land, and of personal estate, the following, namely

Five per cent loan of the State of Pennsylvania, of the par value of	$91,399 91
Five per cent loan of the City of Philadelphia, of the par value of	52,103 18
Six per cent loan of the City of Philadelphia, of the par value of	21,300 00
Five per cent loan of the Schuylkill Navigation Company,	2,175 22
Loan to the Franklin Institute,	1,000 00
Germantown and Perkiomen Turnpike Company stock,	200 00
Philadelphia Exchange Company stock,	10,000 00
Four thousand shares in the Danville and Pottsville Railroad Company,	200,000 00
Two thousand and two hundred shares in the Schuylkill Navigation Company,	110,000 00
Loan to Ridge Road Turnpike Company, par $10,000 certificates of interest, $900,	10,900 00
One hundred and two shares in the Chesapeake and Delaware Canal Company,	20,400 00
One hundred and two shares in the Susquehanna and Lehigh Turnpike Company,	100 00
	$519,578 31

The defendants say, that since their possession of the said devised and bequeathed estate, they have kept the real estate in good repair, improved the same whenever opportunities presented, by altering existing buildings to meet the increased wants of business or occupants, and erecting new ones on vacant ground, and have let out the same to tenants at as advantageous rents as was received by private owners of similar property. The real estate in that part of the city, which was the District of Moyamensing and the Township of Passyunk, has been and still is rented and occupied for farming purposes, and for these purposes must continue to be rented and occupied for many years, as there is no demand for such improvements as would authorize their occupation by houses for residences or for business purposes. The lands in Schuylkill County have remained, as they were left by the testator, unimproved and without tenants. A number of years ago, a lease of a large portion of that part of them supposed to contain coal was made to the Danville and Pottsville Railroad Company at a small rent, with a view to assist the said company in the prosecution of their improvement, and in the expectation that when their road was completed a market could be reached by it, at which the coal mined could be sold. But the effort proved abortive, and the company very soon abandoned their enterprise. The lands have been, until very recently remote from improvements which would enable their products to be brought to market. However, lately in the neighborhood of the lands railroads have been built, and the lands have been advertised for rent and the subject of accepting certain offers to lease them are now under the consideration of the proper committees or agents of the defendants.

The greater portion of the personal property remains in the same state, as to its investment, as it was left by the testator. This property (exclusive of the Delaware avenue fund and the fuel fund) is of the par value of $519,578 31, though its real value is of a far less sum. The investment in the stock of the Danville and Pottsville Railroad, amounting to the par value of 200,000 dollars, is worthless, the company having become extinct some years ago. The investment in the stocks of the Schuylkill Navigation Company, the Chesapeake and Delaware Canal Company, the Susquehanna and Lehigh Turnpike, and the loan to the Ridge Road Turnpike Company, amounting to the total sum of $141,400, are without market value. Of the entire investments of this personal property, of the par value of $519,578 31, but the sum of about 178,000 dollars is, in interest or dividend, paying loans or stocks.

The gross income of the residuary estate, consisting of all of the testator's real estate held by the defendants, and the personalty, except that which has been set aside for the Delaware avenue fund, and for the fund to supply poor house and room keepers with fuel, was, in the year 1857, when the largest income ever realized from the estate was received, as follows:

Rent of real estate in the City of Philadelphia,	$155,709 61
Income of real estate in Schuylkill county,	64 00
Dividends and income from investments in stocks and loans,	8,643 92
	$164,417 53

The expenses chargeable against the same for the same year, were

Annuities,	$1,100 00	
Taxes and water rents,	32,343 88	
Salaries,	3,700 00	
Repairs,	13,990 12	
Incidental and miscellaneous,	3,191 09	
Lands out of the city, taxes, law expenses, &c.,	4,950 33	
Improving real estate		
Papering,	$2,976 49	
Outside painting,	1,474 99	
Inside painting,	2,148 74	
	$6,600 22	
Permanent improvements		
Improvement on vacant lot,	2,932 63	
Erecting buildings,	3,000 00	
		71,858 27
Leaving net income,	.	$92,559 26

The sum expended for the purposes of the college for the same year, was $95,538 59, being upwards of $3,000 beyond the net income of the estate. From whence this excess was obtained, will be presently shown. The annual gross and net income of the residuary estate, and the application of the surplus, from the year 1832 to the present time, is hereafter exhibited in answer to one of the plaintiffs' interrogatories. An explanation of the mode of keeping the account of the estate is necessary to show why in some of the years the surplus has not been expended, and why in others a greater sum than such surplus has been disposed of. In the commencement of the year the defendants caused estimates to be made of the probable income of the estate, and an estimate of the expenses of charge of administration and for taxes, repairs, and improvements. The amount so estimated for expenses, they appropriated for such purposes, and the difference between such estimated expenses and the income, they have, since 1847, appropriated, with one or two trifling exceptions, for the support of the College. At the end of the year the accounts are closed, and all sums unpaid, though appropriated, are carried to the next year's income. Thus, if an improvement be commenced, and not completed or paid for, the balance unpaid is so carried to the subsequent year's income. The amount of the balance is re appropriated during the new year to the original object. When a series of years is examined, it will appear that the income and the expenditures balance, which, as has been stated, will not appear in each year's account.

In some instances the defendants have invested part of the income. They judged this proper, in order to replace, to the extent of the investments so made, in the capital of the residuary, which had been seriously impaired, in consequence of some of the corporations, in whose loans or stocks it was invested, having become bankrupt.

The defendants say, that the beneficiaries of the college will be limited only by the means to support them. Since its opening the number of applicants for admission have far exceeded the ability to maintain them. The whole number of orphans who have applied for admission since 1847 has been 1,673, and there have been admitted 705. The number of inmates at present is 330; the number awaiting admission is 221. The whole, or nearly the whole, of the applicants, hitherto, have been orphans born in the present city. Whenever the means at the command of the managers of the college will justify them in extending its benefits to orphans born *in the State*, outside of the city, the applications for admission will be largely increased.

The defendants deny that there is any sum of money in their hands, being accumulations of surplus unexpended income, except the sum invested as they have before stated. But they say that they have appropriated and applied the income of the said estate in the manner directed by the will of the testator. And they further deny that they, or the corporation of The Mayor, Aldermen, and Citizens of Philadelphia have wrongfully or unnecessarily expended any of the moneys of the estate.

And the defendants, in reference to that part of the plaintiffs' bill as represents that the prospective value of the lands in Schuylkill and Columbia counties is so great as to justify the conclusion that their annual rent will far more than suffice for the wants of the College in any event, say, that although they are justified in believing that the land is of large value, and that it will eventually yield a very considerable income, yet they believe that the value is much overstated. The number of acres of said lands is not 29,000 and odd, as stated by the plaintiffs, but is actually but 17,000, and of this number, but one-third is supposed to contain coal. Their annual value, in rent for coal leave, is uncertain, depending upon the quality of the coal, freedom of the mines from faults, the absence of water, and the demands of trade.

To the interrogatories which the defendants are required to answer, thus say:

To the first. That they admit the fact of the death of Mr. Girard as inquired of therein, to be as is alleged in the bill, and that he died possessed of real and personal estate estimated to be of the value of several millions of dollars, and they are content to admit that the plaintiffs are of kindred to him, as in the bill stated.

To the second. That they admit the fact inquired of herein to be as is in the bill alleged, and that the exhibit marked "A" to the bill annexed, is a true copy of his will and the codicils thereto.

To the third. They admit that the municipality called by the corporate name of The Mayor, Aldermen, and Citizens of Philadelphia, was established and chartered with the boundaries as stated in the bill. And that the said corporation was enlarged by force of the Act of the General Assembly of the Commonwealth of Pennsylvania, approved February 2, 1854, so as to embrace the territory governed by certain other corporate and quasi corporate bodies mentioned in the bill. That so far as the interrogatory refers to the franchises, debts, taxes, and administrations thereof, they refer to the said Act of Assembly; at the same time they deny that any of the franchises of the corporation of The Mayor, Aldermen, and Citizens of Philadelphia, were abrogated by the said Act, but that the same were continued and remain in full force and effect.

To the fourth. That what is called in the said interrogatory "the consolidated charter," was not accepted by the corporators mentioned in the said interrogatory by any formal or public act. It was imposed upon them by the legislative authority. It was a matter of public notoriety, that some of the said corporators petitioned the General Assembly of the Commonwealth therefor, and some protested against it. They admit that nearly all of the members of the Legislature from the City and County of Philadelphia voted in favor of the said charter, as they ascertain from the published proceedings of the said Assembly. That the proceedings of the Select and Common Councils of the corporation of The Mayor, Aldermen, and Citizens of Philadelphia, show that the last-mentioned body did by a majority vote, approve of the proposed amended or extended or altered charter, but that the latter body did not. And for a further answer to the inquiry as to the proceedings of the municipal authorities of the said corporation they refer to so much of their answer to the plaintiffs' bill as relates thereto.

To the fifth. That they have submitted to the Court whether they are entitled to hold the property mentioned in the said interrogatory as absolute owners, or whether they hold in trust for the purposes mentioned in the interrogatory. If they are decreed to hold it in trust, they claim to hold in trust to improve the police and property, and to diminish taxation in that part of the City of Philadelphia which before the 2d of February, 1854, was comprised within the territorial limits of the corporation of The Mayor, Aldermen, and Citizens of Philadelphia.

To the sixth. That they have not applied any portion of the property mentioned or referred to in the said interrogatory to the municipal purposes therein mentioned, because the same has been required for the purposes and the support of the Girard College.

To the seventh. That they hold of the property which was of the said Stephen Girard, the following real estate, namely, in the City of Philadelphia 152 dwelling houses and store houses, the Girard College and its grounds, 3 vacant lots of land, 2 wharves, and 567 acres of farm land in that part of the city which was formerly the Township of Passyunk and the District of Moyamensing. In the counties of Schuylkill and Columbia, in the State of Pennsylvania 43 tracts of land containing about 17,000 acres of land, about one third of which is supposed to contain anthracite coal, and in the State of Kentucky about 1,000 acres of land Beside the above-named they hold no other realty of the estate of Mr. Girard

The gross annual income of the real estate in the City of Philadelphia is about one hundred and fifty six thousand dollars, and not more, and the clear annual income is eighty-six thousand dollars, and not more

To the eighth That they hold of personal property, which was of the testator, that which they have specifically set forth in their answer, (exclusive of $10,000 and $500,000, appropriated and held for the Delaware Avenue improvement, and the fuel fund,) amounting to the par or nominal value of $519,578 31, though the real value thereof is of a much less sum The annual income of the said property is about $9,000, and no more They hold no other personalty of the said estate, except that in this answer mentioned

To the ninth They answer in the affirmative

To the tenth That the sums assumed in the said interrogatory as to the income of the personalty and realty are incorrect—the net income of both being less than therein stated, as they have before shown That the sum mentioned as the one required for the annual expenses of the college is the sum now appropriated, because there is no further sum in their hands for that purpose; but the increased demands of the College, in consequence of the number of orphans applying for admission, require a much larger amount for its annual maintenance And they are informed that there is hardly a limit to the amount which would be required for the maintenance of the College, if all the orphans applying for admission could be received That there is no other deduction or abatement to be made from the net income of said real and personal estate, except the payment of certain annuities of no great amount, after providing for the wants of the College, to precede the application of the income to the objects of improving the police, and the property of the city, the general appearance of the city itself and diminishing the burden of taxation. And whether, if the said objects are not attainable, the said income should be enjoyed by the heirs at-law of the said testator the defendants submit to the judgment of the Court.

To the eleventh. They answer in the negative.

To the twelfth. That to so much of the said interrogatory as inquires concerning accumulations of surplus income they answer in the negative. And to so much thereof as inquires if they can or not apply surplus income for the municipal purposes mentioned in the said interrogatory they answer that they can so apply such income.

To the thirteenth. That if the coal lands in the counties of Schuylkill and Columbia were worked and rented, the income of the estates of the said testator would be increased, but to what extent they are unable to form any estimate. But they believe that the necessities of the College will absorb nearly any amount of income which the estate may produce.

To the fourteenth. That the estates and income of the testator are not liable by the terms of the said will to any other charge except the annuities mentioned in the said interrogatory, and that the said annuities are from time to time falling in at the deaths of the respective annuitants.

And the defendants hereto annex accounts showing the yearly income of the residuary estate, and its annual appropriation.

1832 Income of real estate. $44 907 60

                    $44 907 60

 Appropriations
  Annuities, $3,500 00
  Salaries and incidentals,   3 413 79
  Taxes and water rents,   9,890 77
  Repairs, &c,   2 629 65
  Lands out of the county, taxes, &c, 6 000 00
                   $25,434 21

1833 Income real estate, $55 607 66
   ' personal estate 12 343 78

                    $67 953 44

 Appropriations
  Annuities, $4 300 00
  Salaries and incidentals   7,801 61
  Taxes and water rents,   9 611 79
  Repairs to real estate,   10,858 89
  Building stores and wharf, 5 470 64
   " culvert,   1,877 95
   ' railroad,   1 800 00
  Paving,   7,741 98
  Lands in Louisiana,   1,026 55
                   $50,489 41

1834 Income real estate, $62,856 38
   ' personal estate 11,348 20

                    $74,204 58

 Appropriations
  Annuities, $4,300 00
  Salaries and incidentals,   5,656 95
  Taxes and water rents,   10,473 42
  Repairs,   12,141 12
  Building stores and wharves 12,529 36
  Lands in Pennsylvania and Kentucky 1,192 15
   ' Erie,   279 29
   ' Louisiana,   1,231 14
  Building culvert,   2,122 05
   " railroad,   4,228 55
  Paving,   9,229 47
  Police,   26,322 53
                   $89,706 03

1835	Income real estate,	$72 317 36	
	" personal estate	17,406 80	
			$89 721 16
	Appropriations		
	Annuities,	$4,750 00	
	Salaries, &c,	5,994 16	
	Taxes and water rents,	13,175 80	
	Repairs,	7,581 65	
	Lands out of the county	2 035 32	
	" in Louisiana,	1 140 00	
	Building stores	8 487 21	
	Police	27,831 74	
			$70 995 88
1836	Income real estate,	$86,081 69	
	" personal estate,	21 970 63	
			$108 052 32
	Appropriations		
	Annuities,	$3,100 00	
	Salaries, &c,	6,744 20	
	Taxes and water rents	12 655 69	
	Repairs,	6,101 23	
	Lands out of the county	3 847 74	
	Building stores	13 092 95	
	" market houses	20,000 00	
	Police,	31 651 90	
			$97,193 71
1837	Income real estate,	$97,604 44	
	personal estate,	27,747 24	
			$125 351 68
	Appropriations		
	Annuities,	$4 250 00	
	Salaries, &c,	7,227 66	
	Taxes	13,180 92	
	Repairs,	12,676 51	
	Lands out of the county,	5,303 73	
	Building stores,	25,680 90	
	" wharf,	12,000 00	
	Police,	32,950 00	
			$113 275 72

D W S—38

1838	Income real estate,	$108 505 26	
	" personal estate	25 000 24	
			$133,505 50
	Appropriations		
	Annuities,	$2 950 00	
	Salaries, &c,	8,769 60	
	Taxes,	15,977 44	
	Repairs,	16,982 11	
	Lands out of the county	2 866 19	
	Building stores	104 90	
	' wharf,	7,000 00	
	' tobacco warehouse	7,000 00	
	offices,	3 656 29	
	Iron main	23 000 00	
	Police,	33 190 00	
			$121,496 53
1839	Income real estate,	$112,576 46	
	" personal estate	21 595 24	
			$134 171 70
	Appropriations		
	Annuities,	$4 050 00	
	Salaries, &c	7,027 97	
	Taxes,	16,291 00	
	Repairs,	14 881 35	
	Lands out of the county	1 911 55	
	Public Squares	5 000 00	
	Wharves	2,050 00	
	Lamps and lamp posts,	10 950 00	
	Paving.	8 000 00	
	Improvements at Fairmount	14,000 00	
	Building offices,	5,741 80	
	Police,	33,055 75	
			$122 959 42
1840	Income real estate,	$111 312 24	
	' personal estate,	14,889 98	
			$126,212 22
	Appropriations		
	Annuities,	$3 600 00	
	Salaries, &c,	5,216 44	
	Taxes,	18 451 95	
	Repairs,	8,321 88	
	Lands out of the county	4,401 65	
	Squares,	4,000 00	
	Wharves,	1,000 00	
	Lamps and posts	6,000 00	

	Paving	$10,000 00	
	Improvements at Fairmount	14,000 00	
	Culverts,	5,000 00	
	Repairing streets,	16,000 00	
	Police,	33,248 50	
			$128,240 42
1841	Income real estate,	$113 410 34	
	" personal estate,	8,949 03	
			$122 359 27
	Appropriations		
	Annuities	$3,600 00	
	Salaries, &c.,	4 908 16	
	Taxes,	19,442 61	
	Repairs,	13,089 53	
	Lands out of the county	2,060 56	
	Police	33,107 00	
			$76,207 86
1842	Income real estate,	$94,919 36	
	" personal estate,	3 722 69	
			$98,642 05
	Appropriations		
	Annuities,	$3,100 00	
	Salaries, &c	5 749 17	
	Taxes,	19,089 14	
	Repairs,	14,173 01	
	Lands out of the county	3,100 73	
	Squares,	2,000 00	
	Wharves	700 00	
	Lamps and posts,	4,000 00	
	Paving	6 000 00	
	Culverts,	3,300 00	
	Repaving	9,000 00	
	Police,	6 945 00	
			$77 157 05
1843	Income real estate	$80,571 01	
	" personal estate	1 853 18	
			$82 424 19
	Appropriations		
	Annuities,	$3,300 00	
	Salaries, &c.,	7,515 41	
	Taxes,	19,443 75	
	Repairs,	14,978 13	
	Lands out of the county	2,353 12	
			$47,590 41

1844	Income real estate,	$86,081 97		
	" personal estate	1,766 68		
				$87,850 65
	Appropriations			
	Annuities,		$4,400 00	
	Salaries, &c		17,286 48	
	Taxes,		19,862 00	
	Repairs,		14,990 90	
	Land out of the county		3,542 24	
				$60,081 62
1845	Income real estate,	$88,776 88		
	" personal estate,	3,310 91		
				$92,087 79
	Appropriations			
	Annuities,		$3,300 00	
	Salaries, &c		4,982 33	
	Taxes,		19,155 41	
	Repairs,		14,710 02	
	Lands out of the county		1,984 28	
	Insurance,		5,922 71	
	Building stores,		28,986 25	
	Police,		45,000 00	
				$124,041 00
1846	Income real estate	$104,360 60		
	" personal estate	6,815 50		
				$111,176 10
	Appropriations			
	Annuities		$2,300 00	
	Salaries &c,		5,086 49	
	Taxes,		19,113 04	
	Repairs,		15,000 00	
	Lands out of the county,		4,090 47	
	Rebuilding,		7,000 00	
	Tax Fund		43,000 00	
				$95,590 00
1847	Income real estate	$105,584 10		
	" personal estate	7,110 87		
				$112,694 97
	Appropriations			
	Annuities,		$2,300 00	
	Salaries, &c,		5,983 78	
	Taxes,		22,228 62	
	Repairs,		15,000 00	
	Land out of the county,		3,484 81	

Wharves,	$7,600 00	
Improvement of property, Jones' alley,	31,000 00	
Building College,	5,788 60	
Furnishing "	6,910 00	
Tax Fund,	1,750 00	
		$102,045 81

The excess of income over appropriations in the years 1832, 1833, 1835, 1836, 1837, 1838, 1839, 1841, 1842, 1843, 1844, 1846, and 1847, was,		$249,696 00
The excess of appropriations over income in the years 1834, 1840 and 1845, was		49,482 86
Net excess of income over appropriations		$200,213 14
This excess was thus absorbed.		
By advancing to the executors of Mr Girard funds to aid them to complete the buildings on the square between Market Chestnut, Eleventh, and Twelfth streets. To obtain the funds so advanced the City Corporation borrowed money and repaid the same with its interest out of the income of the residuary estate, to the amount of		$134,119 78
And by the investments in Pennsylvania 5 per cent loan, all the balance in their hands, except the sum of $13,805 77		

1848	Income from real estate	$109,742 36	
	" Sch l co	192 55	
	" personal estate,	8,283 22	
	" sundries,	925 00	
			$149,143 13
	Balance from 1847,		13,805 77
			$162,948 92

Appropriations		
Annuities,	$1,900 00	
Taxes, &c.,	24,300 00	
Salaries,	3,700 00	
Repairs to real estate,	12,059 95	
Lands out of the county,	4,736 10	
Incidentals and miscellaneous	1,728 95	
Improvements real estate, Jones alley	5,000 00	
" " 66 S Third st	8,000 00	
" " 25 N Front st	800 00	
" " 26 "	200 00	
Extending wharf,	400 00	
Culvert for use of houses belonging to esta	1,396 16	
Purchase of right of way	1,500 00	
College,	31,821 83	
		$97,542 99

1849	Income real estate	$115,355 96		
	" Sch'l co,	526 48		
	" personal estate	17,310 29		$133,392 73

Appropriations
Annuities	$1,900 00	
Taxes, &c	24,662 87	
Salaries	3,700 00	
Repairs,	18,000 00	
Incidentals	4,408 50	
Lands out of the county	5,000 00	
Painting real estate,	848 95	
College	72,743 78	
		$131,264 10

1850	Income real estate	$120,507 49	
	" personal estate	8,157 17	$128,664 66

Appropriations
Annuities,	$1,900 00	
Taxes, &c,	23,197 57	
Salaries,	3,700 00	
Repairs,	6,843 10	
Incidentals,	2,709 39	
Lands out of the county	6,752 86	
Permanent improvements real estate,	3,962 57	
Footway, Northern Liberties,	381 69	
Tax Fund	9,000 00	
College,	81,368 81	
		$151,269 29

1851	Income real estate	$123,166 50	
	personal estate	8,531 96	$131,698 46

Appropriations
Annuities	$1,900 00	
Taxes,	23,822 33	
Salaries,	3,700 00	
Repairs,	6,120 94	
Incidentals	9,445 42	
Lands out of the county	5,025 31	
Papering and painting,	5,035 00	
Permanent improvements,	1,928 35	
Curbing and paving around College,	4,389 74	
Gas in College	3,444 66	
College	67,544 11	
		$132,355 86

1852 Income real estate $122,523 26
          "   Sch'l co,   586 38
          '   personal estate   9,080 96
                                              $132,190 80

   Appropriations
     Annuities $1,650 00
     Taxes,   24,554 25
     Salaries,   4,200 00
     Repairs,   5,593 85
     Incidentals,   3,798 72
     Lands out of the county   5,392 68
     Painting and papering   8,821 56
     Permanent improvements   2,350 00
     Improvements North Water street   1,732 83
     Curbing, paving, and water pipes Gi-
        rard College,   1,928 00
     Improvement Third and Chestnut sts 57,843 43
     Permanent improvement at Girard Col-
        lege,   5,058 21
     College,   60,512 37
                                                $183,435 95

1853 Income real estate $136,907 69
          '   Sch'l co   1,303 72
              personal estate,   8,458 96
                                              $146,670 37

   Appropriations
     Annuities, $1,400 00
     Taxes,   27,406 81
     Salaries,   4,050 00
     Repairs,   8,965 85
     Incidentals   9,053 21
     Lands out of the county   3,283 33
     Papering and painting   3,075 14
     Repairs at College,   1,500 00
     Permanent improvements   1,980 00
     Permanent improvement at Third and
        Chestnut sts   41,708 99
     Permanent improvement at College   441 79
     Outfits for pupils at College.   2,595 85
     Curbing and paving   2,739 02
     College,   63,809 76
                                                $173,985 86

1854	Income real estate,	$152,277 90	
	" personal estate,	9,154 71	
			$161,432 61
	Appropriations		
	Annuities,	$1,250 00	
	Taxes,	26,480 52	
	Salaries,	5,049 89	
	Repairs,	7,871 36	
	Incidentals,	2,078 91	
	Lands out of the county,	3,145 18	
	Papering and painting	3,778 28	
	Ice house at College,	1,289 68	
	College,	71,402 37	
			$122,346 19
1855	Income real estate,	$153,199 33	
	" " Sch'l co,	1,034 20	
	" personal estate,	8,318 32	
	" sundries,	363 87	
			$162,915 72
	Appropriations		
	Annuities,	$1,100 00	
	Taxes,	25,276 08	
	Salaries,	4,800 00	
	Repairs,	8,696 03	
	Incidentals,	2,498 26	
	Lands out of the county	3,828 16	
	Papering and painting,	7,048 81	
	Permanent improvements	3,000 00	
	College,	81,754 84	
			$138,002 08
1856	Income real estate,	$152,462 61	
	" " Sch'l co,	877 79	
	" personal estate,	9,050 92	
			$162,391 32
	Appropriations		
	Annuities,	$1,100 00	
	Taxes,	30,175 81	
	Salaries,	4,125 00	
	Repairs,	12,096 45	
	Incidentals	6,973 16	
	Lands out of the county,	2,936 60	
	Papering and painting	11,718 91	
	Permanent improvements,	1,985 08	
	Buildings at College,	4,493 83	
	College, . . .	49,288 50	
			$124,893 34

1857	Income real estate,	$155 709 61	
	" Sch'l co	64 00	
	" personal estate	8 643 92	
			$164,417 53

Appropriations
Annuities	$1,100 00	
Taxes,	32 343 88	
Salaries	3,700 00	
Repairs,	13 900 12	
Incidentals	3 191 09	
Lands out of the county	4 950 33	
Papering and painting,	6 600 22	
Permanent improvements,	2 982 63	
Improvement at Coates st	3 000 00	
New buildings at College,	4 856 18	
College,	90 682 41	
		$167,396 86

1858	Income real estate.	$152 606 20	
	" Sch'l co,	12 50	
	personal estate,	8 661 29	
			$161,279 99

Appropriations
Annuities	$1 100 00	
Taxes,	29 941 01	
Salaries	3 700 00	
Repairs,	12,990 07	
Incidentals	3 236 22	
Lands out of the county,	6 014 17	
Papering and painting,	7 013 92	
Permanent improvements,	2,488 91	
Improvement at Coates street	33,115 91	
College,	88,767 86	
		$188,367 66

1859	Income real estate,	$148 550 38	
	" lands Sch'l co,	50 00	
	" personal property	8,567 14	
			$157 168 12

Appropriations
Annuities,	$1 100 00	
Salaries,	3,700 00	
Taxes and water rents,	28,361 55	
Repairs	15,382 10	
Lands out of the county,	3,960 42	
Permanent improvements,	{ 40,980 98	
	{ 2,176 79	
Miscellaneous,	3 016 25	
Insurance,	722 00	
Law expenses, lands out of the county	666 67	
College,	96,907 02	
		$196 973 78

To the Fifteenth That they refer to their answers hereinbefore

To the Sixteenth The total amount expended in building the said college was $1,935,737 46 This sum was the whole product of the income of the $2,000,000 set apart for the said college, and of the sale of the principal

The amount expended in fitting and furnishing the same, before it was opened for the reception of pupils was $5,886 80

To the Seventeenth The college was built, as has been stated in the last answer, exclusively from the proceeds of the income and sale of the capital of the $2,000,000 There was expended as has been stated the sum of $5,886 80 in fitting and furnishing, before it was opened Since the college was opened in 1847, it has been maintained out of the income of the whole of the residuary estate, which has been always treated by the defendants as being composed of all of the testator's real and personal estate, except that set apart for the Delaware avenue improvement fund, and the fuel fund This fund is styled on the defendants books, the residuary fund It is credited with rents of real and income of personal estate, and charged with annuities, taxes, repairs, and expenses of management, and the balance has been treated as applicable for the purposes of the college The defendants are unable to say how much of the income of the real estate in the city and county of Philadelphia has been applied for college purposes as contradistinguished from the income of the personalty, for the reason that the income from both is blended on their books The Schuylkill Navigation stock has paid no dividend since the college was opened

To the Eighteenth The amount received by the corporation of the Mayor Aldermen and citizens of Philadelphia, as their portion of the purchase money of the land sold under proceedings in partition, as mentioned in the said interrogatory, was $54,099 It was received September 19th 1851, and invested, temporarily, in six per cent loan of the city of Philadelphia. The whole amount, with its interest, namely, $59,506 50, was finally appropriated in January, 1852, to improve the real estate which was devised by the said will to the defendants Nos. 102 and 104 Chestnut street, and Nos. 50 and 52 South Third street. So much of the docket entries mentioned in the interrogatory, as the defendants are required to furnish, are as follows:

"In the Court of Common Pleas of Schuylkill county
March Term, 1849. No. 121.

Plaintiff — Christopher Loeser,
vs.
Hughes and E. Olmsted for the Mayor, etc. — The Mayor, Aldermen, and Citizens of Philadelphia, and Cornelius Stevenson.

Sum's, in Partition issued 19th Dec., 1848
For return, see writ

30th March 1849 nari filed.'

To the Nineteenth. The proceeds of the sales of the lands in Kentucky are as follows:

1847, June 9,	$120 79
1848, June 12,	100 00
1851, July 31,	158 21
1854, May 15,	385 24
Total amount received,	$764 24

Which was invested as follows:

1848, Aug. 18, City 6 per cent loan	$200 00
1854, Jan. 10, " " " "	99 25
June 8,	380 00
Balance to credit,	84 99
	764 24

To the Twentieth. There are no entries in the Journals of the Councils mentioned in the interrogatory, other than those of the dates in the said interrogatory concerning the proposal to consolidate into one the various municipal bodies of the county of Philadelphia.

To the Twenty first. There has been invested, of the

income of the residuary estate, and there yet remains in the hand of the defendants, the following

City loan	$3,300 00,	invested April 17 1847	
	9,800 00	" June 8, 1847	
	800 00,	" June 24, 1847	
	17,300 00,	July 19 1847	
State 5 per cent loan,	53,608 25,	July 17, 1843,	costing $26 000
	26,315 80,	Sept 11, 1843, "	15 000
	10,796 30,	Jan 26 1841	6,909 63

To the Twenty-second That since the death of the testator, the following investments of the capital of his estate have been made by the Mayor, etc —

The mortgage of the Mount Carbon Railroad Company amounting to $20 000, having been paid off, has been invested $10,000 in Loan of the Guardians of the Poor and $10,203 18 in 5 per cent Loan of the county of Philadelphia

The proceeds of the sale of the lands in Kentucky have been invested as mentioned in the answer to the nineteenth interrogatory

The proceeds of the sale of lands in Schuylkill county was invested as has been mentioned in the answer to interrogatory eighteenth

To the Twenty third The testator, in his life time, had made arrangements to cover his square of ground between Chestnut and Market and Eleventh and Twelfth streets. To this end, he had formed his plans of buildings and consulted and employed various mechanics Immediately after his death the residuary legatees, by their Select and Common Councils, authorized and requested the executors, as such, to cause the square of ground mentioned "to be built upon and improved agreeably to the plan, contracts, and arrangements of the testator,' and authorized them "to pay for the same out of the fund that may be in their hands as executors," and stipulated, that the "receipts which they shall obtain, for all payments made by them in the prosecution of the said improvement, shall be accepted by the

Mayor, Aldermen, and Citizens of Philadelphia as a part to the amount of said receipts of the residuary estate devised and bequeathed, by the said testator, to the said Mayor Aldermen, and Citizens of Philadelphia."

The executors accordingly undertook the business of improving the square as above mentioned, and paid for the expenses of the same out of the funds of the estate in their possession. Finally, however, in 1836, the executors found themselves without funds in their hands to complete the improvements they having paid previously to the residuary legatees, without retaining sufficient to meet the demands on them for the cost of the improvement. The residuary devisees and legatees borrowed money and advanced it to the executors, to enable them to complete the buildings. The money so borrowed the said legatees repaid out of the income of the residuary estate.

The whole cost of the improvement upon the square was $814,506 04 of this, the amount paid by the executors, out of the funds of the estate in their hands was $680,386 62 and out of the income of the residuary estate, the corporation of the Mayor, Aldermen, and Citizens paid $134,119 78

How much of the sum so paid by the executors was paid from capital, and how much from interest or income on investments, or sums at interest, the defendants are unable to state. The sum paid by the Mayor, Aldermen and Citizens of Philadelphia was entirely from income.

The defendants are not able to state at what times the payments by the executors were made. They were necessarily very numerous, and commenced in the spring of 1832, and terminated in the spring of 1837.

To the Twenty-fourth. The following-named sums have been expended for the erection of buildings upon the testator's real estate, (excepting the college and the buildings upon the square of ground between Chestnut and Market, and Eleventh and Twelfth streets) at the times hereinafter named, viz —

1835–6	For stores on Delaware avenue, north of Market street,	$22,603 83
1837	For stores on Front, north of Market streets,	24,765 96
1838–9	For offices on Fifth street, above Chestnut,	9,398 09
1845	For 4 stores on Water street.	28,986 25
1857	For buildings on lot, Coates street	3,000 00
1857–8–9	For buildings on lot on Brown street,	74,096 89

And the following named sums for improving and rebuilding real estate, which was of the testator viz —

1837	For extending wharves,	$12,000 00
1838	For extending and rebuilding wharves opposite 5 and 6, Delaware avenue,	7,000 00
1846	For rebuilding property, No. 100 Chestnut street,	7,000 00
1847	For rebuilding property in Jones alley,	36,000 00
"	For extending and capping wharves	8,000 00
1848	For improving property front of 66 South Third street,	1,000 00
"	For improving property rear of 66 South Third street	7,000 00
1848	For improving property 26 and 28 North Front street,	1,000 00
1850	For improving property 5 and 6 North Wharves,	962 57
"	For improving foot-way, property, Northern Liberties,	381 69
1852	For improving property 13 and 15 North Water street,	1,800 00
1852–3	For rebuilding property 102 and 104 Chestnut, and 50 and 52 South Third street,	99,552 42
1853	For repairing damages by fire, 28 North Front street,	512 60

To the Twenty fifth Interrogatory The total amount expended upon the said college, for the year 1859, was $96,907 02, as follows —

Appropriations from the Residuary Fund, for the Use of the Directors of the Girard College, for the year 1859

	Appropriated	Expended	Balance
Appropriation to the Committee on Household, for			
Subsistence, Item No 1,	$23,000 00	$22,958 30	$41 70
Clothing, Item No 2	17,000 00	16,815 94	184 06
Salaries, Items Nos 3, 4, 5, 6, 7, & 9	6,700 00	6,700 00	
Wages Item No 10	9,000 00	8,553 03	446 97
Furniture, Item No 11,	1,500 00	1,423 13	76 87
Fuel, Item No 12,	2,500 00	1,908 54	591 46
Gas, Item No 13,	1,800 00	1,430 97	369 03
Repairs and Imp'm'ts Item No 14	2,500 00	2,484 66	15 34
Imp'm't of Grounds Item No 15,	2,500 00	2,418 93	81 07
Incidentals, Item No 16,	15,000 00	14,903 43	96 57
Appropriation to the Committee on Instruction for			
Salaries, Items Nos 17, 18, 19, 20, 21, 22, 23, 24, 25, 26, 27	13,800 00	13,800 00	
School Philosophical Apparatus, Item No 28,	500 00	490 40	9 60
Books and Stationary,	1,200 00	1,189 50	10 50
School and Chapel Furniture, Item No 30,	500 00	498 96	1 04
Utensils and Materials for Chemical Laboratory, Item No 31,	250 00	234 33	15 67
Additional instruction, and to supply Teachers in case of Sickness, Item No 32,	300 00		300 00
Appropriation to Committee on Accounts, for			
Salaries, Items Nos 33, 34,	1,650 00	1,650 00	
Printing, Advertising, and Newspapers Item No 35,	480 00	476 19	3 81
Appropriation to Committee on Library, for			
Library, Books, and Furniture, Item 36,	1,000 00	992 58	7 42
Appropriation to Committee on Discipline and Discharge, for			
Expenses Binding Out, Advertising, &c, Item No 37,	200 00	81 66	118 34
Reward of Merit, No 38	300 00	251 76	48 24
Expenses of Admission, Advertising, &c Item No 39	250 00		250 00
Beds, Bedding, and other Furniture, for additional Pupils at College, Item No 40	2,500 00	1,282 58	1,317 42
Deficiencies of appropriation, 1858 Item No 41,	117 31	117 31	
New Buildings at College Balance Jan y 1st, 1859, $7,432 21,		7,426 38	5 83
Appropriation, approved April 28 1859, Certain Alterations in Main Buil'g,	2,500 00	2,418 44	81 56
Balance of former Approp'ns, $7,432 21	$93,547 31	$96,907 02	$4,072 50

To the Twenty sixth That on the 20th day of April, 1833, they set apart as the fund of $2,000,000 for erecting and maintaining the said college the following stocks and loans, viz.

6,331 shares of stock in the Bank of the U States,
    valued at $644,715
870,000 par Pennsylvania, 5 per cent loan, valued at 994,418
199,305   "   "   '   '   "   227,367
100,000   " City of Philadelphia,   "   "   113,500

The above fund, as has been before stated, was all absorbed in building the said college. The annual cost of its maintenance is defrayed from the income of the residuary of the estate, which comprises, as the defendants are advised, the whole of the testator's estate, except so much thereof as is appropriated to the Delaware avenue improvement fund of $500,000, and the fuel fund of $10,000.

To the Twenty-seventh The only sums, portions of the residuary estate which have been expended on improvements of real estate outside of the corporate limits, which were of the Mayor, Aldermen, and Citizens of Philadelphia, were—

In 1839, the sum of $14,000; in 1840, the sum of $14,000, on the Water Works of the said Corporation at Fairmount.

In 1857, for buildings on lot in Coates street, the sum of $8,000 and in 1857, 1858, and 1859, the sum of $74,096 89, for buildings on the lot on Brown street.

The sum of $28,000, above mentioned, is the only sum which has been expended on the improvement of property not part of the residuary estate, out of the corporate limits of the Mayor, Aldermen, and Citizens of Philadelphia.

To the Twenty-eighth The five hundred and sixty-seven acres of farm-land in the late districts of Moyamensing and

Passyunk are leased for farms or gardens. The annual rent received therefor is $6,662 50.

To the Twenty-ninth. That many alterations in the charters mentioned in the said interrogatory have been made by the Legislature, but they are not able to specify whether the same were at the instance or against the remonstrance of the said corporation, or whether the said alterations were made without either the application or remonstrance aforesaid.

And the defendants answer, and specially insist to be available to them in such manner as may be according to the practice in equity and the rules of this honorable court, that Etienne Girard, the father of the plaintiffs, was one of the objects of the testator's bounty, and that a legacy was given to him by his said will, as by reference to the same will appear, and that the said Etienne Girard, before the filing of the plaintiff's bill claimed his said legacy from the executors of the said will under the same, and according to the same, and received his said legacy, to wit on the 2d January, 1833, or thereabouts from the said executors, under and according to the said will, and not otherwise. And the defendants say that the plaintiffs who claim under the said Etienne Girard, and as his heirs at-law, are concluded by the election of their ancestors, and cannot now claim against the said will.

And the defendants further answering say, and specially insist to be available as aforementioned, that the said Etienne Girard and Francoise Fenelon Vidal, claiming to be respectively a brother, and niece of the said Stephen Girard, filed their bill in this Court to October Sessions, 1836, No 1, against the defendants by their then corporate name of the Mayor, Aldermen and Citizens of Philadelphia, and against the executors of the will of the said Stephen Girard, wherein they prayed the Court to declare the devise of the residue and remainder of the real estate to the defendants to be void, wherein said bill, upon final hearing on answer, replication, and proof, was dismissed by the said Court, and upon appeal to the Supreme Court of the United States, to January Term, 1844, after argument and consideration, the said decree dismissing the said bill was affirmed. And the defendants say, that by the said decree the trusts created and declared in the said will were decreed to be valid and lawful, and they pray leave to refer to and produce the record of the said suit, with the same effect as if the same were herein at large set forth.

The defendants further answering say, and here show to the Court, that the plaintiffs claim to be decreed to be entitled to the possession and ownership of the said estate in inconsistent rights, for that in one part of their said bill they so claim because, as they allege, by reason of the effect of the said Act of Assembly of February 2d, 1854, the defendants are disabled from executing the trusts of the said will, and in another part they say that the devise to them is an attempt to create a perpetuity, and therefore void. And they submit that the plaintiffs cannot in the same bill claim under the will and against the will, and they pray that the plaintiffs may be required to elect in which of the said rights they will claim.

All which matters and things are true, without this, that there are any other matters or things in the said bill contained, and not herein well and sufficiently confessed and avoided, traversed and denied, are true, as these defendants will maintain and prove.

And these defendants pray that they may be hence dismissed, with their reasonable costs and charges in this behalf most wrongfully sustained.

ALEX. HENRY,
Mayor.

[Seal of the City of Philadelphia]

Opinion.

And afterwards, to wit, on the seventh day of October Anno Domini, 1861, the opinion of the Court was delivered by Mr Justice Grier, which opinion is in the words and of the tenor following, to wit

MADELEINE H. GIRARD, ET AL, *vs* THE CITY OF PHILADELPHIA } In C C U S, E D of Pa In Chancery Submitted on Bill and Answer

The heirs-at law of the late Stephen Girard have again come into Court, claiming a portion of the property devised by him to the city of Philadelphia

The case of Vidal *vs* The Executors of Girard (2 How 17) has put an end to any further controversy as to the validity of the trusts, and the power of the city to execute them

Nor do the heirs, who are complainants in this bill, pretend to call in question the matters finally and conclusively settled by that case. The facts which are supposed to rehabilitate their claim have occurred since its decision. Admitting that the will of Stephen Girard entirely excluded them from any claim of right to the property in question they now contend, that the Consolidation Act has made it impossible for any to execute the trusts for municipal purposes, and, as a consequence, the heirs are entitled to that portion of the estate appropriated by the testator for such uses

If it shall appear that the effect of the Consolidation Act is not that which the bill alleges, it may be unnecessary to discuss the question whether, if it were, the consequences assumed from it be legitimate. The will of Stephen Girard after sundry bequests to his relatives and friends, and to certain specified charities announces (§ xx) his great and favorite charity to be the establishment of a college for the education of poor orphans It then proceeds "Now, I give, devise and bequeath all the residue and remainder of my real and personal estate,' &c unto the "Mayor, Aldermen and Citizens of Philadelphia, in trust for the several uses, intents and purposes hereinafter mentioned and declared'

The attempt to restrain the alienation of the realty, being inoperative, cannot affect the validity of this devise After many and very special directions as to the college, its construction and government, it further directs, that two millions of the personal estate be appropriated to the building and if this sum should not be sufficient, the remainder should be taken "from the final residuary fund hereinafter expressly referred to,' and which is found in the XXIVth section, as follows

"And as it regards the remainder of said residue of *my personal estate*, to invest the same in good securities, and in like manner to invest the interest and income thereof, from time to time, so that the whole shall form a permanent fund, and to apply the income of the said fund,

' *First.* To the further improvement and maintenance of the aforesaid College as directed in the last paragraph of the twenty-first clause of this my Will

' *Second* To enable the Corporation of the city of Philadelphia to provide more effectually than they now do for the security of the inhabitants of the said city, by a competent police, including a sufficient number of watchmen, really suited to the purpose, and to this end, I recommend a division of the city into watch districts, or four parts, each under a proper head

" *Third* To enable the said Corporation to improve the city property, and the general appearance of the city itself, and, in effect, to diminish the burden of taxation, now most oppressive especially on those who are least able to bear it

"To all which objects the prosperity of the city, and the health and comfort of its inhabitants, I devote the said fund as aforesaid, and direct the income thereof to be applied yearly, and every year forever, after providing for the college as hereinbefore directed, as my primary object.'

The realty had before been devised, subject to the trusts of the will, and considering that portion of the fund as already invested in the best manner (as appears from his forbidding its alienation) the income of the whole is then devoted to these three objects, the college being "the primary object." So long as any portion of this fund shall be found necessary for ' its improvement and maintenance,' on the plan and to the extent declared in the will, the second and third objects can claim nothing. The bill admits this to be a valid charity, and claims only the residue after that is satisfied. Now it is admitted (for it has been so decided) that, till February 1854, the corporation was vested with a complete title to the whole residue of the estate of Stephen Girard, subject to these charitable trusts, and consequently, at that date his heirs at law had no right title or interest whatsoever in the same; but the bill alleges that the act of the Legislature of that date (commonly called the "Consolidation Act") which purports to be a supplement to the original act incorporating the city, has either dissolved or destroyed the identity of the original corporation, and it is consequently unable any longer to administer the trust. Now, if this were true, the only consequence would be, not that the charities or trust should fail, but that the Chancellor should substitute another trustee.

It is not insisted that the mere change or abbreviation of the name has destroyed the identity of the corporation. The bill even seems to admit that a small addition to its territory and jurisdiction might not have that effect; but that the annexation of twenty nine boroughs and townships has smothered it to death or rendered it utterly incapable of administering trusts or charities committed to it when its boundaries were Vine and South streets and the two rivers. There is nothing to be found in the letter or spirit of this act, which shows any intention in the Legislature to destroy the original corporation, either by changing its name, enlarging its territory, or increasing the number of its corporators. On the contrary, "all its powers, rights, privileges and immunities, &c., are continued in full vigor and effect." It provides, also, that "all the estates, &c.," held by any of the corporations united by the act shall be held ' upon and for the same uses, trusts, limitations, charities and conditions, as the same were then held."

By the act of 4th of April, 1852, the corporation was 'authorized to exercise all such jurisdiction, to enact all such ordinances, and to do and execute all such acts and things whatsoever, as may be necessary for the full and entire acceptance, execution and prosecution of any and all the devises bequests, trusts and provisions contained in said will.' It may also "provide, by ordinance or otherwise, for the election and appointment of such officers and agents as they may deem essential to the due execution of the duties and trusts enjoined and created by the will of the late Stephen Girard.'

Now, it cannot be pretended that the Legislature had not the power to appoint another trustee if the act had dissolved the corporation, or to continue the rights, duties, trusts, &c., in the enlarged corporation. It has done so, and has given the widest powers to the trustee to administer the trusts and charities according to intent of the testator, as declared in his will.

The Legislature may alter, modify, or even annul, the franchises of a public municipal corporation, although it may not impose burthens on it without its consent. In this case the corporation has assented to accept the charges, assume the burthens, and perform the duties imposed upon it; and it is difficult to conceive how they can have forfeited their right to the charities, which the law makes it their duty to administer. The objects of the testator's charity remain the same, while the city, large or small, exists, the trust is an existing and valid one, the trustee is vested by law with the estate and the fullest power and authority to execute the trust

Whatever the fears or fancy of the complainants may be as to the moral ability of this overgrown corporation, there is no necessary or natural inability which prohibits it from administering this charity as faithfully as it could before its increase. In fact, it is a matter in which the complainants have no concern whatever, or any right to intervene. If the trust be not rightly administered, the *cestui que trust* or the sovereign may require the courts to compel a proper execution.

In the case of Vidal (2 How. 19), the Supreme Court say, that "if the trusts were in themselves valid in point of law, it is plain that neither the heirs of the testator or any other private person would have any right to enquire into or contest the right of the corporation to take the property or execute the trust; this would exclusively belong to the State in its sovereign capacity and as *parens patriæ*, and its sole discretion."

This is not an assertion that the Legislature, as *parens patriæ*, may interfere by retrospective acts to exercise the *cy pres* power, which has become so odious from its application in England to what were called superstitious uses. Baxter's case (Vernon), and other similar ones, cannot be precedents, where there is no established church which treats all dissent as superstition. But it cannot admit of a doubt that, where there is a valid devise to a corporation, in trust for certain charitable purposes, unaffected by any question as to its validity because of superstition, the sovereign may interfere to enforce the execution of the trusts, either by changing the administrator, if the corporation be dissolved, or, if not, by modifying or enlarging its franchises, provided the trust be not perverted and no wrong done to the beneficiaries. Where the trustee is a corporation, no modification of its franchises or change in its name, while its identity remains, can affect its rights to hold property devised to it for any purpose. Nor can a valid vested estate in trust lapse or become forfeited by any misconduct in the trustee or inability in the corporation to execute it, if such existed. Charity never fails, and it is the right, as well as the duty, of the sovereign, by its courts and public officers, as also by legislation (if needed), to have the charities properly administered. Now, there is no complaint that the charity, so far as regards the primary and great object of the testator, is not properly administered; and it does not appear that there *now* is, or ever will be, any residue to apply to the secondary objects. If that time should ever arrive, the question, whether the charity shall be so applied as to have the "effect to diminish the burden of taxation" on all the corporation, or only those within the former boundaries of the city, will have to be decided. The case of Soohan *vs* The City (9 Casey) does not decide it. Nor is this Court bound to decide it. The answer shows *how* it may be done, and the corporation has ample power conferred on it to execute the trust according to either hypothesis; and if further power were necessary, the Legislature, executing the sovereign power, can certainly grant them. In the mean time, the heirs-at-law of the testator have no concern in the matter, or any right to interfere by a bill *quia timet*. Their anticipations of the future perversion of the charity by the corruption or folly of the enlarged corporation, and the moral impossibility of its just administration, are not sufficient reasons for the interference of this Court, to seize upon the fund, or any part of it and to deliver it up to the complainants who never had, and by the will of Stephen Girard were not intended to have, any right, title or claim whatsoever to the property.

In fine, the bill must be dismissed, because

1st. The residue of the estate of Stephen Girard, at the time of his death, was by his will vested in the corporation on valid legal trusts, which it was fully competent to execute.

2d. By the supplement to the act incorporating the city (commonly called the 'Consolidation Act'), the identity of the corporation is not destroyed. Nor can the change in its name, the enlargement of its area, or increase in the number of its corporators, affect its title to property held at the time of such change.

3d. The corporation under its amended charter has every capacity to hold, and every power and authority necessary to execute, the trusts of the will.

4th. That the difficulties anticipated by the bill as to the execution of the secondary trusts are imaginary. They have not arisen and most probably never will.

5th. And if they should, it is a matter, whether probable or improbable with which the complainants have no concern, and cannot have, on any possible contingency.

AN ACT

To enable the Mayor, Aldermen, and Citizens of Philadelphia to carry into effect certain improvements, and execute certain trusts

WHEREAS, By the last will and testament of Stephen Girard, late of the City of Philadelphia, deceased, the sum of five hundred thousand dollars is bequeathed to the Mayor, Aldermen, and Citizens of Philadelphia, in trust among other things, to apply the income thereof "First, to lay out, regulate, curb, light, and pave a passage or street on the east part of the City of Philadelphia, fronting the river Delaware not less than twenty-one feet wide, and to be called Delaware avenue extending from South or Cedar street, all along the east part of Water street squares, and the west side of the logs which form the heads of the docks, or thereabouts, and to this intent, to obtain such acts of assembly, and to make such purchases or agreements as will enable the Mayor, Aldermen, and Citizens of Philadelphia to remove or pull down all the buildings, fences, and obstructions which may be in the way, and to prohibit all buildings, fences, or erections of any kind to the eastward of said avenue, to fill up the heads of such of the docks as may not afford sufficient room for the said street, to compel the owners of wharves to keep them clean, and covered completely with gravel or other hard materials, and to be so levelled that water will not remain thereon after a shower of rain, to completely clean and keep clean, all the docks within the limits of the city, fronting on the Delaware, and to pull down all platforms carried out from the east part of the city, over the river Delaware, on piles or pillars." 'Second To pull down and remove all wooden buildings, as well as those made of wood and other combustible materials as those called brick paned, or frame buildings, filled in with bricks, that are erected within the limits of the City of Philadelphia, and also to prohibit the erection of any such building within the said city's limits at any future time. "Third To widen, pave, and curb Water street, and to distribute the Schuylkill water therein, upon" a certain plan therein set forth. Now, for the purpose of enabling the Mayor, Aldermen, and Citizens of Philadelphia aforesaid, to effect the improvements contemplated by the said testator, and to execute in all other respects the trusts created by his will, to enable the constituted authorities of the City of Philadelphia to carry which into effect, the said Stephen Girard has desired the legislature to enact the necessary laws.

SECT. 1. Be it enacted by the Senate and House of Representatives of the Commonwealth of Pennsylvania, in General Assembly met, and it is hereby enacted by the authority of the same, That it shall and may be lawful for the Mayor, Aldermen, and Citizens of Philadelphia, by ordinance lawfully enacted, or the intervention and act of authorized officers or agents, to lay out, regulate, curb, light, and pave a passage or street, not less than twenty one feet in width on the east part of the City of Philadelphia, fronting the river Delaware, at such distance or distances in the several parts thereof from the eastern line of Water street as they shall judge proper, extending from Vine to Cedar street, to be called the Delaware avenue; and that, having laid out such street, they shall cause a record of the same to be made in the Court of Quarter Sessions for the County of Philadelphia.

SECT. 2. And be it further enacted by the authority aforesaid, That it shall be lawful for the Mayor, Aldermen, and Citizens of Philadelphia aforesaid, in manner aforesaid, to lay out Water street, in the said city, anew, in such manner as that the same shall be as nearly straight as conveniently may be, and of a uniform, or as near as may be uniform width throughout, not less than thirty nine feet, if practicable, and the same to open and keep open for ever, as a common and public highway; and that having laid out said Water street of such increased width, they shall cause a record of the same to be made in the Court of Quarter Sessions for the County of Philadelphia.

SECT. 3. And be it further enacted by the authority aforesaid, That it shall be lawful for the Mayor, Aldermen, and Citizens of Philadelphia aforesaid, to pass ordinances, or take other measures for regulating adjusting, and determining the easternmost line to which wharves may thereafter lawfully be constructed on the river Delaware fronting said city, and to cause a record of such regulated line to be made in the Court of Quarter Sessions for the County of Philadelphia, to fix and decide on, or cause their officers to fix and decide on the levels of all wharves fronting the said city, and to declare the regulation thereof, to require the owners thereof to pave the same or to lay them with gravel, according to such regulation so as effectually to drain and pass off the water from the same and to require all persons owning and occupying or using docks or wharves, to cleanse the same and to keep the same in repair, and to prescribe the form, materials, and character of workmanship of all wharves hereafter to be constructed, and to require all platforms now projecting into the river Delaware, and supported on piles pillars, or piers, to be removed, and to prohibit the construction in future, of any such projecting platforms, and to require the removal, and prohibit the construction, in future of all buildings, fences, and other obstructions, to the eastward of Delaware avenue, above mentioned, and to declare all erections and constructions whatsoever, contrary to the said ordinances, whether erected before or after the passage of the same to be nuisances, and generally to devise, ordain and execute whatever other things shall by them, the said Mayor, Aldermen, and Citizens of Philadelphia aforesaid, be deemed necessary or convenient for the good arrangement, security and government of the said wharves. *Provided*, That the easternmost line of the said wharves shall not be held to be finally determined, and the record thereof shall not be made, as aforesaid, unless the board of wardens, of the port of Philadelphia, shall decide and make their certificate in writing, that such easternmost line is not inconsistent with the public interests, which certificate shall also be recorded in the said Court of Quarter Sessions: but if the said certificate shall not be granted by them, within three months after application made therefor, the refusal or omission of the said board of wardens to grant such certificate, shall when duly verified by affidavit, be esteemed the judgment and decision of the said board of wardens, that such easternmost line is inconsistent with the public interests, and in case such a decision shall in any wise be made, an appeal shall lie therefrom to the said Court of Quarter Sessions as in other cases, and the judgment of the said Court, in favor of such regulated line, shall be, for all purposes, equivalent to a similar decision by the said board of wardens. *Provided* That nothing herein contained shall be construed to give authority to any one to erect wharves or piers extending out as far as the said regulated easternmost line, without license from the said board of wardens as heretofore.

SECT. 4. And be it further enacted by the authority aforesaid, That it shall be lawful for the Mayor, Aldermen, and Citizens of Philadelphia aforesaid, to pass ordinances, prohibiting the construction within the said city or any parts thereof, of all framed or brick paned or other buildings the walls whereof are not wholly composed of incombustible materials, determining the thicknesses of which walls of buildings of different dimensions and characters shall hereafter be made in the said city, and in making all such other legal provisions as they shall think expedient for preventing the extension of injuries from fire in the said city, and to declare all buildings the walls whereof are not wholly composed of incombustible materials, to be nuisances.

SECT. 5. And be it further enacted by the authority aforesaid, That when any of the said ordinances shall have been passed, or other proceedings had in relation to the said Delaware avenue and Water street, or either of them, and the record thereof shall have been made as aforesaid, it shall be lawful for the Mayor, Aldermen, and Citizens of Philadelphia aforesaid, to proceed, from time to time, to open for public use, any part or parts thereof, and the same to keep open as common and public highways for ever, and to that end, to enter upon such property as may be found to be within the same, construct wharves extending into the river, within the lines of said Delaware avenue, and to a reasonable distance beyond the same, and to fill up all docks within the limits thereof, and remove all obstructions, of whatever kind from within the limits of said avenue and street or any parts thereof and level, drain pitch, and pave the same, as other streets in the said city And from and after the passing of such ordinances, and the record of the said avenue and street all buildings, thereafter erected or rebuilt on the said avenue and street shall conform to the recorded limits of the same and the Mayor, Aldermen, and Citizens of Philadelphia aforesaid, may pass ordinances, declaring all obstructions within the same to be nuisances

SECT 6 And be it further enacted by the authorty afore said, That it shall at all times be lawful for the Mayor, Aldermen and Citizens of Philadelphia aforesaid, to remove and abate any building, erection or obstruction whatever, which, by this Act, or by any ordinance to be hereafter passed by virtue of it, may be declared a nuisance *Provided*, That if such building, erection or obstruction shall have been in existence at the time of the passage of this Act, or of such ordinance passed by virtue hereof, the Mayor, Aldermen, and Citizens aforesaid shall give at least three months' notice of their intention to remove the same to the persons having the ownership, occupation or use thereof, or in case no such persons shall be known to them, then they shall affix a copy of such notice to and upon such building, erection, or obstruction three months before proceeding to remove the same.

SECT 7 And be it further enacted by the authority aforesaid, That it shall be lawful for the said the Mayor, Aldermen, and Citizens of Philadelphia aforesaid, to provide for the punishment of any person or persons who shall commit any nuisance contrary to the intent and meaning of this Act, and of the ordinances which may be passed by virtue thereof, and of any person or persons who having committed any such nuisance, shall, after notice, refuse or neglect to remove the same.

SECT. 8. And be it further enacted by the authority aforesaid, That all persons whatsoever who shall receive damage to their property by reason of any thing which shall have been done by the Mayor, Aldermen, and Citizens of Philadelphia, under this Act, or any ordinance passed by virtue hereof, may, after ten days notice of such their intention, to the Mayor, Aldermen, and Citizens aforesaid, apply by petition in writing, to the Court of Quarter Sessions for the County of Philadelphia, who shall thereupon appoint a jury of twelve disinterested freeholders, citizens of the City of Philadelphia, which jury shall assemble, after ten days' notice of their meeting, given as aforesaid, and shall be sworn or affirmed to inquire what damages the petitioners, or any of them, have sustained by reason of any thing so done, considering as well the advantages which may accrue to such petitioners as the injuries by them complained of, and the said jury having viewed the premises and heard the parties or their counsel, shall report in writing, under the hands of at least ten jurors, and their report having been considered and confirmed by the Court, the damages thereby found shall be paid by the Mayor, Aldermen, and Citizens aforesaid, in six months after the confirmation of the said report.

SECT. 9. And be it further enacted by the authority aforesaid, That if the Mayor, Aldermen, and Citizens aforesaid, shall deem it expedient that the damages should be legally ascertained before proceeding to enter on premises for the purpose of removing obstructions, and before appropriating to public use any property of individuals, or otherwise injuriously affecting the rights and interests of any proprietor, the Mayor, Aldermen, and Citizens aforesaid may, from time to time, apply to the Court of Quarter Sessions for the county of Philadelphia, by petition, in writing, specifying therein as nearly as may be the persons and property in regard to which they desire that the damages should be ascertained, and thereupon the said Court shall appoint a jury of twelve disinterested freeholders, citizens of the City of Philadelphia, which jury shall assemble, after ten days' notice of their meeting given to the owners or occupiers of the property, and shall be sworn or affirmed, as is provided in the foregoing section of this Act, and having viewed and heard, as is therein provided, shall report in writing, under the hands of at least ten jurors, specifying in their said report, as well the causes for which damages, if any, should be paid, as the amounts of such damages, and in such case the Mayor, Aldermen, and Citizens aforesaid, may, within one year after the confirmation of such report by the Court of Quarter Sessions, tender to any owner of property named therein the amount of damages thereby found in his favor, or may pay the same into Court, for his use and benefit, and may thereafter proceed to enter upon the premises, and remove the obstructions, or appropriate the property for which damages shall have been so paid or tendered, first giving three months' notice to the tenant in possession, if any. *Provided, however*, That if the amount so found by such jury in favor of any owner, shall not be so tendered or paid within one year after the confirmation of such report, then the proceedings had upon the said position of the Mayor, Aldermen, and Citizens aforesaid, shall, so far as relates to the said owner, be null and void, and the Mayor, Aldermen, and Citizens aforesaid, may thereafter present their petition, in writing, anew, under this section, as if no proceedings had before been had. *And provided also*, That when a report shall have been made by a jury, under the provisions of this section, and damages shall have been tendered or paid, in accordance therewith, if thereafter any other damage than that reported on shall be sustained, the party aggrieved may thereafter apply, in regard to such other damages, for a jury to assess the same, under the eighth section of this Act. *Provided further*, That it shall at all times be competent to the Mayor, Aldermen, and Citizens aforesaid, to agree with any owner or owners of property, so to be taken, removed, or affected for the damages thereby to be occasioned, and such agreement shall be instead of any of the proceedings detailed in this or the foregoing sections of this Act. And, forasmuch as in the course of time it may appear that powers are not vested in the said the Mayor, Aldermen, and Citizens of Philadelphia, which may be yet required to the full execution of those parts of the said will of the said Stephen Girard, for the carrying of which into effect he has in his said will requested legislative provision, and it is the object and intent of this Act fully to confer all such powers.

SECT. 10. Be it further enacted by the authority aforesaid, That it shall be lawful for the Mayor, Aldermen, and Citizens of Philadelphia, to exercise all such jurisdiction, enact all such ordinances, and do and execute all such acts and things whatsoever as may be necessary and convenient for the full and entire acceptance, execution, and prosecution of any and all the devises and bequests, trusts and provisions contained in the said will which are the subjects of the preceding parts of this Act, and to enable the constituted authorities of the City of Philadelphia to carry which into effect, the said Stephen Girard has desired the legislature to enact the necessary laws.

SECT. 11. And be it further enacted by the authority aforesaid, That no road or street shall be laid out, or passed through the land in the County of Philadelphia, bequeathed by the late Stephen Girard, for the erection of a college, unless the same shall be recommended by the Trustees or Directors of said college, and approved of by a majority of the Select and Common Councils of the City of Philadelphia.

APPROVED—The twenty-fourth day of March, A. D. one thousand eight hundred and thirty-two.

Pamphlet Laws, 176–182

A SUPPLEMENT

To the Act entitled 'An Act to enable the Mayor, Aldermen, and Citizens of Philadelphia to carry into effect certain improvements and to execute certain trusts."

Sect. 1. Be it enacted by the Senate and House of Representatives of the Commonwealth of Pennsylvania, in General Assembly met, and it is hereby enacted by the authority of the same, That the Select and Common Councils of the City of Philadelphia, shall be and they are hereby authorized to provide by ordinance or otherwise, for the election or appointment of such officers and agents as they may deem essential to the due execution of the duties and trusts enjoined and created by the will of the late Stephen Girard.

Approved—The fourth day of April, Anno Domini eighteen hundred and thirty-two.

Pamphlet Laws, 275.

EXEMPLIFICATION OF PARTS OF THE CASE OF

VIDAL, et al

vs

THE CITY OF PHILADELPHIA.

Reported in 2 Howard, 17

And referred to in the opinion of Judge GRIER, in his opinion [p 311]

Docket Entries

In the Circuit Court of the United States for the Eastern District of Pennsylvania, on the Third Circuit of October Sessions, 1836 No 1.

<small>Kittera, Broom, Perkins</small>

ETIENNE GIRARD and FRANCOISE FENELON VIDAL, aliens, and citizens and subjects of the monarchy of France,

vs

<small>Chauncey, for Girard Exec

Olmsted and Sergeant for Mayor et al</small>

THE MAYOR, ALDERMEN AND CITIZENS OF PHILADELPHIA, TIMOTHY PAXSON, THOMAS P COPE, JOSEPH ROBERTS, WILLIAM J DUANE and JOHN J BARCLAY Executors of STEPHEN GIRARD, deceased, MARK RICHARTS, Trustee of CAROLINE HASLEM, JOHN HEMPHILL and MARIA A, his wife, JOHN Y CLARK and HENRIETTA, his wife, and JOHN B HASLEM and CAROLINE, his wife all citizens of the State of Pennsylvania

In Equity

1836 Oct 22d Recog of Jacob Tuse as security for costs filed

1836 Aug t 26   Bill filed and subpœna ext Returnable eleventh of October next

"   Oct 11   Subpœna ret'd, " served on all the defendants " but John Y Clark and Henrietta, his wife and John B Haslem and Caroline, his wife as to whom ret'd " Nil habent

1837 Jan'y 20   Several answer of the Mayor, Aldermen and Citizens of Philadelphia filed

D W S—43

1837 Jan'y 31   Answer of Thomas P Cope and al, exe'rs of S Girard, filed
" May 8   On motion of Mr Kittera, for complainants leave is given to file an amended bill
1838 March 8   Amended bill filed, and subpœna exit, ret'ble to April 8, 1838
" April 11.   Subpœna ret d "Served on the Mayor and al, on T Paxson, T P Cope, J Roberts, W J Duane, J A Barclay J Hemphill and wife, and M Richards, and nil habent as to J Y Clark and wife, and Caroline E G Haslam'
" Sept 5   Answer of the executors of Stephen Girard to the amended bill filed
1839 Apr 10   Bill of revivor filed 11 Exit subpœna on bill of revivor, ret ble Rule day of May next
" Apr 29   Death of T Paxson suggested, and Mr Chauncey appears for the other executors
" Apr 29   Joint and several answer of John Hemphill and M Antoinette, his wife, filed.
" Apr 30   Subp a sur bill of revivor ret'd, "Served on the Mayor, &c, Trustees, on all the ex rs of S. Girard, and service accepted for the other defendants'
" June 20   Interrog s, e p compl ts, filed and rule for comm n to Perigneux, in France Sec Reg
" Aug't 7   Exit comm'n to Perigneux
" Oct 11   Comm'n ret'd and filed
" Nov 18   Translation of return to comm n filed
1840 May 18   On motion of complainants counsel, the Court appoint Oliver Hopkinson, Esq, examiner, to take dep ns of witnesses, e p compl ts
" May 23   Decree of revivor (See minutes and files)
" " 29   Replication filed
" Aug't 31   Dep'ns of D Greland, Jno Ducoing, Thos U Walter, A D Bache, B Jones, Jr, James Bayard, Esq, and Wm Strickland, taken before the examiner under rule of 18th May last, filed By

329

  writing filed, the complainants' solicitor directs the cause to be set down for argument at the October Session of the Court

1841 Feb'y 1 By order of Mr Broom, for complainants this cause is put down for argument at the special session in March

  April 27 Argument for filing the answer of the Mayor, Aldermen and Citizens of Philadelphia and for setting down the demurrer of the executors of Girard for arg't filed Answer to Mayor, &c filed Replication to answer of Mayor, &c filed

" April 28 Bill dismissed with costs

" May 3 Appeal entered and allowed

" June 30 Bond of Samuel P Griffiths Jr and James G Clark, as security on the appeal, filed Record returned

1844 August 30. Mandate of Supreme Court of the U S filed affirming the decree of this Court with costs and that the respondents recover for their costs against the complainants, the sum of $273 14 and have execution therefor

UNITED STATES OF AMERICA
 EASTERN DISTRICT OF PENNSYLVANIA sc'

I certify the foregoing to be a true and faithful transcript from the docket entries in the above case

Witness my hand and the seal of the Circuit Court of the
  United States for the Eastern District of Pennsylvania, in the third circuit, at Philadelphia
 [SEAL] this seventeenth day of March A D 1860 and in the eighty-fourth year of the Independence of the said United States

       BENJN PATTON,
         Clerk C C

Bill.

Pleas before the honorable the Judges of the Circuit Court of the United States for the Eastern District of Pennsylvania, on the third circuit, of October Sessions, 1836. No. 1. In equity.

It is thus contained.

Be it remembered, that heretofore, to wit, on the twenty-sixth day of August, in the year of our Lord one thousand eight hundred and thirty-six, Etienne Girard and Françoise Fenelon Vidal, aliens, and citizens and subjects of the monarchy of France, by their solicitors T. Kittera and James M. Broom, Esqs., filed of record in the said Court their bill of complaint against The Mayor, Aldermen and Citizens of Philadelphia, Timothy Paxson, Thomas P. Cope, Joseph Roberts, Wm. J. Duane, and John A. Barclay, executors of Stephen Girard, deceased; Mark Richards, trustee of Caroline Haslem, John Hemphill and Maria A., his wife, John Y. Clark and Henrietta, his wife, and John B. Haslem and Caroline, his wife, all citizens of the State of Pennsylvania, which bill of complaint is in the words and of the tenor following, to wit:

To the Honorable the Judges of the Circuit Court of the United States for the Eastern District of Pennsylvania sitting in Equity.

Humbly complaining showeth unto your honors, your orator and oratrix, Etienne Girard and Françoise Fenelon Vidal aliens to the United States of America, and citizens and subjects of the monarchy of France, that Stephen Girard late of the city of Philadelphia, in the State of Pennsylvania banker and merchant a native born subject of the former kingdom of France, but at the time of his death, and for more than fifty years preceding, a citizen of the United

States and of the State of Pennsylvania and there domiciled, departed this life at Philadelphia aforesaid, on the twenty sixth day of December, in the year one thousand eight hundred and thirty one, having first duly made and published his last will and testament bearing date on the sixteenth day of February, in the year one thousand eight hundred and thirty with a certain writing thereto annexed bearing date on the twenty fifth day of December in the same year, purporting to be a republication thereof also a certain other paper writing, purporting to be a codicil to his last will and testament and a second republication thereof, bearing date on the twentieth day of June, one thousand eight hundred and thirty one, of which last will, &c., the said testator therein and thereby named and appointed Timothy Paxson, Thomas P Cope, Joseph Roberts, William J Duane and John A Barclay, the executors, all of whom duly proved the said will, &c., obtained letters testamentary thereon, and took upon themselves the burthen of the execution thereof and all of whom were then and yet are citizens of the State of Pennsylvania aforesaid. And your orator and oratrix pray they may be made defendants to this bill that the said testator in and by the said will, after sundry legacies and devises of very inconsiderable value and amount compared with the bulk of his estate to his next of kin and heirs-at-law, and after sundry other legacies and devises to various other persons and institutions corporate and unincorporate devised and bequeathed to " The Mayor, Aldermen and Citizens of Philadelphia" (all of whom are citizens of the State of Pennsylvania aforesaid, and who your orator and oratrix pray may be made defendants to this bill), their successors and assigns, two undivided third parts of certain large and valuable estates in Louisiana, and in addition thereto all the residue and remainder of all his real and personal estate of every sort and kind wheresoever situate, in trust to and for the several uses, intents and purposes mentioned and declared of and concerning the same in the said will, and so far as regards his real estate in Pennsylvania in trust that no part thereof shall ever be sold or alienated by the said "Mayor, Aldermen and Citizens of Philadelphia," or their successors, but that the same be forever thereafter let from time to time, to good tenants at yearly or other rents and upon leases of not more than five years duration, and that the rents, issues and profits thereof be applied towards keeping that part of the real estate situate in the city and liberties of Philadelphia constantly in good repair, and towards improving the same whenever necessary by erecting new buildings, and that the net residue of such rents and profits (after paying the several annuities in the said will before provided for) be applied to the same uses and purposes as are in the said will declared of and concerning the residue of his personal estate and so far as regards his real estate in Kentucky, in trust to sell and dispose of the same whenever expedient to do so, and apply the proceeds to the same uses and purposes declared of the residue of his personal estate as aforesaid that among such uses and purposes the primary and preferred object is the erection and endowment of a college, for the construction, constitution and discipline whereof numerous and detailed rules and directions are prescribed or recommended in said will, the site of which college was originally fixed by the said will on a certain square of ground in the said city of Philadelphia, but by the last codicil to the said will was removed to a certain country seat called "Peel Hall," situate on the Ridge Road, in Penn Township, Philadelphia County, containing forty-five acres and some perches of land, which the testator, after the publication of his said original will, had purchased from one William Parker, the whole of which country seat with the lands thereto appertaining is expressly devoted by the said codicil to the purpose of constituting the site of the said college and its appendages, in lieu of the said square of ground in the city of Philadelphia, which is consequently thrown into the residuum of the estate devised in trust as aforesaid, that the ultimate and only intent and object of said college is declared by the said will to be the education of "such a number of poor male white orphan children as can be trained in one institution" and among other directions for the execution of the plan and management of said college, especially in regard to the particular objects and the selection of the objects of the charity which the said will imports an intent to institute, and for whose sole and exclusive benefit such charity purports to be instituted, the testator further directs in his said will that "as many poor white male orphans, between the ages of six and ten years, as the said income shall be adequate to maintain, shall be introduced into the college as soon as possible, and for the selection of such orphans, if there be more applications for admission than vacancies he further directs that priority of applications shall entitle the applicant to preference in admission, all other things concurring but if there be at any time more applications than vacancies, and the applying orphans shall have been born in different places, a preference shall be given first, to orphans born in the city of Philadelphia, secondly, to those born in any other part of Pennsylvania, thirdly, to those born in the city of New York, and lastly, to those born in the city of New Orleans, without there being found in the body of said will any more certain or definite description or limitation of the objects of said charity than as herein above recited and mentioned. That the said testator, in and by his said will, has appropriated, in the first instance, two millions of dollars out of the said residue of his personal estate for the erection and endowment of the said college, and has directed the method of disbursing and husbanding that fund for such objects, and has in like manner dedicated the whole of the said residuum of his real and personal estate (with certain exceptions hereinafter to be mentioned), so devised to the said Mayor, Aldermen and Citizens of Philadelphia, in trust as aforesaid, to the progressive enlargement of said college and its establishment, so that in effect there are no other limitations to the number of orphans to be ultimately admitted into the said college, nor to the extent or cost of the said establishment, but the number and extent of the collegiate buildings and their appendages that may from time to time be erected within the entire area of the said forty-five acres and some perches of land, and the sum total of the said residuum of the real and personal estate as devised in trust as aforesaid, after deducting two other appropriations of the same, forming the exceptions above referred to, to wit the sum of five hundred thousand dollars expressly devised out of the said residuum to the said Mayor, Aldermen and Citizens of Philadelphia, in trust as a capital to be invested, and the yearly income thereof appropriated to certain local improvements and public conveniences in the city of Philadelphia, enumerated under three several heads in the twenty-second clause of said will, and then by the twenty-third clause of said will, he makes a substantial devise to the Commonwealth of Pennsylvania of the sum of three hundred thousand dollars, for the purpose of internal improvement by canal navigation, to be paid into the State treasury by his executors, as soon as such laws shall have been enacted by the constituted authorities of said Commonwealth as shall be necessary and amply sufficient to carry into effect, or enable the constituted authorities of the city of Philadelphia to carry into effect, the several local improvements in that city specified in the said twenty-second clause of the will and recapitulated in the said twenty third clause, without any designation of the particular fund out of which the last mentioned sum shall be paid, though from the next succeeding clause of said will it may be plainly inferred that it is to be paid out of the said residuum of his personal estate, and as it regards the remainder and residue of his personal estate, he further devises by the twenty-fourth clause of said will, that the same be held in trust by the said Mayor, Aldermen and Citizens of Philadelphia, to be invested, both the principal and accruing income thereof, in good securities &c, that the whole, that is, the invested principal and income, shall form a permanent fund, the income whereof to be applied as follows first, to the further improvement and maintenance of said college as before directed in said will secondly, to provide by a competent police more effectually for the security of the persons and property of the inhabitants of said city and thirdly, to improve the city property and the general appearance of the city itself, and in effect diminish the burthen of taxation &c all which last two appropriations of the income of the last mentioned fund are made in the said will, and by the last mentioned clause thereof secondary and subordinate to the said college and its establishment which is therein expressly declared to be the primary object of the testator, and further the said testator, in and by his said will directed his banking establishment to be speedily settled and closed, and the balance accruing from that establishment to be paid over to his executors, and to go into the said residue of his estate, all which will more particularly and at large appear, reference being had to the said last will and testament and the said other testamentary papers, copies of all which, and of the probate of the same, your orator and oratrix now here produce and annex as exhibit or exhibits to this their bill marked A, and pray that the same may be taken and referred to as part and parcel of this bill And your orator and oratrix are well advised, and do verily believe, and so they charge, that upon due consideration of the contents of the said will, and the sum and substance and true effect of its various provisions, it appears that no part or parcel whatever of the said residuum of the real estate, so devised to the said Mayor Aldermen and Citizens of Philadelphia, in trust as aforesaid, is dedicated or in any manner devised or appropriated by the said will to any use, purpose or object whatever, but to the erection, establishment and endowment of a college for the education of orphan children as aforesaid and that no part or parcel of the said residuum of the personal estate, in like manner devised in trust as aforesaid (except the said sum of five hundred thousand dollars, devised to the said Mayor, Aldermen and Citizens for the purpose of accomplishing certain objects of local improvement in the said city, and the said sum of three hundred thousand dollars devised to the Commonwealth of Pennsylvania) is dedicated or in any manner devised or appropriated by said will to any other use purpose or object than the charity connected with the establishment of said college, except it be contingently in case that establishment do not or be not made, as it is contemplated to be, capable of absorbing the whole of said fund. And your orator and oratrix are credibly informed and believe, and so they charge, that the value of the whole real estate left by the said testator at his death, and deviseable by his said will and codicils, amounted to two millions of dollars or upwards. And that so much of the same, whereof the said will purports to devise the residuum to the said Mayor, Aldermen and Citizens, as lies within the State of Pennsylvania, alone of the value of one million four hundred thousand dollars, or upwards, and that the whole of the personal estate left by the testator at his death, and which has come or will come to the hands of his said executors, to be administered, is of the value of seven millions of dollars, or upwards, and the residuum thereof, devised or which the said will purports to devise to the said Mayor, Aldermen and Citizens, is of the value of   dollars or upwards. And your orator and oratrix are further well advised and believe, and so they expressly charge, that the supposed devise of the residue and remainder of the said real estate to the said Mayor, Alderman and Citizens of Philadelphia, in trust as aforesaid, is void, for want of capacity in such supposed devisees to take lands by devise—or if capable of taking generally by devise for their own use and benefit, for want of a capacity to take such lands as devisees in trust—and so, that the whole of the lands supposed to be devised to the last-named defendants in trust as aforesaid, have, for want of good and effectual devise of the same, descended to the heirs-at law of the said testator, Stephen Girard, according to the laws of Pennsylvania prescribing the course of descents, and to the treaty stipulations between France and the United States, according as such laws and treaty stipulations respectively affect the rights of such of the said heirs as are citizens of the said State, or of such as are aliens and French subjects or citizens: and further, that whatever be the capacity of the said last named defendants to take lands by devise in trust, the objects of the charity for which the said lands are so devised in trust, as aforesaid, are altogether indefinite, vague and uncertain, and so no trust is created by the said will that is capable of being executed or of being cognizable at law or equity, nor any trust estate devised that can vest at law or equity in any existing or possible cestui que trust: so that the only trust upon which the said last mentioned defendants can hold the said residue of the said real estate [if they be capable of holding the same upon any trust] is a trust for the alien and citizen heirs of the said testator, Stephen Girard, according to their respective rights of inheritance and succession; and further, that the whole residue of the personal estate supposed to be devised by the said will to the last mentioned defendants in trust for the objects of charity aforesaid, in like manner results to the next of kin of the said testator, Stephen Girard, both citizen and alien, according to their several distributive rights, by reason of the same defect of definite and certain objects or the charities for benefit of which the said devise was supposed to be made.

And your orator and oratrix further show that the said testator left at his death the following persons, and no others, entitled as his heirs at law and next of kin to the inheritance and succession of his real estate, and to a due distribution of his personal property, in so far as the same remain undisposed of or ineffectually disposed of, by his said will, to wit: Your orator, Etienne Girard, brother of the whole blood of the testator, Stephen Girard, and your oratrix, Françoise Fenelon Vidal, widow of Lewis Vidal, deceased, and niece of the said testator, Stephen Girard, being the same person named and described by the said testator in his said will as his niece Victorine Fenelon, daughter of his late sister, Sophia Girard Capayron, both of them being aliens and citizens and subjects of France, as aforesaid, and each of them entitled as alien and French heirs of the said testator, Stephen Girard, to one third part or to sell and dispose of one third part, of such undevised lands, and each of them in like manner entitled to one third part of such personal estate as aforesaid, in a due course of distribution,—and the following citizens, heirs and next of kin, to wit: Maria Antoinetta wife of John Hemphill, Henrietta, wife of John Y. Clark, and Caroline, wife of John B. Haslem, which said Maria Antoinetta, Henrietta and Caroline are daughters of John Girard, deceased, brother of the said Stephen Girard, of the whole blood, and they and their said husbands are all citizens of the said State of Pennsylvania, and your orator and oratrix pray that they and their said husbands be made defendants to this bill. That, by a deed of indenture dated the 24th day of April, in the year 1833, between the said John B. Haslem and Caroline his wife, of the one part, and Mark Richards, of the city of Philadelphia, of the other part [a copy of which is hereto annexed, marked B, as an exhibit, and which your orator and oratrix pray may be taken and referred to as part of this their bill], the said John and Caroline granted and conveyed to the said Mark Richards, his heirs and assigns, all and singular the real estate belonging to her, the said Caroline, or to which she is in any wise entitled, in trust to pay the rents, issues and income thereof to the said Caroline, during her life, and after her death to hold the said estate for the use of such persons or purposes as the said Caroline might, by an instrument in nature of a last will and testament, appoint, and, in default of any such appointment, then in trust for such persons to whom the said real estate would have gone according to the laws of Pennsylvania, had the said deed not been executed, and the said Caroline had died unmarried, seized in fee of the premises, and your orator and oratrix aver that the said Mark Richards is a citizen of the State of Pennsylvania, and pray that the said Mark Richards may be made a defendant to this bill.

And your orator and oratrix further show, that they have applied themselves in a friendly manner to the said defendants, requesting the said Mayor, Aldermen and Citizens of Philadelphia to let them into the enjoyment of their respective shares of the said real estate, by entering into the possession of the same, or selling and disposing of the same, and to account to your orator and oratrix for the rents issues and profits of the same since the death of the said Stephen Girard, also requesting the said executors to account with your orators for the said personal estate of the said testator Stephen Girard, which has come to their hands to be administered, &c., and to make due distribution of the surplus of the same among the next of kin of the said testator and especially to pay and distribute to your orator and oratrix their due shares and proportions of the same, and requesting the other defendants the said citizen heirs of the said testator, and their said husbands respectively and the said Mark Richards, trustee to join and co operate with your orator and oratrix in a due partition and division among all the said heirs, or their assigns, of the said real estate

But now so it is, may it please the Court, that the said defendants, nowise regarding the said reasonable requests of your orator and oratrix, but combining and confederating together and artfully and subtilly contriving how to aggrieve and defraud your orator and oratrix in the premises, altogether refuse to comply with such their reasonable requests and instances And forasmuch as your orator and oratrix are remediless in the premises in and by the strict rules of the Common Law, and can have relief in this Court only as a Court of Equity, where matters of this sort, and especially of fraud, trust, partition, distribution and account, are properly cognizable and relievable To the end therefore that the said defendants may, upon their several corporal oaths, full true and perfect answers make to all and singular the matters and things in this bill contained, as fully and particularly as if the same were herein repeated and particularly interrogated—especially, that they may answer and discover whether your orator, Etienne Guard, and your oratrix, Françoise Fenelon Vidal be not such heirs at-law and next of kin of the said testator, as they have above described themselves, and whether they and the defendants, above named and described as being the citizen heirs and next of kin of the said testator be not the sole and only persons entitled to claim, as heirs-at law and next of kin of the said testator, such partition of his real estate and such distribution of his personal estate as aforesaid, in case any such estate, real or personal, should be found not disposed of, or not effectually disposed of by his said will. That the said defendants, the said Mayor, Aldermen and Citizens of Philadelphia, may answer and discover what real estate the testator died seized of and where the same is situate and the value of the same more especially what real estate he died seized of within the limits of Pennsylvania, the aggregate value thereof, and yearly income and value thereof, what of such real estate they claim or have entered into the possession of, as claiming the same under the said supposed residuary devise in trust to them, the aggregate value thereof, where situate in the said State, and the yearly rents issues and profits of the same, what monies, effects, securities, assets, and personal or mixed property or estate they have received from said other defendants, the executors, as in fulfilment of such supposed residuary devise and what has become of such real and personal estate, and the interest and income thereof that they be compelled, by the order or decree of this Court to set apart and surrender to your orator and oratrix respectively their due shares and proportions of such real estate and to account to them for their due shares and proportions respectively of the rents, issues and profits of the same since the death of the said testator, and that the other defendants, the said citizen heirs of the said testator, be decreed to quit claim, and release to your orator and oratrix such parts and parcels of the said real estate as, upon a due partition thereof, shall be found the just shares and proportions of your orator and oratrix respectively; and that the other of the said defendants, the above-named executors of the said will answer and discover what monies, stocks, securities, effects, personal property, or assets of any kind or description, were left by the said testator at his death; what and how much of the same have come to their hands to be administered, or are like to fall as assets into their hands to be administered hereafter; what has become of the same; in whose hands the same now be; of what consisting, and how administered and disposed of since the death of said testator; and that the last mentioned defendants be decreed to account and pay to your orator and oratrix, respectively, their due shares and proportions of all such assets present and future, and of all the increment of the same since the death of the said testator; and that your orator and oratrix may have such further and other relief in the premises as to this Court may seem agreeable to equity and good conscience.

May it please the Court to grant them the proper and usual writ or writs of subpœna, &c. to be directed to the Mayor, Aldermen and Citizens of Philadelphia, to the said Timothy Paxson, Thomas P. Cope, Joseph Roberts, William J. Duane, and John J. Barclay, executors as aforesaid, to the said Mark Richards, trustee as aforesaid, and to the said John Hemphill and Maria A. his wife, John Y. Clark and Henrietta, his wife, and John B. Haslem and Caroline, his wife,—commanding them severally and respectively to be and appear at a certain day, and under a certain pain, therein to be specified, personally to be and appear before your honours in this honourable Court, and then and there to answer all and singular the premises aforesaid, and to stand to perform and abide such order, direction and decree therein as to your honours shall seem meet. And your orator and oratrix shall ever pray, &c., &c.

JAMES M. BROOM,
Solicitor for Complainant, Etienne Girard.
TH. KITTERA,
Solicitor for Complainants.

Afterwards to wit, on the 26th day of August, A D 1836, writ of subpœna issued

Afterwards, to wit, on the 11th day of October, A. D 1836, the said writ of subpœna is returned "served on all the defendants but John Y Clark and Henrietta, his wife, and John B Haslem and Caroline, his wife, as to whom returned, 'nil habent'"

The answer of the Mayor, Aldermen and Citizens of Philadelphia.

Afterwards, to wit, on the 20th day of January, in the year of our Lord, 1837, the several answer of the Mayor, Aldermen and Citizens of Philadelphia is presented by their solicitors, John Sergeant and Edw Olmsted, Esquires, which being read and filed is in the words following, to wit

Answer.

To the Honorable the Judges of the Circuit Court of the United States, in and for the District of Pennsylvania

The several answer of the Mayor, Aldermen and Citizens of Philadelphia, to the bill of complaint of Etienne Girard and Françoise Fenelon Vidal, aliens

These respondents saving and reserving to themselves now and at all times hereafter, all and all manner of exception to the various errors, imperfections and uncertainties, in the said bill of complaint contained, for answer thereto or unto so much thereof, as they are advised it is material for them to answer, they answer and say, that it is true as therein stated that the late Stephen Girard, esquire, died at his domicil, in the city of Philadelphia, on the 26th day of December, A D 1831, that during his lifetime he duly made a last will and testament, bearing date the 16th February, A D 1830, and a paper purporting to be a republication thereof, bearing date the 25th December, A D 1830, and also a codicil thereto bearing date the 20th June, A D

1831, and that he appointed the executors named in the said bill of complaint, who proved his said will, and took upon themselves the execution thereof, that your respondents do not deem it necessary to answer whether or not the contents of the said will are truly stated and set forth in the said bill of complaint, referring to a copy of the said will, and so far and no further, as the same may be cognizable by this Honorable Court, submitting it to the Court for the exposition and construction thereof, and of all and every part thereof. And your respondents admit that the said Stephen Girard, in and by his will aforesaid, bequeathed a large personal estate and also that he devised a considerable real estate within the State of Pennsylvania, being the only part of his real estate subject to the laws of that State or to the jurisdiction of this Court, that the amount and nature of the personal estate are not exactly known to your respondents but so far as can now be known will appear upon the inventory and accounts of the executors filed and remaining in the said Register's office or in the Orphans Court of the City and County of Philadelphia where the said accounts are undergoing an investigation according to law, as to the charges and discharges thereof, and where the exclusive jurisdiction of all matters touching the said accounts and the distribution of the balance which shall hereafter appear upon them, as well as the propriety of all payments heretofore made, do of right belong, that your respondents have entered upon and are now in the possession of all the real estate in the State of Pennsylvania devised by the said will, and are holding the same for the purposes and uses and in the manner directed by the testator in his said will, so that the same may be fully carried into effect according to his intention as therein plainly expressed and in conformity with an Act of Assembly of the Commonwealth of Pennsylvania, bearing date the 24th day of March, A D 1832 entitled "An Act to enable the Mayor, Aldermen and Citizens of Philadelphia to carry into effect certain improvements and execute certain trusts" and a supplement thereto, passed the 4th day of April, A. D 1832, which several Acts of Assembly your respondents pray may be taken as part of this their answer, as if the same were herein at large set forth

And your respondents further answering say that they are not able to state the value of the said real estate, but, if so required by this Honourable Court, will cause a list of the same to be furnished and filed, submitting, however, that the expense of making the same out should be provided for by the complainants a part of the said real estate has been improved since the death of the testator by the expenditure thereon of a very large sum of money, in completion of plans, arrangements and contracts of the testator, the particulars of which they reserve to themselves a right to exhibit, if it should become necessary

And your respondents further answering say, that they have no knowledge whether the heirs and next of kin of the testator were or were not as set forth in the said bill, further than as the same may be supposed to appear by his will, or by several suits, which will be presently referred to, though they have no reason to believe to the contrary But these respondents answer and specially insist to be available to them, in such manner as may be according to the practice in Equity and the rules of this Honourable Court, that each and every of the persons named in the said bill as heirs at-law and next of kin of the testator, including all the complainants, were objects of the bounty of the testator, to whom legacies were given by his said will, as by reference to the said will will appear, that the complainants, and the said several other persons named as heirs and next of kin in the said bill of complaint, before the said bill of complaint was filed, claimed their several legacies from the executors, under the said will and according to the said will, and severally received the said legacies from the executors, under and according to the said will, and not otherwise

And these respondents further answering say, and specially insist, to be available as aforementioned, that certain real estate in the State of Pennsylvania having been purchased by the testator after the date of his said will, and after the date of the last codicil thereto, the said complainants, together with the other heirs and next of kin named in the said bill of complaint, after the death of the testator and after the probate of the said will and codicils, and also after your respondents had entered upon the real estate devised to them and were executing the trusts thereof made a claim specifically to the said after purchased real estate upon the ground that being after-purchased, it did not pass by the said will, and upon no other ground whatever Your respondents not being willing to take upon themselves to decide what was the law of the case in relation to estates held by them in trust, did not yield to the claim There upon ejectments were brought against your respondents, in the Supreme Court of Pennsylvania by the complainants and the said other persons named, and judgments were by the said Court rendered against your respondents for the said after-purchased lands, that afterwards your respondents, being informed that doubts were expressed whether the said cases had been as fully presented as they ought to have been for the consideration of the Court determined to have them again submitted, and for that purpose brought one or more ejectments, in which the subject was again deliberately considered by the said Court and judgments rendered against your respondents And your respondents aver, that in making said claims, no pretension was set up by the complainants or the other heirs or next of kin of a right or claim to any part of the real estate devised to your respondents by the said will or codicils, nor that the devises therein were illegal, invalid or void, but only to the lands purchased after the date of the said will and codicils and your respondents understood and believe that as well the said complainants and other heirs and next of kin in making their claim, as the said Court in rendering its judgment admitted the right of your respondents to the lands devised to them Your respondents never heard anything to the contrary, until the filing of the present bill of complaint in this Honourable Court. And your respondents further say, and specially insist to be available in such manner as may be according to the practice in Equity and the rules of this Honourable Court that before the filing of the bill of complaint of the complainants and before any proceedings in this Honourable Court the executors named in the will of the said Stephen Girard had duly and according to the course of the law in Pennsylvania filed and settled their account of the administration of the personal estate of the testator, in the office of the Register for the Probate of Wills and granting of Letters of Administration for the City and County of Philadelphia, that the said settlement had been duly reported and presented for confirmation to the Orphans' Court for the County of Philadelphia, and by the said Court, in due course of law, referred to auditors appointed by the said Court to examine and report thereon, before which said auditors, for the purpose aforesaid, the same was pending when the complainants filed their bill of complaint and still is pending. By reason whereof the said Orphans' Court had and has according to the laws of Pennsylvania, the sole and exclusive jurisdiction of the personal estate of the testator, as well for the settlement of the accounts of the executors as for the distribution of the said personal estate, and the determination to whom the same or any part thereof belongs, and to give relief to the complainants, if they be entitled to relief, in relation to the said personal estate, and this Honourable Court has no jurisdiction of the same nor of any part thereof.

And your respondents further say and especially insist to be available according to the practice in Equity and the rules of this Honourable Court, that the complainants have no equity to be heard in this Honourable Court as to the real estate in Pennsylvania, because their title to the same, if any they have, is a legal title, and their remedy is at law and not in equity, inasmuch as there is nothing in their case, even upon their own showing, which makes it necessary that they should have relief in equity, or shows that they may not have full, plain and adequate relief at law.

And your respondents further say, and specially insist to be available according to the practice in Equity and the rules of this Honourable Court, that the complainants are not entitled to relief upon their own showing in their bill of complaint, inasmuch as in addition to the several matters hereinbefore contained and set forth and independently thereof, it plainly and manifestly appears in the said bill of complaint, that according to the laws of Pennsylvania, which govern as to the whole personal estate of the testator and govern as to all the real estate he died seized of in the State of Pennsylvania the said Stephen Girard made a good and valid disposition by will of all his personal estate and of all his real estate (excepting the said after-purchased lands already recovered at law by the complainants and others as hereinbefore stated), that the same personal and real estate sufficiently passed by his said will, and, according to the laws aforesaid, have become vested in your respondents as the legal owners thereof, and that the said complainants have no right or title to the said personal estate or the said devised real estate, nor to any part of the same, nor any interest in the said personal estate and devised real estate or any part thereof, nor any power or right of control over or interference with the same, and therefore that they have no equity whatever to ask the aid of this Honourable Court or to entitle them to be heard therein.—Wherefore your respondents pray that they may be hence dismissed with their reasonable costs in this behalf expended, and they will pray, &c.

[L S]   JOHN SWIFT, *Mayor*
JOHN SERGEANT,
EDW OLMSTED,
For Respondents

The Demurrer, Plea and Answer of the Executors of Stephen Girard.

Afterwards, to wit, on the thirty-first day of January, in the year of our Lord one thousand eight hundred and thirty-seven, the demurrer plea, and answer of Timothy Paxson, Thos P Cope, Joseph Roberts, William J Duane, and John A Barclay, executors of Stephen Girard, deceased, is presented by their solicitor, Charles Chauncey, Esq, which answer, being read and filed, is in the words and of the tenor following, to wit

In the Circuit Court of the United States for the District of Pennsylvania, in the Third Circuit—in Equity

The Demurrer, Plea and Answer of Timothy Paxson, Thomas P Cope, Joseph Roberts, William J Duane, and John A Barclay, executors of Stephen Girard, deceased, to the bill of complaint of Etienne Girard and Françoise Fenelon Vidal, complainants

These defendants, by protestation, not confessing or acknowledging all or any of the matters and things in the said bill of complaint to be true in such sort and manner as the same are therein expressed and contained, as to so much of the said bill as seeks to set aside or impeach, or have any relief against the will of Stephen Girard, in the bill named and the codicils thereto as to the personal estate of the said Stephen Girard, or that seeks any discovery or account from these defendants of their administration thereof, or any decree against them as to the same, these defendants do demur thereto and for cause of demurrer show—that it appears by the Complainants' own showing, that the said will and codicils were duly proved by these defendants, as executors therein and thereby appointed and letters testamentary obtained thereon, and that these defendants took upon themselves the burden of the execution thereof, that these proceedings were had before the Register of Wills for the city and county of Philadelphia, to whom these defendants are advised, that the probate of wills relating to estates, and particularly relating to personal estates properly belongs, and that the same ought not to be called into question in this Honourable Court, and for further cause of demurrer these defendants show that there is not as they are advised any matter or thing set forth in and by the said bill as a foundation of equity for this court to interpose in relation to the said will and the disposition therein made of the personal estate of the testator but what is properly cognizable at law and that the said complainants may have the benefit of, by proceeding at law if the same is true for which reason and for divers other causes, these defendants do demur to so much of the said bill as aforesaid and humbly pray the judgment of this Honorable Court, whether they shall make any further or other answer thereto, and as to so much of the said bill as seeks to have a distribution of the personal estate or effects of the said Stephen Girard, and payment to them, the complainants and certain other persons named as defendants in said bill, as being next of kin of the said Stephen Girard, as in case of intestacy, these defendants do plead thereunto and for plea these defendants say that the said Stephen Girard did in his lifetime, on or about the sixteenth day of February, A. D. 1830, as these defendants believe, duly make and publish his last will and testament, in writing, and also did, on the twenty fifth day of December, 1830, and on the twentieth day of June 1831, make and publish codicils to his said will and by said will and codicils after having given several legacies therein particularly mentioned gave and bequeathed all the residue and remainder of his estate to the Mayor, Aldermen and Citizens of Philadelphia, in trust to and for the several uses, intents and purposes mentioned and declared of and concerning the same in the said will as appears by the copy of said will and codicils annexed to the complainants' bill of complaint and therein and thereby appointed these defendants executors thereof that these defendants as executors duly proved the said will and codicils before said "Register of Wills for the City and County of Philadelphia," obtained letters testamentary thereon, and took upon themselves the burden of the execution thereof, that these defendants as executors as aforesaid have proceeded in the execution of said will and in the administration of the estate of the said testator, according to the said will and codicils, without any notice whatever of any claim by them other than that of legatees from the said complainants, and have made payments of legacies and of large sums of money to the said residuary legatees, and have filed their accounts of their said administration in the office of the Register of Wills for the City and County of Philadelphia, from where they have in due course of legal proceedings passed to the Orphans' Court in the City and County of Philadelphia, to whom it properly belongs to have cognizance of the same. That the said court having said accounts under their jurisdiction and notice, have referred the same to auditors appointed by said court to audit, adjust and settle the same and that the said accounts are at this time depending before the said auditors to be audited, adjusted and settled, and reported upon to the said Orphans' Court, for their adjudication thereon, all which said matters and things these defendants do aver, and are ready to prove as this honorable court shall direct, and do plead the same in bar to so much of said bill as for that purpose is hereinbefore mentioned, and humbly crave the judgment of this Honourable Court, whether they shall make any further or other answer thereto

And as to so much of the said bill as these defendants have not before demurred, or pleaded to, these defendants in no sort waiving the benefit of their demurrer or plea, or either of them but wholly relying and insisting thereon, these defendants for answer to the residue of the complainants' said bill, or unto so much thereof as these defendants are advised is material, or necessary for them to make answer unto, they, these defendants answer and say, that they admit to be true that Stephen Girard departed this life at Philadelphia, on the twenty-sixth day of December in the year one thousand eight hundred and thirty one having first made and published his last will and testament, together with the codicils to said will and republications mentioned in the complainants' said bill of complaint, copies of which and of the probate of the same are annexed thereto, as exhibit marked A, and that said copies are as these defendants believe true copies of the originals thereof. For the matter contained in the said will and codicils these defendants respectfully refer to the said instruments themselves, and for the construction thereof they submit themselves to this Honourable Court. The defendants admit that they were as alleged in the complainants' said bill appointed executors, that they duly proved the said will and codicils and obtained letters testamentary thereon and took upon themselves the burden of the execution thereof.

These defendants further answering say that they have heard and believe it to be true, that the complainants and the defendants who are described as being the citizen heirs of Stephen Girard are of kindred to the said Stephen Girard, as alleged in said complainants' bill of complaint.

And further answering the defendants say that the inventories and accounts hereto annexed and marked A B C D E & F contain a full and true statement of the monies, stocks, securities, effects, personal property and assets of any kind or description which were left by the testator Stephen Girard, at the time of his death, so far as they have come to the knowledge of these defendants, and also of what has come to their hands to be administered (or like to fall as assets into their hands to be administered hereafter) and also of what has become of the same, of what consisting and how administered or disposed of since the death of the said testator to the time of filing the last of said accounts, and further that the said accounts hereto annexed are true copies of the accounts settled by these defendants as Executors in the office of the Register of Wills for the City and County of Philadelphia, and now before auditors appointed by the Orphans' Court for the City and County of Philadelphia to audit and settle the same, and they further say, that the several sums of money charged in their accounts as paid to the Mayor, Aldermen and Citizens of Philadelphia or their treasurer, as residuary legatees have been paid upon receiving a refunding bond executed according to law, and without any notice or knowledge of the claim thereto set up in the complainants' said bill of complaint, and as these defendants were advised and believed in conformity with the disposition and direction made of and concerning the same in and by the said will of Stephen Girard deceased—without that that there is any other matter or thing in the complainants' said bill of complaint contained material or effectual for these defendants to make answer unto, and not hereinbefore pleaded or answered, confessed or avoided, traversed or denied is true, all which matters and things these defendants are ready to aver, justify, maintain, and prove, as this Honourable Court shall award and direct and humbly pray, to be hence dismissed with their reasonable costs and charges in this behalf sustained

CHARLES CHAUNCEY,
Solicitor

Timothy Paxson, Thomas P Cope—two of the respondents in the foregoing answer named, being duly affirmed, and Joseph Roberts, William J Duane, and John A Barclay, three of the respondents being duly sworn, according to law, do each of them on his several and respective oath or affirmation say, that the several matters and things contained in said answer, so far as they relate to his own knowledge or belief are true, and so far as they relate to the knowledge of others he believes them to be true

TIMOTHY PAXSON,
THOMAS P COPE,
JOSEPH ROBERTS,
W J DUANE,
JOHN A BARCLAY

Affirmed and subscribed by Timothy Paxson and Thomas P Cope, and sworn to and subscribed by Joseph Roberts, William J Duane and John A Barclay, this twenty sixth day of January, A D 1837, before me

    WILLIAM MILNOR,
      Alderman

Motion for Amended Bill.

Afterwards, to wit on the 8th day of May, A D 1837, on motion of Th Kittera, Esquire for complainants, leave is granted to file an amended will

Amended Bill

Thereupon afterwards, to wit, on the 8th day of March A D 1839, the complainants by their solicitors Th Kittera and James M Broom, Esquires, file their amended bill in the words following, to wit

To the Honourable the Judges of the Circuit Court of the United States, in and for the Third Circuit, in the Eastern District of Pennsylvania, sitting in Equity

The petition of Etienne Girard and Françoise Fenelon Vidal, aliens to the United States and citizens and subjects of the Monarchy of France, humbly complaining showeth to this Honourable Court, that your orator and oratrix, on the twenty sixth day of August, Anno Domini one thousand eight hundred and thirty six, exhibited their original bill of complaint, in this Court, against the Mayor Aldermen and Citizens of Philadelphia, as trustees, and against Timothy Paxson, Thomas P Cope, Joseph Roberts, William J Duane and John A Barclay, executors of the last will and testament of Stephen Girard, late of the city of Philadelphia, deceased, and also against John Hemphill and Maria Antoinette, his wife, John Y Clark and Henrietta, his wife, Caroline E G Haslem, wife of John Haslem, and Mark Richards, trustee of the said Caroline E G Haslem, all of which the said defendants are citizens of the United States and of the State of Pennsylvania, as by a reference to the said original bill will more fully appear

And your complainants further show, that the said Mayor, Aldermen and Citizens of Philadelphia, and the said executors, after being served with process of subpœna, appeared and put in evasive answers to said bill. That none of the other defendants in the original bill have answered the same And your complainants further show, that they afterwards, to wit, on the eighth day of May, in the year one thousand eight hundred and thirty seven, obtained leave from this Honourable Court to file an amended bill, and no other or further proceedings have since been had in the suit

Your orator and oratrix further show, that amongst other things in their original bill, they have alleged and charged that the testator, Stephen Girard, by a supposed devise in his last will and testament, has in the first place appropriated two millions of dollars to the Mayor, Aldermen and Citizens of Philadelphia, in trust, for the erection and endowment of a college for the maintenance and education of a class of orphans, attempted to be described by the said testator in his will

And your orator and oratrix further state, that in their original bill they set out that the said testator, in and by his will, after appropriating the two millions of dollars as aforesaid, by another supposed devise dedicated the whole of the residuum of his real and personal estate, with certain exceptions mentioned in the said original bill, to the Mayor, Aldermen and Citizens of Philadelphia in trust, for the progressive enlargement of said college, and that there are no other limitations to the number of orphans to be ultimately admitted into the said college nor to the cost nor extent of the establishment, but the number and extent of the collegiate buildings and their appendages that may from time to time be erected within the entire area of forty-five acres and some perches of land, being a country seat called Peel Hall, so that in effect there is no devise over of any part of the said residuum of the real and personal estate of the testator to any other use, purpose or object, after deducting the appropriations that are excepted in the original bill, than the charity connected with the establishment of said college except it be contingently, in case the said college establishment be not made, as it is contemplated to be capable of absorbing the whole of the said residuum of the real and personal estate intended to be devised in trust as aforesaid, as by a reference to the said original bill and exhibits which your complainants pray may be taken as part of this bill will more fully appear.

Your complainants suggest and insist to be available that it will be decided from a true exposition and construction of said will, which is submitted to the Court, that it was the intention of the testator to dedicate the whole of the rents, issues and profits of his real estate in the city and county of Philadelphia in trust, exclusively to the uses and purposes of the charity connected with said college and not that the said real estate, or the rents, issues and profits thereof, are to be contingently applied to any other use or purpose, unless it be to the payment of a rateable proportion of certain annuities charged on the real estate of the testator in the State of Pennsylvania by the eighteenth clause in his will.

And your orator and oratrix further aver and expressly charge, that the charity connected with the college if the establishment is erected and managed according to the directions of the testator, and the necessary buildings constructed so as to fill up and improve the whole area of forty five acres and some perches of land, will require and consume the whole of the residuum of his real and personal estate attempted to be devised as aforesaid for the purposes of erecting, progressively enlarging and perpetually maintaining said collegiate establishment for the support and education of as great a number of orphans as the testator directs to be admitted therein, so that there will be no surplus of said residuum of his real and personal estate supposed to be devised in trust as aforesaid to be appropriated to any other objects or purposes designated by the testator in his will. And your orator and oratrix aver, that there is no devise over for any other purpose, upon any contingency of the said two millions of dollars supposed to be devised to the Mayor, Aldermen and Citizens of Philadelphia, in trust, for the erection and endowment of said college, and that no part of said two millions of dollars, according to the will of the testator, can be applied in any event to any other use, purpose or object, except to the charitable objects depending upon the erection, endowment and perpetual support of said college. And your orator and oratrix aver and insist to be available, that the said supposed devise of two millions of dollars to the Mayor, Aldermen and Citizens of Philadelphia, in trust, for the erection and endowment of said college, for the benefits of uncertain objects of charity, supposed to be intended by the testator, is void.

And your complainants maintain that the Mayor, Aldermen and Citizens of Philadelphia were, at the death of the testator, incapable of executing any such trust, or of taking and holding a legal estate for the benefit of others, and that, whatever may be the capacity of said Mayor, Aldermen and Citizens of Philadelphia to hold property for the use of others, or to execute a trust, the objects for whose benefit the said devise in trust is supposed to have been made are indefinite, vague and uncertain, as will appear from an examination of said will, so that no trust is created that is capable of being executed, or is cognizable either at law or in equity, and no estate passed by said supposed devise that can vest in any existing or ascertainable cestui que trusts; that if the objects or persons for whose benefit the said devise is supposed to have been made were susceptible of ascertainment, yet such beneficiaries, when ascertained, would be wholly incapable of transmitting their equitable title in perpetual succession, so that the said two millions of dollars, for want of a good and effectual devise, has descended, by operation of the law governing descents in the State of Pennsylvania, and the treaty stipulations between France and the United States to the heirs at law of Stephen Girard the testator according as such laws and treaty stipulations affect the rights of such of the heirs as are aliens and such as are citizens of the United States.

Your orator and oratrix expressly charge, in their original bill that the said supposed devise to the Mayor, Aldermen and Citizens of Philadelphia, in trust, of the whole of the residuum of the real and personal estate of the testator, for the erection, progressive enlargement and perpetual support of said college, is void and that your complainants were heirs at law of said testator, and each entitled to one third part of the estate of the testator, undisposed of or ineffectually disposed of by his last will, according to the law governing descents in the State of Pennsylvania and the treaty stipulations between France and the United States, and that the testator, at the time of his death, left certain other heirs namely, Maria Antoinetta wife of John Hemphill, Henrietta wife of John Y Clark and Caroline, wife of John Haslem, which said Maria, Henrietta and Caroline are neices of the said testator and daughters of John Girard, late of Philadelphia, deceased, and they and their husbands, except the husband of said Caroline, are all made defendants to said bill, together with Mark Richards, who is the trustee of said Caroline, all of which said defendants are citizens of the State of Pennsylvania. And your orator and oratrix further allege that the last named heirs are the only persons entitled besides your complainants to any part of the real or personal estate of which the said testator died seized or possessed, and which remained undisposed of or ineffectually devised by his will.

And your complainants, as they are informed, verily believe and expressly charge, that notwithstanding the invalidity of said supposed devise or devises in trust, the said Mayor, Alderman and Citizens of Philadelphia, soon after the death of the testator, entered upon and possessed themselves of the two millions of dollars, supposed to be devised to them in trust for the erection and support of said college, and also of the whole of the residuum of the real and personal estate of the testator, supposed to be devised to them for the same purposes, and have ever since continued to hold and manage the same according to the terms of said supposed trust, or under the pretext of applying the said two millions of dollars, and the said residuum of the real and personal estate of the testator, to the supposed objects and purposes of said trust, that they have altogether refused to account with your complainants, or to pay over to them any part of their distributive shares, either of the said two millions of dollars or of the residuum of the real and personal estate, to which they are entitled, but intending, artfully and fraudulently to evade and baffle the reasonable and just claims of your complainants, and the relief prayed for in their original bill, they have neglected to answer fully either as to the amount or value of the real or personal estate they have entered upon or received from the estate of the testator, under colour of said trust, and your complainants pray that in order to obtain the relief and equity prayed for, the said Mayor, Aldermen and Citizens of Philadelphia, be compelled to answer and discover,

1.—Whether they have not received the two millions of dollars, supposed to be appropriated in the first instance by the testator, to the erection and endowment of said college?

2.—How much of said two millions of dollars they have already expended in erecting said college?

3.—How much of said residuum of real and personal estate, supposed to be devised to them in trust, they have already received, and how much in value and amount they expect to receive in a due course of administration?

4.—In what counties and townships the real estate of the testator in Pennsylvania is situate, into how many distinct tracts of land the same is divided, with the patented name of each tract, and the number of acres it contained, and the value of each tract according to the estimate they have fixed upon it?

5.—In what county or counties the real estate left by the testator in Kentucky is situate, the number of acres in the whole, and whether there are more tracts than one, and the probable or estimated value of such real estate, whether they did not enter into possession of said real estate in Kentucky, whether they have sold the same or part thereof, if not all, how much they have sold and for what price, how much money they have received from such sale or sales, and how much is still due from such sales as they have made

6.—What is the number of acres, where situate, and the estimated value of the real estate of the testator, in the State of Louisiana, devised to them in trust, and whether they have not taken possession of the same under colour of supposed trust?

7.—What amount of money they have expended in improving and building upon the square of ground in the City of Philadelphia, between High and Chestnut Streets, and Eleventh and Twelfth Streets, and what is the annual amount of the rents, issues and profits thereof?

8.—Whether the expenses incidental to the said college establishment, in erecting buildings on the whole area of forty-five acres and some perches of land, at Peel Hall, and on the square of ground in the City of Philadelphia, according to the directions of the testator, and all the other expenses necessary for the perpetual maintainance of said college, and the objects of charity connected therewith, will not consume the whole of the residuum of the real and personal estate of the testator, and also the two millions of dollars supposed to be devised in trust for the uses of the college, without leaving any surplus to be applied to the contingent uses designated in the will of the donor?

9.—What amount of money or other property they have received from the Executors since the death of the testator, under said supposed trust, and the balance now remaining in their hands, or how much of the same is loaned out, and to whom or where deposited for safe keeping?

And your orator and oratrix further pray that the said Timothy Paxson, Thomas P. Cope, Joseph Roberts, William J. Duane, and John A. Barclay, upon their several oaths or affirmations, be compelled to answer and discover.

1.—What amount of money they have received as executors from the trustees appointed by the testator during his lifetime, to wind up and settle his banking concern

2.—What amount of money or other property they have paid over to the Mayor, Aldermen and Citizens of Philadelphia, to go into the residuum of the real and personal estate supposed to be devised to them in trust

3.—What amount of money remains in their hands to be paid over to said Mayor, Aldermen and Citizens of Philadelphia, according to the directions of the testator?

4.—Whether the Mayor, Aldermen and Citizens of Philadelphia have not possessed themselves of all or part of the residuum of the real and personal estate, and what part in Pennsylvania, Louisiana, and Kentucky, supposed to be devised to them in trust by said testator, and are not now engaged in managing the same for the purposes of said trust?

5.—Whether your orator and oratrix are not related to the testator in the manner and in the degrees of consanguinity stated in this bill, to the best of their knowledge and belief

And your complainants pray that the said Mayor, Aldermen and Citizens of Philadelphia, the said Timothy Paxson, Thomas P. Cope, Joseph Roberts, William J. Duane and John A. Barclay, Mark Richards, and the other defendants to this bill, answer

1.—Whether the matters and things charged in this bill

are not true to the best of their knowledge and belief, and also the matters and things charged in the original bill.

2.—Whether your orator is not a brother to the said testator, Stephen Girard?

3.—Whether your oratrix is not a niece of the said testator, Stephen Girard?

4.—Whether the said Maria Antoinetta, Henrietta and Caroline are not nieces to the said testator, Stephen Girard?

4.—Whether your orator is not the same person described by the testator in the ninth and tenth clauses of his will as his brother Etienne Girard, residing in France?

5.—Whether your oratrix is not the same person described by the testator in the ninth and eleventh clauses of his will as his niece Victorine Fenelon, residing in France, and daughter of his late sister, Sophia Girard Capayron, and whether the said Sophia is not deceased?

6.—Whether the said Maria Antoinetta, wife of John Hemphill, of Philadelphia, who, with her husband, is one of the defendants in this bill, is not the same person described by the testator in the twelfth clause of his said will as his niece Antoinetta, married to Mr Hemphill?

7.—Whether the said Henrietta, who, with her husband, Dr John Y Clark, is one of the defendants to this bill, is not the same person described by the testator in the fourteenth clause of his will as his niece Henrietta, married to Dr Clark?

8.—Whether the said Caroline, wife of John B Haslem, who, with her trustee, is made one of the defendants to this bill, is not the same person described by the testator in the thirteenth clause of his will as his niece Caroline, married to Mr Haslem?

9.—Whether the said orator, Etienne Girard, is not the only brother of the testator now living?

10.—Whether the said oratrix, Françoise Fenelon Vidal, is not the only surviving child of said Sophia, the sister of the testator?

11.—Whether the said Maria Antoinetta, Henrietta and

Caroline are not the only surviving daughters or children of John Girard, late of Philadelphia, deceased, brother to the testator?

12.—Whether your orator and oratrix, and the said Antoinetta, Henrietta and Caroline, were not the next of kin to the testator, Stephen Girard, at the time of his death?

13.—Whether the testator, Stephen Girard, left any child or children, or brother or sister, or child or children of deceased brothers or sisters, other than those named in this bill?

And your orator and oratrix pray that the said Mayor, Aldermen and Citizens of Philadelphia be compelled, by order or decree of this Court, to surrender to your complainants their respective shares and proportions of said two millions of dollars, and also their due proportions and shares of the residuum of the real and personal estate of the testator, that may or has come into their possession under colour of said void trust, as well as their proportional shares of the real estate of the testator in the city and county of Philadelphia, and that the said executors be ordered and decreed to account and pay to your orator and oratrix, respectively their due shares and proportions of all such assets, present and future, as prayed in their original bill, and that your orator and oratrix have such other and further relief in the premises as to this Court may seem agreeable to equity and good conscience.

And that the United States Writ of Subpœna may issue, directed to the Mayor, Aldermen and Citizens of Philadelphia, as trustees, and to Timothy Paxson, Thomas P. Cope, Joseph Roberts, William J. Duane, and John A. Barclay, executors of the last will and testament of Stephen Girard, late of the city of Philadelphia, deceased, and also to John Hemphill and Maria Antoinetta his wife John Y. Clark and Henrietta, his wife, Caroline E. G. Haslem, wife of John Haslem, and Mark Richards, trustee of the said Caroline, all of whom are citizens of the State of Pennsylvania, commanding them, at a certain day and under a certain penalty therein to be named, to be and appear before this Honourable Court, then and there to answer the premises and to stand and abide such order and decree therein as this Honourable Court shall deem agreeable to equity and good conscience, and your orator and oratrix shall ever pray

TH KITTERA,
Solicitor for Complainants
JAMES M BROOM,
Solicitor for E Girard

Afterwards, to wit, on the eighth day of March, A D 1838, on the amended bill filed, the writ of subpœna issued.

Afterwards, to wit, on the 11th day of April, A D 1838, the said writ of subpœna is returned, " Served on the Mayor, Aldermen and Citizens of Philadelphia, on T Paxson, T P Cope, J Roberts, W J Duane, J A Barclay, J Hemphill and wife, and M. Richards, and nil habent as to J Y Clark and wife, and Caroline E G Haslem "

Answer of Executors of Stephen Girard to Amended Bill.

Afterwards, to wit, on the 5th day of September, A D 1838, the answer of Timothy Paxson, Thomas P Cope, Joseph Roberts, William J Duane, and John A Barclay executors of Stephen Girard, deceased, to amended bill of complainants, is presented, which, being read and filed, is in the words following, to wit

In the Circuit Court of the United States, in and for the District of Pennsylvania in the Third Circuit

The answer of Timothy Paxson, Thomas P Cope, Joseph Roberts, William J Duane, and John A Barclay, executors of Stephen Girard, deceased, to the amended bill of complaint of Etienne Girard and Françoise Fenelon Vidal, complainants

These defendants, saving and reserving to themselves all and all manner of benefit and advantage of exception to the errors, insufficiencies, uncertainties and other imperfections and defects in the said complainants' said amended bill of complaint contained, for answer thereunto, or unto so much thereof as they are advised is material or necessary for them to make answer unto, they, these defendants, answer and say, that to all and singular the matters and things alleged and charged in the complainants' said amended bill of complaint, and to all the interrogatories therein propounded to these defendants, so far as they know, have heard or believed, they, these defendants, have already answered and without evasion, in their answer to the complainants' bill of complaint, and the exhibits annexed to their said answer and prayed to be taken as part thereof, save and except that the further doings of the said executors are herewith presented, in the two accounts of their administration, which have been filled by them since their former answer, true copies of which are hereto annexed, marked A and B, which they pray may be taken as part of this their answer, without that, that any other matter or thing in the said complainants' said amended bill of complaint contained, material or effectual for these defendants to make answer unto, and not already before pleaded and answered, confessed or avoided, traversed or denied, is here, all which matters and things these defendants are ready to aver, maintain, &c., and prove, as this Honourable Court shall award and direct, and humbly pray to be hence dismissed with their reasonable costs and charges in this behalf sustained.

TIMOTHY PAXSON,
THOMAS P. COPE,
JOSEPH ROBERTS,
W. J. DUANE,
JOHN A. BARCLAY.

Timothy Paxson and Thomas P. Cope, being duly affirmed, and Joseph Roberts, William J. Duane and John A. Barclay, being duly sworn, according to law, severally say that the foregoing answer by them subscribed is, as they verily believe, just and true

TIMOTHY PAXSON,
THOMAS P COPE,
JOSEPH ROBERTS,
W J DUANE,
JOHN A BARCLAY

Sworn and affirmed to and subscribed, the fourth day of September, A D 1838

WILLIAM MILNOR, *Alderman*

Bill of Revivor.

Afterwards, to wit, on the 10th day of April, A D 1839 the complainants, by their solicitors, James M. Broom and Th Kittera, Esquires, file their bill of revivor in the words following, to wit .

To the Honourable the Judges of the Circuit Court of the United States, in and for the Eastern District of Pennsylvania, Sitting in Equity

The bill of François Fenelon Vidal, an alien to the United States of America, and a citizen and subject of the Monarchy of France, John Fabricius Girard, Margueritte Palmiere Girard and her husband Henry Louis Lardy, Anne Henrietta Pelagie Girard and her husband, John Devais Dumaine, John Auguste Girard, Marie Celeste Girard and her husband, François Louis De Roux, and Madelaine Henrietta Girard, Margueritte Chloe Girard, and Anne Stephanie Girard an infant, who appears by her next friend, John A Girard, who is an alien to the United States, and a citizen of France, all of which above named plaintiffs are aliens to the United States of America, and citizens and subjects of the Monarchy of France, and all of the full age of twenty-one years, except the said Anne

Stephanie, and Henry Stump, a citizen of the United States and of the State of Maryland

Humbly complaining, sheweth unto your honors, that the above named François Fenelon Vidal and Etienne Girard, also an alien to the United States of America, and late a citizen and subject of the Monarchy of France, but now deceased, on or about the 26th day of August, in the year 1836, exhibited their original bill of complaint in this Honourable Court, against the Mayor, Aldermen and Citizens of Philadelphia, and against Timothy Paxson, Thomas P. Cope, Joseph Roberts, William J. Duane and John A. Barclay, executors of the last will and testament of Stephen Girard, late of Philadelphia, deceased, and against John Hemphill, and Maria Antoinette his wife, John Y. Clark and Henrietta his wife, Coroline E. G. Haslem, wife of John B. Haslem, and Mark Richards, the trustee of said Caroline, all of which said defendants are citizens of the United States, and of the State of Pennsylvania, which said John B. Haslem has since died, intestate, without leaving any heirs or representatives entitled to any portion of the estate of said Stephen Girard. In which said original bill, the complainants aforesaid stated such several matters and things as are therein for that purpose more particularly mentioned and set forth, as by reference to said original bill, remaining on record in this Honourable Court, will more fully appear; and prayed that said defendants might, upon their several corporate oaths, full true and perfect answers make to all and singular the matters and things in said original bill contained—as fully and particularly as if the same were therein repeated and particularly interrogated, and especially, that they might answer and discover whether said complainants, Etienne Girard and Françoise Fenelon Vidal, were not such heirs at law and next of kin of the said testator as they described themselves, and whether they and the defendants named and described as citizen heirs and next of kin of the said testator were not the only persons entitled to claim as heirs at law a partition of the real estate of said testator, in case any such estate, real or personal, should be found not disposed of, or not effectually disposed of, by his said will. That the said Mayor, Aldermen and Citizens of Philadelphia might answer and discover what real estate the said testator died seized of, and where the same is situate, and the real value of the same, more especially what real estate he died seized of within the limits of Pennsylvania, the aggregate value thereof, what of such real estate they claim or have entered into the possession as claiming the same, under the supposed residuary devise in trust to them, the aggregate value thereof, where situate in said State, and the yearly rents, issues and profits of the same, what moneys, effects, securities and personal or mixed property or estate they have received from the said other defendants, the executors, as in fulfilment of such supposed residuary devise, and what has become of such real and personal estate, and the interest and income thereof, that they be compelled, by order or decree of this Court, to set apart and surrender to said complainants in said original bill, respectively, their due shares and proportions of such real estate, and to account to them for their due shares and proportions respectively of the rents, issues and profits of the same since the death of the testator, and that the said defendants, the said citizen heirs of the testator, be decreed to quit claim to the complainants in said original bill such parts and parcels of said real estate as, upon a due partition thereof, should be found the just shares and proportions of said complainants, respectively, and that the other of said defendants, the above named executors of said will, answer and discover what moneys, stocks, securities, effects, personal property or assets of any kind or description were left by the testator at his death, what and how much of the same had come to their hands to be administered, or were likely to fall as assets into their hands to be administered thereafter, what had become of the same, and in whose hands the same then were, of what consisting, and how administered or disposed of since the death of the testator, and that the last mentioned defendants be decreed to account and pay to the complainants, respectively, their due shares and proportions of all such assets, present and future, and of all the increments of the same since the death of the testator, and that the said complainants might have such further and other relief in the premises, as to this Court might seem agreeable to equity and good conscience

And that it might please the Court to grant them the proper and usual writ or writs of subpœna, &c., to be directed to the Mayor, Aldermen and Citizens of Philadelphia—to the said Timothy Paxson, Thomas P. Cope, Joseph Roberts, William J. Duane and John A. Barclay, executors as aforesaid, to the said Mark Richards, trustee, as aforesaid, and to the said John Hemphill and Maria A. his wife, John Y. Clark and Henrietta his wife, and John B. Haslem and Caroline his wife, commanding them severally and respectively to be and appear at a certain day, and under a certain pain therein to be specified, and personally to be and appear before your Honors in this Honorable Court, and then and there to answer all and singular the premises as aforesaid, and to stand to, abide and perform such order, direction and decree therein, as to your Honors should seem meet

And your complainants further state that process of subpœna was issued from this Honorable Court, against the said defendants to the original bill, to appear in said Court, and answer the premises, and some of them being served therewith, appeared accordingly.

That the said Mayor, Aldermen and Citizens of Philadelphia, after being served with the process aforesaid, appeared, and on or about the twentieth day of January, in the year eighteen hundred and thirty-seven, answered the said original bill, that the said Timothy Paxson, Thomas P. Cope, Joseph Roberts, William J. Duane and John A. Barclay, executors of the said will of said Stephen Girard, being served with the process, appeared, and on or about the thirty-first day of January, in the year eighteen hundred and thirty-seven, answered said bill, as by the said original bill and answers remaining on record in this Honorable Court, relation being thereto had, will more fully and at large appear. That the other defendants, to wit the said John Hemphill and Maria Antoinetta his wife, John Y Clark and Henrietta his wife, John B. Haslem and Caroline his wife, and Mark Richards, trustee of said Caroline, have not appeared and answered the said original bill.

And the complainants in this bill further show, that the complainants in the original bill caused this Honourable Court to be moved, that they might have leave to file an amended bill, and that in pursuance of such leave, on or about the eighth day of March, in the year eighteen hundred and thirty eight, they filed their amended bill for the purpose of stating matters and things inadvertently omitted in their original bill, and not for the purpose of making any new parties to the bill, or introducing any matter that had happened since the filing of the original bill, thereby stating such several matters and things as are therein for that purpose more particularly mentioned and set forth, as by the said amended bill remaining on record in this Honourable Court reference being thereto had, will more fully appear.

And praying this Honourable Court that the said Mayor, Aldermen and Citizens of Philadelphia be compelled, by order or decree of this Court, to surrender to your complainants their respective shares and proportions of two millions of dollars, and also their due proportions and shares of the residuum of the real and personal estate of the testator that may, or has, come into their possession, under colour of said void trust, as well as their proportional shares of the real estate of the testator in the city and county of Philadelphia, and that the said executors be ordered and decreed to account and pay to your complainants in said amended bill, respectively, their due shares and proportions of all such assets, present and future, as prayed in their original bill, and that said complainants to said amended bill have such other and further relief in the premises as to this Court might seem agreeable to equity and good conscience.

And that the United States writ of subpœna might issue,

directed to the Mayor, Aldermen and Citizens of Philadelphia, as trustees, and to Timothy Paxson, Thomas P Cope, Joseph Roberts, William J Duane, and John A Barclay, executors of the last will and testament of Stephen Girard, late of the city of Philadelphia, deceased, and also to John Hemphill and Maria Antoinetta his wife, John Y Clark and Henrietta his wife, Caroline E G. Haslem, wife of John B Haslem, and Mark Richards, trustee of the said Caroline, all of whom are citizens of the State of Pennsylvania, commanding them at a certain day, and under a certain penalty therein to be named, to be and appear before this Honourable Court, then and there to answer the premises, and to stand and abide such order and decree therein, as this Honourable Court should deem agreeable to equity and good conscience, all which will more particularly, and at large appear, reference being had to the said original bill, and the answers thereto, and the said amended bill, and the proceedings in said cause as of record or on file in this Court, to all and singular of which these complainants refer, and pray that the same be taken as parcel and part thereof. But so it is, may it please the Honourable Court, before any other proceedings were had in the cause, the said Etienne Girard, one of the complainants in the original bill, died intestate, whereby the said suit and proceedings became abated, leaving at the time of his death, no widow, but the following children, who are his heirs-at law, namely· John Fabricius Girard, Margueritte Palmire Girard, who intermarried with Henry Louis Lardy, Anne Henrietta Pelagie, who is intermarried with said John Devais Dumaine, John Auguste Girard, Marie Celeste, who intermarried with François Louis De Roux, Madelaine Henrietta Girard, who is a feme sole, Margueritte Chloe Girard, who is a feme sole, and Anne Stephanie Girard, who is a feme sole, all of which said children of Etienne Girard and their Barons aforesaid, the complainants in this bill, are aliens to the United States of America, and citizens and subjects of the Monarchy of France, and are the only children and heirs-at law, that the said Etienne Girard left at the time of his death. And your complainants further show to this Honourable Court, that since the death of said Etienne Girard, to wit: On the seventh day of July, in the year eighteen hundred and thirty-eight, Letters of Administration of the personal goods and chattels, rights and credits, which were of the said Etienne Girard, at the time of his death, in the Commonwealth of Pennsylvania, have been granted to the said Henry Stump, attorney at law, of the city of Baltimore, who is a citizen of the State of Maryland by the Register for the Probate of Wills and granting Letters of Administration in and for the City and County of Philadelphia, in the Commonwealth of Pennsylvania, by virtue whereof the said Henry Stump is become entitled to the personal estate of the said Etienne Girard, in the State of Pennsylvania, and your plaintiffs are advised that they are entitled to have said suit and proceedings revised, and to be put in the same plight and condition as they were at the time of the abatement thereof, as aforesaid. To the end, therefore, that the said bills and answers, and all the proceedings thereon, so abated as aforesaid, may stand revived against the said defendants, and be in the same plight, state and condition as the same were at the time of the abatement thereof,—may it please this Honourable Court, to grant unto these plaintiffs writs of subpoena ad revivendum, to be directed to the said Mayor, Aldermen and Citizens of Philadelphia, to the said Timothy Paxson, Thomas P. Cope, Joseph Roberts, William J. Duane and John A. Barclay, executors as aforesaid to the said John Hemphill and Maria Antoinetta, his wife, John Y. Clark and Henrietta, his wife, to Caroline E. G. Haslem, widow of John B. Haslem, and Mark Richards, the trustee of said Caroline, thereby commanding them, respectively, at a certain day, under a certain pain therein to be limited, personally to be and appear before this Honourable Court, then and there to show cause (if any they can) why the said proceedings, so abated as aforesaid, should not be revived and be in the same plight, state and condition as the same were in at the time of the abatement thereof, and your said plaintiffs be further relieved in the premises, as to this Court may seem agreeable to equity and good conscience

TH. KITTERA,
for Compts.
JAMES M. BROOM,
for J. F. Girard and others.

Afterwards, to wit, on the 11th day of April, A. D. 1839, the writ of subpœna issued on the bill of revivor.

Afterwards, to wit, on the 29th day of April, 1839, the death of T. Paxson is suggested.

Answer of John Hemphill, et al.

Afterwards, to wit, on the 29th day of April, A. D. 1839, the answer of John Hemphill et al., defendants is presented by their solicitor, Thomas A. Budd, Esquire, which answer, being read and filed, is in the words and of the tenor following, to wit:

To the Honourable the Judges of the Circuit Court of the United States, in and for the Eastern District of Pennsylvania—sitting in Equity.

The joint and several answer of John Hemphill and Maria Antoinetta, his wife, John Y. Clark and Henrietta, his wife, Caroline E. G. Haslem, widow of John B. Haslem, and Mark Richards, trustee of said Caroline, six of the defendants to the original and amended bill of Etienne Girard, late a citizen of France, but since deceased, and Françoise Fenelon Vidal, a citizen of France, and also their answer to the bill of revivor of said Françoise Fenelon Vidal, John Fabricius Girard, Margueritte Palmiere Girard and her husband Henry Louis Lardy, Anne Henrietta Pelagie Girard and her husband John Devais Dumaine, John Auguste Girard, Marie Celeste Girard and her husband François Louis De Roux, Madelaine Henrietta Girard, Margueritte Chloe Girard, Anne Stephanie Girard and her next friend, John A Girard, and Henry Stump, administrators of Etienne Girard

These respondents answer and say, that true it is as stated in the original bill of said complainants Etienne Girard and François Fenelon Vidal, that Stephen Girard, late of Philadelphia, died at his residence in said city on the 26th day of December, in the year Anno Domini 1831, that during his life time he made a paper writing purporting to be his last will and testament, bearing date the 16th day of February, A D 1830, and also a paper purporting to be a republication thereof, bearing date on the 25th day of December, A. D. 1830, and also a writing purporting to be a codicil thereto, bearing date the 20th day of June, A D 1831, and that he appointed the executors named in said bill who took upon themselves the execution of said will

That your respondents believe that all the matters of fact set forth in said original, and also in the said amended bill and bill of revivor, are true as therein stated, and these respondents submit to the opinion of this Honourable Court for the true exposition and construction of said will and every part thereof, whereas they are advised such matters are properly cognizable

These respondents further say, that true it is as stated in the original bill, that said Etienne Girard, one of the complainants therein, was the brother of the said Stephen Girard, of the whole blood, and entitled, as they are advised, to one third part of the real and personal estate of the said testator in the State of Pennsylvania so far as the same remains undisposed of or ineffectually disposed of by the will of said testator, according to the descent law of the State of Pennsylvania and the treaty stipulations betwixt the United States and France, that said Etienne Girard was the only brother that the said testator left at the time of his death, and that he was an alien to the United States and a citizen and subject of the Monarchy of France, that said Etienne Girard is since deceased, leaving the children named as such in the bill of revivor and no others, his heirs-at-law, all of whom, with their husbands and next friend also therein named, are aliens to the United States and citizens and subjects of the Monarchy of France. That the said Henry Stump named in the bill of revivor is the administrator of said Etienne Girard, deceased, and entitled, as these respondents are advised, to the personal estate of said Etienne in the Commonwealth of Pennsylvania, which said Henry is a citizen of the State of Maryland and of the United States of America.

And these respondents further state that the said Françoise Fenelon Vidal, the other complainant in the original and amended bill and also one of the plaintiffs in the bill of revivor filed in this cause, is a niece of the said testator, Stephen Girard, being the only living child and heir-at-law or descendant of Sophia Girard Capayron, a sister of said Stephen Girard of the whole blood, which said Françoise is the widow of Louis Vidal, deceased, and at this time a feme sole and an alien to the United States and a citizen and subject of the Monarchy of France, and entitled, as these respondents are advised, to one-third of the estate of said Stephen Girard, the testator, undisposed of or ineffectually disposed of by his will, according to the descent law of Pennsylvania and the treaty stipulations betwixt the United States and France.

And these respondents further state to this Honourable Court, that the said Maria Antoinetta, wife of John Hemphill, Henrietta, wife of John Y. Clark, and Caroline E. G. Haslem, are nieces of said testator, Stephen Girard, being the only remaining children or descendants of John Girard, deceased, a brother of the whole blood aforesaid of Stephen the testator, and entitled, as they are advised, to one third of the real and personal estate of said testator undisposed of by his will, according to the descent laws of the Commonwealth of Pennsylvania, which said Maria Antoinetta, John Hemphill, Henrietta, John Y. Clark, Caroline E. G. Haslem, and Mark Richards, trustee of said Caroline mentioned in said original and amended bills and in the bill of revivor filed in this cause, are all citizens of the United States and of the State of Pennsylvania.

And these respondents further answering state, that the said Etienne Girard, now deceased, Françoise Fenelon Vidal, Maria Antoinetta Hemphill, Henrietta Clark, and Caroline E. G. Haslem, were the only heirs at-law and next of kin to the said Stephen Girard, the testator, at the time of his death, who, together with the children of the said Etienne Girard named in the bill of revivor filed in this cause, are the only heirs at-law and next of kin to the said testator at the present time. These defendants not denying but admitting the allegations and charges in the said original and amended bills contained, for greater certainty crave leave to refer to the said will and codicils of the said Stephen Girard, exhibited with the said bills, and submit themselves to such order and decree in the premises as this Court in its wisdom may think fit to pass, &c., &c.

THOMAS A. BUDD,
Solicitor for Defendants, as above stated.

Replication.

To the Honourable the Circuit Court of the United States for the Eastern District of Pennsylvania, sitting in Equity.

The replication of Françoise Fenelon Vidal, John Fabricius Girard, Margueritte Palmire Girard and her husband Henry Louis Lardy, Anne Henriette Pelagie Girard and her husband John Devais Dumaine, John Auguste Girard, Maria Celeste Girard and her husband François Louis de Roux, Madelaine Henriette Girard, Margueritte Chloé Girard, and Anne Stephanie Girard, an infant, who appears by her next friend, John A. Girard, all of which above named parties are aliens to the United States, and Henry Stump, a citizen of the United States and of the State of Maryland, to the answer of the Mayor, Aldermen and Citizens of Philadelphia to the original bill of complaint of Etienne Girard and Françoise Fenelon Vidal, aliens.

These repliants, saving and reserving unto themselves all and all manner of advantage of exception to the manifold insufficiencies of the said answer, for replication thereunto say, that they will aver and prove the original bill of said Etienne Girard and Françoise Fenelon Vidal to be true and certain and sufficient to be answered unto, and that the answer of said defendants is uncertain, untrue and insufficient to be replied unto by these replants, without this that any other matter or thing whatsoever in said answer contained material or effectual in the law to be replied unto, confessed and avoided, traversed or denied, is true; all which matters and things, these replants are and will be ready to aver and prove as this Honourable Court shall direct, and these replants humbly pray as the said Etienne Girard and Françoise Fenelon Vidal in their said original bill have already prayed, &c., &c.

SAMUEL H. PERKINS, JAMES M. BROOM,
Solicitor. *Solicitor.*

To the Honourable the Circuit Court of the United States for the Eastern District of Pennsylvania, sitting in Equity.

The replication of Françoise Fenelon Vidal, John Fabricius Girard, Margueritte Palmire Girard and her husband Henry Louis Lardy, Anne Henriette Pelagie Girard and her husband John Devais Dumaine, John Auguste Girard, Marie Celeste Girard and her husband Françoise Louis de Roux, Madelaine Henriette Girard, Margueritte Chloé Girard, and Anne Stephanie Girard, an infant who appears by her next friend John A. Girard, all of which above named parties are aliens to the United States, and Henry Stump, a citizen of the United States, and of the State of Maryland, to the answer of Timothy Paxson, Thomas P. Cope, Joseph Roberts, William J. Duane, and John A. Barclay, executors, &c., to the original bill of complaint of Etienne Girard and Françoise Fenelon Vidal, aliens

These repliants saving and reserving unto themselves all, and all manner of advantage of exception to the manifold insufficiencies of the said answer for replication thereunto say, that they will aver and prove the original bill of said Etienne Girard and Françoise Fenelon Vidal, to be true and certain and sufficient to be answered unto, and that the answer of said defendants is uncertain, untrue and insufficient to be replied unto by these repliants, without this that any other matter or thing whatsoever in said answer contained material or effectual in the law to be replied unto, confessed and avoided, traversed or denied, is true, all which matters and things these repliants are and will be ready to aver and prove, as this Honourable Court shall direct, and these repliants humbly pray as the said Etienne Girard and Françoise Fenelon Vidal, in their said original bill have already prayed, &c, &c

SAMUEL H. PERKINS,
Solicitor.

JAMES M BROOM,
Solicitor

To the Honourable the Circuit Court of the United States for the Eastern District of Pennsylvania, sitting in Equity.

The replication of Françoise Fenelon Vidal, John Fabricius Girard, Margueritte Palmire Girard and her husband Henry Louis Lardy, Anne Henriette Pelagie Girard and her husband John Devais Dumaine, John Auguste Girard, Marie Celeste Girard and her husband Françoise Louis de Roux, Madelaine Henriette Girard, Margueritte Chloé Girard, and Anne Stephanie Girard, an infant who appears by her next friend John A Girard, all of which above named parties are aliens to the United States, and Henry Stump, a citizen of the United States, and a citizen of Maryland, to the answer of Timothy Paxson, Thomas P Cope, Joseph Robert, William J. Duane, and John A Barclay, executors, &c, to the amended bill of complaint of Etienne Girard and Françoise Fenelon Vidal, aliens

There repliants saving and reserving unto themselves all, and all manner of advantage of exception to the manifold insufficiencies of the said answer for replication thereunto say, that they will aver and prove the amended bill of said Etienne Girard and Françoise Fenelon Vidal, to be true and certain and sufficient to be answered unto, and that the answer of said defendants is uncertain, untrue and insufficient to be replied unto by these repliants, without this, that any other matter or thing whatsoever in said answer contained material or effectual in the law to be replied unto, confessed and avoided, traversed or denied, is true, all which matters and things these repliants are and will be ready to aver and prove, as this Honourable Court shall direct, and these repliants humbly pray as the said Etienne Girard and Françoise Fenelon Vidal, in their said amended bill have already prayed, &c., &c.

SAMUEL H. PERKINS,   JAMES M. BROOM,
  Solicitor.   *Solicitor.*

Replications Filed, 29th May, 1840.

Agreement for Argument.

And thereupon, afterwards, to wit: on the 27th day of April, A. D. 1841, the agreement, for filing the answer of the Mayor, Aldermen and Citizens of Philadelphia, and for setting down the demurrer of the executors of S. Girard for argument, is filed in the words following, to wit:

  GIRARD, ET AL., Complainants,
       vs.
  THE MAYOR, &c., of Phila., Defendants.

It is agreed by the parties on the above cause:

1. That the separate answer of the Mayor, Aldermen and Citizens of Philadelphia, and the replication of the complain-

ants thereto, be filed as at the rules next after the filing of the said amended bill.

2 That the demurrer and plea of Timothy Paxson and al, executors of the last will &c, of Stephen Girard, deceased, be set down for argument at the final hearing of the cause, and that such rule for argument be entered as at the rules next after the filing of the demurrer, plea and answer of the said executors

EDWARD OLMSTED,
Solicitor of The Mayor, &c, of Phila.

CH. CHAUNCEY,
For the Exe'rs of S Girard.

J H MARKLAND,
For Hemphill et ux, Clark et ux., C. Haslem and M. Richards

JAMES M. BROOM,
Solicitor for Compl'ts.

SAML. H. PERKINS,
Solicitor for Compl'ts.

ENDORSED.

Circ't C'rt, Oct S 1836.

Girard & al
vs
The Mayor, Ald'n & Citizens of Philad'a & al

Agreement for filing answer of Mayor & al, and for setting down demurrer of the executors for argument.

Filed 27th April, 1841.

Answer to Amended Bill.

And thereupon afterwards, to wit, on the twenty-seventh day of April, A. D. 1841, the several answer of the Mayor, Aldermen and Citizens of Philadelphia, by their solicitor, is filed in the words following, to wit:

In the Circuit Court of the United States in and for the District of Pennsylvania, in the Third Circuit

The several answer of the Mayor, Aldermen and Citizens of Philadelphia to the amended bill of complaint of Etienne Girard and Françoise Fenelon Vidal, aliens

These respondents saving and reserving to themselves, now and at all times hereafter, all and all manner of exception to the manifold errors, uncertainties and inconsistencies in the said amended bill of complaint contained, for answer thereunto, or unto so much thereof as it is advised it is material for them to answer unto, say, that these respondents, in answer to the said amended bill, crave leave to refer to, and do specially insist upon, all such matters and things as in their answer to the complainants' original bill of complaint they have already insisted to be available to them against the relief sought by the complainants, as well in their said amended as in their original bill of complaint, in such manner as may be according to the practice in Equity and the rules of this Honourable Court, without this, that there is any other matter or thing in the said amended bill of complaint material or necessary for these respondents to answer unto, and not already sufficiently answered unto, and these respondents pray to be hence dismissed with their reasonable costs and charges in this behalf sustained

EDW OLMSTED,
Solicitor for the Mayor, Ald'n & Citizens of Philadelphia.

Replication to Answer to Amended Bill.

And thereupon afterward, to wit, on the said 27th day of April, A. D 1841, the replication of complainants, by their solicitors, is filed in the words following, to wit·

To the Honourable the Circuit Court of the United States for the Eastern District of Pennsylvania, sitting in Equity

The replication of Françoise Fenelon Vidal, John Fabricius Girard, Margueritte Palmire Girard and her husband Henry Louis Lardy, Anne Henriette Pelagie Girard and her husband John Devais Dumaine John Auguste Girard, Marie Celeste Girard and her husband François Louis de Roux, Madelaine Henriette Girard, Margueritte Chloe Girard, and Anne Stephanie Girard, an infant, who appears by her next friend, John A Girard, all of which above named parties are aliens to the United States and Henry Stump, a citizen of the United States and a citizen of Maryland,—to the answer of the Mayor, Aldermen and Citizens of Philadelphia to the amended bill of complaint of Etienne Girard and Françoise Fenelon Vidal, aliens

These repliants, saving and reserving unto themselves all and all manner of advantage of exception to the manifold insufficiencies of said answer, for replication thereunto say, that they will aver and prove the said amended bill of said Etienne Girard and Françoise Fenelon Vidal to be true and certain and sufficient to be answered unto, and that the answer of said defendants is uncertain, untrue and insufficient to be replied unto by these repliants, without this, that any other matter or thing whatsoever in said answer contained, material or effectual in law to be replied to, confessed or avoided, traversed or denied, is true

All which matters and things these repliants are and will

be ready to aver and prove as this Honourable Court shal direct, and these repliants humbly pray as the said Etienne Girard and Françoise Fenelon Vidal in their said amended bill have already prayed, &c.

JAMES M. BROOM,
Solicitor for Comp'ts.
SAML H. PERKINS,
Solicitor for Comp'ts.

Decree.

And now, April 28th, 1841, this cause having come on for hearing upon the bill, amended bill and bill of revivor, answers, replications, depositions and exhibits, and counsel on both sides having been heard, it is ordered, adjudged and decreed that the complainants' bill be dismissed with costs